0002153424

ST. JOSEPH'S COLLEGE OF EDUCATION LIBRARY

This book is issued in accordance with current College
Library Regulations.

DATE DUE AT LIBRARY LAST STAMPED BELOW

D1429451

INTERPRETING HUMAN EXPERIENCE

By the same author

NOW IS THE TIME

INTERPRETING
HUMAN EXPERIENCE

A Philosophical Prologue to Theology

PAUL ROWNTREE CLIFFORD

COLLINS

ST JAMES'S PLACE, LONDON, 1971

William Collins Sons & Co Ltd
London · Glasgow · Sydney · Auckland
Toronto · Johannesburg

First published 1971
© Paul Rowntree Clifford 1971

ISBN 0 00 215342 4

Set in Monotype Bembo
Made and Printed in Great Britain by
William Collins Sons & Co Ltd Glasgow

CONTENTS

�֍

PREFACE

This is not another book about religious experience. On the contrary, it is an attempt to come to grips with philosophical issues which, largely under the influence of Continental theology, were so long regarded as irrelevant to the understanding of the Christian faith and are now in danger of being uncritically by-passed by many who are seeking to explore a new direction in theological thinking related to the presuppositions of a secular age. In doing this, I believe these theologians have manifested a disturbing tendency to take for granted the narrowest empiricist assumptions, which rule out *ab initio* any dimension of transcendental mystery, with the result that the Christian Gospel has been accommodated to the spirit of the age to the point of becoming almost indistinguishable from an enlightened humanism. It is my conviction that a proper perspective may be recovered by a critical analysis of philosophical empiricism, not with a view to discarding it in favour of some alternative approach, but in order to show that it implies a dimension of reality which its more extreme exponents have thought they could exclude. In other words, I believe that an open-minded empiricism, pursued within strictly philosophical terms of reference, leads to the acknowledgement of a dimension of mystery to which the Christian faith has direct relevance. The following pages, therefore, are an attempt to suggest a methodology for bridging the gulf between the questionings of unfettered reason and the insights of revealed religion.

My indebtedness to others will be apparent from the many quotations and footnote references. But there are some whose influence and help I am particularly grateful to acknowledge. I owe my first real interest in philosophy to Lord Morris, formerly Vice-Chancellor of the University of Leeds, who was my tutor at Balliol over thirty years ago, and whose astringent criticism of woolly thinking awakened an undergratuate ambition to wrestle with great themes. His tutorials were reinforced by the lectures of the late H. A. Prichard, and anyone who had the privilege of sitting under him could scarcely fail to be captivated by his enthusiasm for his subject, only matched by the devastating way in which he demolished the arguments of his opponents. Those were memorable years at Oxford, with Collingwood in his prime, 'Sandy' Lindsay expounding Plato, H. H. Price discussing the theory of knowledge, and H. W. B. Joseph still a force in the land. It was an invigorating climate and it was good to be there.

The opportunity to pursue philosophical inquiry was denied by the harsh realities of war and the pressure of ministerial duties, and it was not until I joined the faculty of McMaster University sixteen years ago that I was able to take up again questions which had long been in the back of my mind. Research and writing depend in large measure on the stimulus of an academic community, and I could never repay what I owe to McMaster, and, in particular, to its chief administrative officers. With their encouragement I was able to spend two extended summers in Oxford, the second supported by grants from the Canada Council and the Nuffield Foundation, and on both occasions I enjoyed the hospitality of the Senior Common Room at Regent's Park College through the kindness of the Principal and tutors. This afforded a congenial atmosphere for writing and an opportunity for discussing the manuscript with others, notably Professor Ian Ramsey of Oriel, before his elevation to the bishopric of Durham. I am especially grateful to Dr Ramsey for the generous way in which he put his time at my disposal and for offering detailed criticism of the manuscript in its earlier and later drafts. It has also been reviewed by my friend and colleague at McMaster, Professor George P. Grant, as well as by Professor H. D. Lewis, to both of whom I owe a very great debt of gratitude for their frank and kindly scrutiny. All of them have helped me to clarify some of my arguments and correct certain mistakes which I would otherwise have made.

My thanks are due to the editor of *The Review of Metaphysics* for permission to use again in Chapter 4 the substance of an article I published in the issue of March 1964 under the title 'Knowledge as Trans-sensational'. I am also most grateful to Mrs Moya Barker, Miss Diane Mobley, Miss Kathleen Dyck, all of the secretarial staff of McMaster University, who typed successive drafts of the manuscript, and to Miss Frances Williams of the Selly Oak Colleges who prepared the final version. Last, but not least, I have been spurred and encouraged throughout these years by my brother Hugh, who always believed that this book should be written, and by my wife, who has had to live with the manuscript as well as its author.

Selly Oak Colleges   PAUL ROWNTREE CLIFFORD
Birmingham

CHAPTER ONE

THE FRONTIER OF EMPIRICISM

Belief in God as Creator and Lord of the universe is widely thought to be no longer a viable option for modern man. There is nothing new about this attitude. Explicit exponents of atheism have never been lacking since the dawn of reflective thinking. From ancient times all down the centuries voices have been raised proclaiming that the idea of God is a fanciful illusion, and the intellectual convictions of the few have been matched by the practical atheism of the many who have lived as if God did not exist. This is not the first age of scepticism by a very long way.

Nevertheless, there is something radically different about the present climate of thought to which theologians have to address themselves. In the past atheism was a protest against a generally accepted world view which took the supernatural very much for granted. Today, largely as a result of developments in philosophy, science and technology, increasing numbers of people have come to believe that the universe is a closed system which does not allow for any supernatural dimension. This is what is meant by secularization, defined as 'the historical process by which the world is de-divinized'.[1]

The most striking reaction to this new situation has been the emergence of the so-called secular theologians, who have attempted to come to terms with the secularization of the modern world by abandoning the traditional categories of theism and by reinterpreting the idea of God, freed from all metaphysical and supernatural presuppositions. Popularized by the Bishop of

1. Arnold E. Loen, *Secularization—Science without God?* (London, SCM Press, 1967), p. 7.

Woolwich in *Honest to God*,[2] it has been given more radical expression by such writers as Paul van Buren, Alfred Starratt, Harvey Cox and Ronald Gregor Smith,[3] and has reached its zenith or nadir, according to one's point of view, in the 'death of God' theology of Thomas J. Altizer and William Hamilton.[4] But we are bound to ask whether accommodation to the prevailing climate of opinion has not gone much too far and whether any intelligible concept of God has been left when the secular theologians have done their work of reconstruction. Certainly the sceptics have on the whole remained singularly unimpressed. Alasdair MacIntyre, for example, in his review of *Honest to God* concluded that Robinson had virtually landed himself in atheistic naturalism, cloaked in religious language,[5] while Marghanita Laski in an outspoken article in *Punch* dismissed the whole approach as having no significance for her. 'What I want to explain,' she wrote, 'is why Radical Christianity has almost no appeal to me, and certainly less than the traditional English Protestantism it seeks to revivify or replace . . . Where the Church of England has, at its best, given superb expression to a full range of experiences and needs, the Radical Christians seem to confine themselves to a range so limited as fairly to be called a cult rather than religion. And I cannot see what it necessarily has to do with Christianity.'[6]

In the face of comments like this and the general confusion in

2. John Robinson, *Honest to God* (London, SCM Press, 1963).

3. Cf. Paul van Buren, *The Secular Meaning of the Gospel* (London, SCM Press, 1965); Alfred B. Starratt, *The Real God* (London, SCM Press, 1965); Harvey E. Cox, *The Secular City* (London, SCM Press, 1966); R. Gregor Smith, *Secular Christianity* (London, Collins, 1966). The parallel school of thought on the European continent is analysed by Heinz Zahrnt in *The Question of God* (London, Collins, 1969).

4. Cf. T. J. Altizer and William Hamilton, *Radical Theology and the Death of God* (Harmondsworth, Penguin, 1968).

5. Alasdair MacIntyre, 'God and the Theologians', *Encounter*, Vol. XXI (September 1963), pp. 3-10.

6. Marghanita Laski, 'Why I am not a Radical Christian', *Punch*, Vol. 248 (23 June 1965).

Christian circles about the precise content that the secular theologians are prepared to give to the idea of God, it is necessary to ask whether the abandonment of the traditional categories of theism, with the assumption that metaphysics and supernaturalism are now finally outmoded, is at all justifiable. If it is, then I am persuaded that the case for belief in God falls to the ground, in any sense that is intelligible for modern man or that provides a foundation for the Christian faith as it has been understood from the apostolic age onwards. On the contrary, I am prepared to maintain that the framework of thought within which the secular or new theologians are operating is far too restricted, and that consequently they have been leading their followers into the heart of a tangled jungle. While much that they have to say is extremely important and points to a new direction in theological thinking, it is bedevilled by a lack of clarity regarding fundamental presuppositions. And if a building is erected on shaky foundations, it is bound to crumble, however good the materials used in the superstructure.

Whatever their differences, those to whom I am referring hold in common the conviction that we have to come to terms with the process of secularization as an established fact, insisting that modern man actually does regard the universe as a closed system and conducts his life without any reference to God as Creator and Lord. In so far as this is the recognition of an actual state of affairs it is obviously not open to question: the outlook of many of our contemporaries is secularized and any attempt to interpret the Christian faith has to reckon with that as the inescapable context within which such interpretation has to be undertaken. If that were all there were to it, the issue would be relatively simple. It could be argued that secularization is an inadequate frame of reference and that the only way in which Christianity can be made intelligible within such a closed world is by making plain that it is a prison out of which man has to break if he is to see the universe as it really is.

But that is precisely what the secular theologians refuse to allow. They hold that the process of secularization is to be welcomed, as delivering man from an other-worldly pietism, setting him free for life in this world. Here and here only is God to be found. He is not to be banished to a supernatural realm, divorced from this one. Nor is he the God of the gaps, filling the lacunae in man's knowledge of his environment or ability to control it. He is to be discerned at the heart of this world's life and concerned with the whole of it. The positive content and importance of this emphasis are well summarized by Heinz Zahrnt in his sympathetic treatment of two of the most influential pioneers of secular theology in Germany: 'Friedrich Gogarten and Dietrich Bonhoeffer raised questions and established positions from which theology can no longer retreat if it is not to fail in the task of preaching in our time. But they are only two voices, albeit two leading voices among a great chorus of theologians and non-theologians in many Churches and countries. However much they may differ individually, they all proceed from the same point and work in the same direction. They all face the question of total secularization, as the decisive challenge to Christianity in our time. They see the sole adequate answer to this challenge not in reversing the process of secularization, but in bearing witness to Christian faith in a secularized world, in such a way that the reality of God and the reality of the world are brought together in faith as a *single* unity.'[7]

With the broad conclusion outlined I have no quarrel whatever; indeed it has close affinities with the main thesis which will be developed in this book. God is revealed nowhere else but at the heart of this world's life and as concerned with the whole of it. But surely that means a radical critique of secularization in so far as it is understood to mean the de-divinization of the universe. You cannot have God at the heart of the world's life and banished from it at the same time. It is here that the confusion of thought to which I want to draw attention begins to become apparent. While the secular theologians are right in maintaining that God is not to be found in another world or on the fringes of this one, but is 'beyond in the midst of our life', to use Bonhoeffer's

7. Zahrnt, op. cit., p. 167.

famous phrase,[8] such a claim cannot be made intelligible by tacitly accepting a scientific and philosophical frame of reference which not only precludes what they reject but also what they are trying to assert. And that is implicit in the cavalier dismissal of metaphysics and the supernatural. Perhaps some clarity could be introduced into the discussion if a distinction was drawn between different types of metaphysics and different ways of conceiving the supernatural. But to accept the allegedly closed universe of the scientist and the philosopher as the context for reinterpreting the Christian faith does not leave even one inch of room for the theologian; still less does it open the door to a Christian interpretation of the universe.

Here is the real nub of the matter. While the fact of secularization is undisputed, is the scientific and philosophical justification for it established beyond all question, and are the secular theologians right in assuming that metaphysical and supernatural categories are now outmoded? In taking for granted the answers to these questions, those of whom I am speaking do not always clearly distinguish between the scientific and philosophical presuppositions which they have chosen to adopt. On strictly scientific grounds there is no justification for the limiting assumption that metaphysics and supernaturalism are outmoded. For the natural scientist in his professional capacity the question of metaphysics does not arise, still less the legitimacy or otherwise of thinking of God as supernatural. He is concerned with a restricted field of inquiry and with the abstraction of certain aspects of that field which are amenable to controlled experiment. The scientific method neither precludes nor does it directly suggest any metaphysical or theological account of the universe. Such issues lie outside the realm of experimental science which, properly understood, is completely neutral in respect to them.

However, the tendency to confuse scientific and philosophical presuppositions arises out of the fact that much recent philosophy has sought to undergird an exclusively scientific world view, and

8. Dietrich Bonhoeffer, *Letters and Papers from Prison* (London, SCM Press, 1967), p. 155.

13

a type of empiricism has developed which precludes any talk of a dimension of reality beyond that which is presented as sense experience. It rests on what Antony Flew calls the Stratonician principle: 'the presumption that all qualities observed in things are qualities belonging by natural right to those things themselves; and hence that whatever characteristics we think ourselves able to discern in the universe as a whole are the underivative characteristics of the universe itself.'[9] In other words, the universe is a closed system, and any idea of the supernatural is automatically ruled out of account.

This is the fundamental question that has to be faced. If the purpose of the secular theologians is to establish that 'God is beyond in the midst of our life', then this cannot be achieved by uncritically accepting a restricted philosophical viewpoint, which appears to be a half-digested amalgam of empiricism and existentialism, and by denying that the traditional categories of theism have any usefulness or validity. Some, like van Buren and Starratt, seem to take a very narrow empiricism as their frame of reference, while others, like John Robinson, are more influenced by the existentialists with their emphasis on man's predicament in trying to make sense of the world in which he finds himself. But common to them all is their repeated insistence on the exclusion of metaphysics and the supernatural which they assume modern philosophy has made inescapable; and this is what I find so stultifying.

On balance, the ultimate questions centre around the nature of empiricism: whether or not it leads to a closed or an open view of the universe, whether it confines us within a naturalistic prison or is the gateway to fathomless depths of reality. If Antony Flew, and many others who think like him, are right, then the answer is clear: not only are metaphysics and supernaturalism ruled out of account, but all theology, including that of the secular theologians, is a meaningless enterprise. If he is wrong, then the pre-

9. Antony Flew, *God and Philosophy* (London, Hutchinson, 1966), p. 69. The Stratonician principle is so called because of its first clear formulation by Strato, next but one in succession to Aristotle as head of the Lyceum.

suppositions and conclusions of the secular theologians are radically called in question.

Therefore it seems to me to be of the very first importance to take the empirical approach seriously as a prolegomenon to theology and see where it leads. The thesis which will be developed in the following pages is that for man reality is fundamentally and in principle mysterious, and that his attempt to eradicate mystery from the universe is a cardinal error. When he tries to do so, he overreaches himself, and, as in the ancient myth of the Tower of Babel, the result is a confusion of languages: a breakdown in communication and a lack of coherence in thought and life. On the contrary, I shall claim that the recognition of mystery for what it is enables us to discern in the totality of our experience a certain pattern or texture which, though far from translucent, begins to make sense without our having to ignore or distort that of which we try to give some account. In other words, I believe that a kind of map of the dimension of mystery in our experience will emerge which exposes any reductionist empiricism as superficial concern with the surface of things. Of itself this will not lead inevitably to any theological conclusions; for it is always possible to argue that mystery is a dimension of this world and so preserve the Stratonician principle intact. But I shall maintain that the pattern of mystery which is disclosed to us is such that it not only opens the door to a theological interpretation, but is illuminated thereby, thus suggesting a way in which philosophical inquiry and Christian revelation meet one another. First, however, it is necessary to ask what is meant by the word 'mystery' in order that we may be clear as to the conceptual status of the category which is to play such a key role in the development of our argument.

In common parlance 'mystery' is generally employed in one of two ways: either to denote a problem which can be unravelled by careful investigation, or as something which transcends understanding and is in principle unknowable. In the first sense we speak of mystery stories. The detective is set a puzzle[10] by the

10. E. L. Mascall distinguishes between a puzzle and a problem, reserving

committal of a robbery or a murder, but by patiently following up all the clues, the pieces fall into place and the pattern of events is made plain. This is a typical problem, and throughout the age of progress there has been a strong and growing tendency to reduce all mysteries to this one common denominator. The expansion of scientific knowledge, carrying with it the technical mastery of man's environment, has led to the widespread assumption that the range of intellectual achievement is virtually unlimited, while in recent years the notable spread of the influence of the social sciences and psychology has extended the scope of man's confidence in his ability to know anything and everything to man himself as well as the world around him. Indeed, it has been almost axiomatic in the disciplines concerned with human behaviour, no less than in those concerned with the natural sciences, that the facts can be ascertained without raising any metaphysical question, in spite of protests, largely unheeded, that Max Weber's famous distinction between fact and value is not the foundation, but the breakdown of any viable approach to sociology.[11] However, as the bounds of scientific knowledge are constantly enlarged, and the results of scientific achievement become increasingly self-evident, many think it ridiculous to claim that there is anything beyond the powers of human comprehension. It is only a matter of time. Ignorance will progressively be dispelled, and in the end mystery will have vanished, since it is simply the equivalent of the as yet unknown.

Those who work amongst undergraduates cannot but be struck by the naïve confidence with which this outlook has come to be adopted throughout the educational process, and there are

---

the former for pseudo-problems which arise from a misuse of words, such as the assertion that a monosyllable eats fish because a cat eats fish, and cat is a monosyllable. But, after all, this is a word problem which can be solved by examining the proper use of terminology, and therefore the distinction is not a basic one. See *Words and Images* (London, Longmans, Green, 1957), p. 77.

11. e.g., Eric Voegelin, *The New Science of Politics* (Chicago, University of Chicago Press, 1952), pp. 13-23.

many university teachers who never seriously question the validity of the assumption. Indeed, philosophers, who have traditionally considered it their function to raise fundamental questions, have joined the chorus of those anathematizing 'mystery' in any sense other than the problematical. This has been one of the principal emphases of those who claim to stand within the analytic tradition, a philosophical approach marked by the determination to reduce all questions to those capable of a clear answer. A typical example may be cited from an essay by Moritz Schlick, a leader of the Vienna Circle forty years ago. Although modern analysts are quick to dissociate themselves from the views of the early positivists, Schlick's words are nevertheless representative of an attitude which persists beyond the abandonment of its more restricted formulation. 'If in any case', he says, 'we find an answer to be logically impossible we know that we really have not been asking anything, that what sounded like a question was actually a nonsensical concatenation of words. A genuine question is one for which an answer is logically possible. This is one of the most characteristic results of our empiricism. It means that in principle there are no limits to knowledge. The boundaries which must be acknowledged are of an empirical nature and, therefore, never ultimate; they can be pushed back further and further; there is no unfathomable mystery in the world.'[12] Thus in this way the rigorous criticism of the logical use of language has been pressed into service to undergird a non-mysterious view of reality, with the result that in certain quarters philosophy has become the linguistic handmaid of a progressively confident scientism.

Over against this determination to reduce all mysteries to problems, which, given sufficient ingenuity, can ultimately be

12. M. Schlick, 'Meaning and Verification' in *Readings in Philosophical Analysis*, ed. H. Feigl and W. Sellars (New York, Appleton-Century-Crofts, 1949), pp. 155 f. For a fuller discussion of the rejection of mystery in analytic philosophy, see M. B. Foster, *Mystery and Philosophy* (London, SCM Press, 1957), pp. 13-28.

solved, is the counter assertion that the mysterious may be defined as that which transcends all finite experience, not merely in practice, but in principle. However far the range of our knowledge may extend, there is a realm beyond our understanding, and this will always remain so, simply because we are subject to earthly conditions which of themselves set the bounds to our comprehension. This is obvious, it may be said, once we realize that we are inextricably involved in the subject-object relationship, which makes it impossible to comprehend anything as it is in itself; and the knowing subject remains unknowable in himself for exactly the same reason. The classic statement of the case is, of course, found in the works of Immanuel Kant, who claimed that it was impossible for man to comprehend anything beyond the sphere of the phenomenal, that 'things-in-themselves' and the 'transcendental ego' were theoretically incomprehensible even though their reality was the very foundation of the phenomenal realm and the *sine qua non* of all finite experience.

The difficulty about such a definition of mystery is that there is nothing whatever that we could comprehend about it and no appropriate language to use in talking about it, since the language we do use is significant only within the realm of finite experience. Hence Kant's arguments against the supposed validity of the traditional proofs for the existence of God—that they employ categories of the phenomenal world to argue illegitimately about that which transcends it—were extended by twentieth-century positivists to the dismissal of metaphysics and theology as meaningless nonsense. Even their more cautious successors amongst contemporary logical analysts for the most part remain unconvinced that it is possible to talk meaningfully about a transcendental realm, and although the cavalier dismissal of metaphysics and theology is now out of fashion and questions are being asked about the logical function of such discourse, it is widely regarded as an odd sort of language game, having at best an ambiguous relation to the real world of science and common sense. At all events, if mystery is equated with a purely transcendental realm, beyond the bounds of human knowledge, the best we can do is to keep silent before it; for there is nothing meaning-ful for us to say.

A third sense in which the word 'mystery' may be used is out-lined in Gabriel Marcel's Gifford Lectures, *The Mystery of Being*.[13] Holding firmly to the distinction between a mystery and a problem, Marcel rejects the Kantian position that mystery is the realm of that which transcends experience as completely un-knowable, and argues that it is the transcendent *within* experience. 'Not only', he says, 'does the word "transcendent" *not* mean "transcending experience", but on the contrary there must exist a possibility of having an experience *of* the transcendent as such, and unless that possibility exists the word can have no meaning.'[14] He explains his position as differentiating between the unknow-able as 'the limiting case of the problematic' and mystery which is recognized through intuition in depth.[15] The contrast is eluci-dated by what Marcel calls being confronted with a presence rather than an object, where I am conscious of myself as in-volved: 'a sphere where the distinction between what is in me and what is before me loses its meaning and its initial validity.'[16]

Now Marcel is a difficult thinker to pin down, and it is by no means clear from what he says wherein he understands mystery precisely to lie. But amidst all the elusiveness of the discussion at least three points of great importance emerge which, taken to-gether, suggest a definition of mystery as an inescapable dimen-sion of all experience, and sharply challenge the extreme forms of reductionist empiricism. In the first place, Marcel maintains that everything is capable of being apprehended in depth and nothing is ever known exhaustively. Attending simply to the phenomenal is to fail to understand anything for what it is or penetrate beyond the mere surface of things. Marcel would reject *toto caelo* the attempt of many within the empirical tradition to equate knowledge with sense experience on the ground that this

13. Gabriel Marcel, *The Mystery of Being* (London, Harvill, 1950-51), 2 vols.
14. Ibid., Vol. I, p. 46.
15. Marcel, *Being and Having* (London, Dacre Press, 1949), p. 118.
16. Ibid., p. 117.

is to mistake the means for the end. The sensible is only the surface of reality, and if we are comprehendingly to perceive anything at all, we have to recognize that the senses are the means whereby we come to know that which can be intellectually grasped only in depth. The point is well made by E. L. Mascall when he says that while there is 'no perception without sensation, . . . the sensible particular . . . is not the terminus of perception, not the *objectum quod*, . . . but the *objectum quo*, through which the intellect grasps, in a direct but mediate activity, the intelligible extramental reality, which is the *real thing*.'[17] And later he argues that 'in order to penetrate beneath the sensible phenomena to the real intelligible things that support them, we need, not an attitude of detachment, ratiocination and attention to the phenomenal surface of things, useful as this is for certain purposes, but an attitude of involvement, contemplation, and penetration into their intelligible depths.'[18] All this is very reminiscent of Marcel, and opens the way to the apprehension of mystery as the fathomless depth of everything; for once we refuse to rest content with the sensible particular and the phenomenal surface of things, we find ourselves on the threshold of a world that stretches far beyond the range of our comprehension and yet is presented to us in everything of which we are aware.

In the second place, Marcel argues that to treat anything, and still more anyone, merely as an object is to deal with an abstraction, failing altogether to understand what it is in itself. The objectification of persons in particular hides the fact that they make claims upon us, that they confront us with 'a presence', and to treat them as things to be docketed, moved around and disposed of is to distort their very nature. This may be taken as an amplification of the conviction that being must be apprehended in depth, applied directly to the sphere of personal relations. 'Each one of us', he writes, 'is being treated today more and more as an agent, whose behaviour ought to contribute towards the progress of a certain social whole, a something rather distant, rather oppressive, let us even frankly say rather tyrannical. This

17. Mascall, op. cit., p. 34.   18. Ibid., p. 71.

presupposes a registration, an enrolment, not once and for all, like that of the new-born child in the registrar's office, but again and again, repeatedly, while life lasts.'[19] He illustrates his point from a novel by a young Rumanian, C. Virgil Gheorgui, who tells the story of a man in the Nazi and post-Nazi period continuously docketed by those who want to classify him according to the ethnic group to which he belongs. 'Not the least account is taken of what the young man himself thinks and feels.'[20] Later Marcel cites the case of a sleeping child, who in his complete unprotectedness 'appears to be utterly *in our power*', for us to treat objectively just as we like. But, Marcel goes on, 'we might say that it is just because this being is completely unprotected, that it is utterly at our mercy, that it is also invulnerable or sacred. And there can be no doubt at all that the strongest and most irrefutable mark of sheer barbarism that we could imagine would consist in the refusal to recognize this mysterious invulnerability.'[21]

It is from this standpoint that the approach of many experimental psychologists and scientific sociologists is subject to philosophical question. Is man, regarded individually or in his social relationships, exhaustively or even adequately understood as a mere object of investigation? As such he is an abstraction, and, although certain things can be learned this way, human beings are not really *understood* except in the depth of their individuality, and then never exhaustively fathomed. Unfortunately, while many physical scientists recognize that they are dealing with abstractions from reality when they are considering things in their quantitative aspects, those who have embarked on the relatively new science of human beings tend to be less critical of their methodology and basic assumptions. This can lead to disastrous results and explains why not a few are becoming concerned lest the development of the social sciences, particularly on the North American continent, may lead to the progressive dehumanization of man and the emergence of the tyranny of the

19. Marcel, *The Mystery of Being*, Vol. I, p. 28.
20. Ibid., p. 29.   21. Ibid., pp. 216 f.

clever—those who have learned the technique of manipulating their fellow-men as if they were mere things. Human beings make claims upon us in the depth of their own individuality, and dynamic intersubjectivity, even more than the analysis of objective experience, compellingly suggests the necessity of penetration beyond a merely superficial empiricism.

Radical empiricism reaches its nemesis, however, when confronted with Marcel's central theme: man's inescapable involvement in the subject-object relationship; for the most obvious weakness of the empirical tradition has been its failure to take full account of the knowing subject and its treatment of objects as if they could be apprehended in sheer detachment. Unfortunately, at this crucial point Marcel is far from clear in drawing out the consequences of his own basic premise. He appears to hold that once we recognize that claims are made upon us within the subject-object relationship, it is impossible to objectify those claims and therefore understand them; we turn the claimant into a problem which he is not. Thus a claimant admits only of response, not of understanding; and being is accordingly mysterious in principle.

If this is the correct interpretation of the essence of Marcel's position, what becomes of the theory of knowledge? Strictly speaking, we could not pretend to know anything, and it is hard to see how such a position would differ from the crudest kind of behaviourist theory of stimulus and response, which in turn is open to the objection that it has no validity save as a response to stimuli, and so on *ad infinitum*. The fact is that human beings cannot escape from the problem of knowledge. Once we claim to know anything at all, we have objectified whatever is alleged to be known, including the mystery which, according to Marcel, is disclosed in our experience of a presence. Existentialist philosophy, whatever its pretensions, cannot avoid objectifying that with which it deals, and thus mystery by definition appears to become a problem. Why, then, is it in principle irresolvable?

The only way out of the difficulty seems to be to assert that we are involved in and at the same time somehow transcend the subject-object relationship; and this explains why we can objectify mystery without it becoming a soluble problem. In a notable passage in the preface to the second edition of *The Critique of Pure Reason* Kant declared it was his purpose 'to abolish *knowledge* to make room for *belief*',[22] his thesis being that we are so enmeshed in the phenomenal that the best we can claim is a qualified apprehension of the things of sense. But we do transcend sense experience in order to be able to reflect upon it and talk about it, however odd that may be. If it were true that we are absolutely imprisoned within the subject-object relationship, we could not possibly be aware of it and it would be impossible to speak about it. Man's intellectual activity presupposes a second order relationship, supervening upon that of organic animal response, and it will not do to argue that this is a logical puzzle that can be solved in linguistic terms. It is not the case that statements about the subject-object relationship are merely second order statements; they express second order *activities* distinguishable from the automatic response of the organism to its environment. Failure to recognize this fact has contributed to the prevailing confusion in theories of perception and knowledge. Radical empiricists have so often tried to reduce perception to sentience, without realizing that this renders a theory of knowledge impossible. It is one thing to say that the capacity to know has evolved over the ages out of the organism's practical adjustment to its environment; it is another to reduce knowledge to this practical adjustment. But once this has been admitted, we have to avoid the opposite—the completely erroneous conclusion that we can know anything exhaustively. Mystery is inherent in whatever is known from the standpoint of involvement.

Thus we have reached a position which, if not exactly that of Marcel, is built upon his major premises. Accepting his contention that mystery is meaningless if it is purely transcendental, we may discern it as that which is in principle unfathomable in the totality

22. Kant, Preface to the second edition of *The Critique of Pure Reason*, trans. J. M. D. Meiklejohn (London, Dent, 1934), p. 18.

of our experience because, involved as we are in the subject-object relationship, our transcendence of it is at best partial under earthly conditions. Mystery, then, is not the 'beyond' of a problem, 'the limiting case of the problematic', in the sense that it is the sphere of the unknowable beyond the frontier of what is known. If this were so, we could claim to know certain things exhaustively, but would stand baffled before that of which we knew nothing at all. It would then be possible to argue that the frontiers could be progressively pushed back, gradually turning mystery into that which could be completely comprehended. On the contrary, mystery confronts us as the depth of all our experience, the unfathomable dimension of everything that is.

This conclusion may be reinforced by recognizing the attitude of awe and wonder as essentially and properly human. It is evoked not merely by what we fail to understand, but by that which overwhelms us, compelling us to realize our finitude and the insignificance of our stature. The sense of the numinous, the '*mysterium tremendum et fascinans*', as Rudolf Otto called it,[23] has always been a feature of religion, but it is also exemplified in the overpowering impression made on poets, artists and quite ordinary people alike as they contemplate the beauty of nature. Wordsworth speaks for many in his famous lines on revisiting the banks of the Wye above Tintern Abbey:

> that blessed mood
> In which the burthen of the mystery,
> In which the heavy and the weary weight
> Of all this unintelligible world
> Is lightened: that serene and blessed mood
> In which the affections gently lead us on
> Until, the breath of this corporeal frame
> And even the motion of our human blood
> Almost suspended, we are laid asleep
> In body, and become a living soul.[24]

23. Rudolf Otto, *Das Heilig* (Breslau, 1917).

24. William Wordsworth, 'Lines Written a Few Miles above Tintern Abbey, on Revisiting the Banks of the Wye during a Tour' (13 July 1798).

The objection will doubtless be raised that this is sheer mystification, invoking confused emotions to obscure an essentially irrationalist position. But is not such a reaction itself fundamentally irrational, claiming in the face of plain facts that man can scale the heights of Olympus and view everything in lordly detachment as translucent to his mind? The Greek tragedians were surely right when they saw that 'hubris', man's overweening pride, was his downfall. To disdain the sense of wonder is not to become emancipated, but to be defective as a human being.

This becomes increasingly clear as we begin to see how our languages, categories and concepts, so far from enabling us to master reality, are shattered by the overwhelming plenitude of whatever we endeavour to grasp. 'Reality', writes John Baillie, 'is what I "come up against", what takes me by surprise, the other-than-myself which pulls me up and obliges me to reckon with it and adjust myself to it because it will not consent simply to adjust itself to me.'[25] Herein lies the difference between the scientist and the metaphysician: the former is concerned with abstracted aspects of reality which are conformable to his own categories, refined to the maximum point of precision, whereas the latter is constantly breaking his categories on the rock of reality itself. What differentiates the metaphysician's yardstick from that of the scientist is that the latter's is adequate to what he is trying to describe (e.g., the measurable aspect of things, ignoring what is not commensurable with it), whereas the metaphysician's yardsticks are never adequate; they are always being broken. 'When I approach my environment', says Austin Farrer, 'yardstick in hand, I do not ask the general question "What have we here?" or even "What here is most important?" but always the narrow question "What will my yardstick tell me about the things that are here?" The true scientist is justly credited with a supreme respect for fact, that is to say for the real world upon which he makes his experiments. He will stubbornly refuse to record what his yardstick does not bring to light, or to construct

25. John Baillie, *The Sense of the Presence of God* (London, Oxford University Press, 1962), p. 33.

in defiance of any least thing that it does. This is rightly called respect for fact: but it can scarcely be called respect for being.'[26] Respect for being is the proper attitude of the metaphysician, who is concerned with reality as such, and whose 'method is to keep breaking his yardsticks against the requirements of real truth'.[27]

The reason for this is not to be found merely in the fact that we are inextricably involved in the subject-object relationship, but in the very character of that relationship itself; for, whatever may have been assumed in the past, we are now becoming more and more aware that we are confronted everywhere with what is dynamic rather than static. No longer is man able to think of himself as standing over against a universe which can be held sterile in his intellectual grasp, waiting to be analysed by the patient investigator. He is in rapport with an environment which is constantly acting and reacting upon him. As P. T. Forsyth once said, 'Modern thought has to do with the process and destiny of a world that lives, and moves and grows, and not with a structure or substance of a world of still life.'[28] The necessity of thinking in this way has been forced upon us by the development of the specialized sciences. Not only have such disciplines as biology and zoology confronted us with a world of life and activity; even those branches of knowledge which hitherto have seemed to be occupied with unresponsive and pliable material have had to adjust to the idea of restless energy as the common characteristic of everything that is. The dynamics of being simply break our yardsticks. However many problems we solve, we remain what we are, dependent on the yardsticks available to us and incapable of the completely transcendental viewpoint from which reality could be comprehended in its wholeness and depth.

This means that mystery can be indicated, but not described, at least in the sense of being exhaustively defined. Analogy, myth

26. Austin Farrer, *The Glass of Vision* (London, Dacre Press, 1948), pp. 65 f.
27. Ibid., p. 68.
28. P. T. Forsyth, *The Principle of Authority* (London, Independent Press, 1952), p. 37. Cf. Karl Heim, *God Transcendent* (London, Nisbet, 1955), pp. 181-5.

and symbol here come into play, not as the conceptual or linguistic 'photographs' of reality, but as more or less valid ways of indicating what cannot be grasped in the wholeness and depth of its being. Our concepts and language are simply inadequate to the richness of the reality of which we may become progressively aware. It is one of the commonest mistakes of those within the analytic tradition to assume that we cannot apprehend that which transcends our comprehension; and this is why they find the language of analogy, myth and symbol so difficult to place. Perhaps we get nearest to the heart of the matter if we say that the metaphysician is concerned to 'map' the mystery of reality, while his descriptions, though more or less illuminating, show the impossibility of fathoming that which he is trying to understand. As Farrer says, 'he can point to the natural mysteries. Without analogizing he can do no more than point to them, or at the most name them: he cannot express or describe them.'[29] In short, then, from the philosophical standpoint mystery can be designated; it cannot be described in any sense that lays bare the nature of that about which we are speaking.

So far we have been discussing the way in which mystery may be held to lie at the heart of reality from a strictly philosophical point of view. There is, however, another usage of the word peculiar to the religious frame of reference. It is found in the writings of the New Testament, where it is intended to denote that which has been hidden from man's natural understanding, but has been disclosed by God through a special act of revelation. Thus the apostle Paul spoke of his commission to preach the word of God, 'even the mystery which hath been hid from ages and from generations, but now is made manifest to his saints' (Col. 1:26), and later in the same letter of 'the mystery of God, and of the Father, and of Christ; in whom are hid all the treasures of wisdom and knowledge' (Col. 2:2-3).[30]

Now we must be careful to define just what this means. The Christian mystery is to be sharply distinguished from the mystery

29. Farrer, op. cit., p. 74.
30. Cf. Mark 4:11; 1 Cor. 13:2; 15:51; Eph. 1:9; 3:3; 6:19; Rev. 17:7; *et al.*

of reality in general in that the Transcendent Lord is believed to have disclosed himself by taking the initiative in revelation. This is not a mystery to be discovered by the analysis of human experience; it is a mystery which breaks in upon the human scene: one that is within God's providence to withhold or disclose, the origin and apprehension of which is rooted and grounded in the divine grace. But in revealing himself he remains the ultimate mystery, for in so far as he discloses himself, he does so in finite terms, and this surely does not imply that the transcendental nature of God is made absolutely transparent. On the contrary, the finite character of the revelation rules out such a conclusion. He remains transcendent in disclosing himself, and thus is known only in the mystery of his being. To use a pregnant phrase of Sergius Bulgakoff, 'God is a self-disclosing Mystery'.[31] Karl Barth goes even further, arguing that the nature of God and the 'worldliness' of the medium make this inevitable. In a note on his discussion of the subject he writes, '*Mysterium* signifies not simply the hiddenness of God, but rather His becoming manifest in a hidden, i.e. in a non-apparent way, which gives information not directly but indirectly. *Mysterium* is the veiling of God in which He meets us by actually unveiling Himself to us: because He will not and cannot unveil Himself to us in any other way than by veiling Himself.'[32]

For Christians, then, the revelation is given in historical events, culminating in the advent of a man amongst men, Jesus of Nazareth. We are not delivered from the contingent world of ordinary human experience and transported into a realm where everything is translucent and unambiguous. So far from that being the case, the question posed by critics is whether we are justified in going beyond the biblical events, regarded as bare occurrences similar to any other occurrences in history, and according to them

31. Sergius Bulgakoff in *Revelation*, ed. John Baillie and Hugh Martin (London, Faber, 1937), p. 126.
32. Karl Barth, *The Doctrine of the Word of God*, trans. G. T. Thomson (Edinburgh, Clark, 1936), p. 188.

any theological significance.[33] In other words, the question is not whether God is absolutely disclosed as God in himself, but whether these events have a mysterious dimension which justifies us in interpreting them as the way by which God has 'visited and redeemed his people'. Thus Christians are ultimately concerned to assert the mystery of Christ over against those who claim that a purely naturalistic version of his life and all the events leading up to it and succeeding it provides us with an exhaustive account of 'the facts'. A more detailed consideration of this question will occupy us later. For the present, it is sufficient to make the point that the particular usage of the word 'mystery' in the New Testament has some affinity (*pace* Barth) with the philosophical definition of the term in the preceding pages: as the depth to a unique series of events, which is inexhaustible for finite man, and yet given in his involvement with them. Thus, for the Christian, something of what is essentially mysterious, i.e. beyond the powers of reason to fathom, has been unveiled, only to disclose the further depths of profundity utterly beyond his grasp.

The difficulty about this distinctively Christian understanding of mystery is that it has been largely expounded within a strictly theological context, divorced from the language and concepts of secular man. For many this has been nothing but gain. Under the influence of modern biblical theology, they have tended to disparage philosophy together with the categories and language of natural man in their insistence on special revelation as the only valid way to the knowledge of ultimate reality. The most influential figure in the propagation of this thesis has, of course, been Karl Barth, whose commentary on the Epistle to the Romans in 1918 and subsequent works have caused what has undoubtedly proved to be a theological revolution. Barth and his followers redirected attention to what they held to be man's incapacity through finitude and sin to attain to any true knowledge of God. Man is utterly dependent on divine revelation, the gracious descent to his condition and conquest of it. Through the

33. Cf. Kai Nielsen, 'Eschatological Verification', *Canadian Journal of Theology*, Vol. IX (October 1963), pp. 271-81.

Word alone, to which the Scriptures bear testimony, is ultimate truth apprehended.

Actually, the references to philosophy as such are oblique, and the subject of metaphysics is virtually ignored. The enemy singled out for attack is natural theology, which rests on the conviction that there is a knowledge of God to be obtained through rational reflection on the natural universe. But the implication is that metaphysical speculation is useless; the mind of man is so limited and infected with sin that the quest for truth is vitiated from the beginning. Faith, the response to God's advent in Christ, is the beginning and the end of knowledge.

Now, in spite of the difficulties inherent in this position, there can be no doubt that it has challenged a great deal of woolly thinking, bringing fresh intellectual vigour and a renewal of spiritual life to the Churches of the Reformation, and it has not left the older Catholic tradition untouched. Karl Barth and his followers have faced us with the absurdity and impiety of human pretensions in any claim to construct a metaphysical system or attain to the knowledge of God through the processes of unaided reason. If God be God and man his finite creature, then it is impossible for us in the nature of the case to produce a metaphysical system from which all mystery has been removed and which gives us a perfectly clear and coherent account of the universe of which we are a part. Here the most sceptical logical empiricist and the biblical theologian find themselves on common ground. Again, we may be grateful for the insistence that if the nature and purpose of God is to be apprehended, this is only possible through a divine disclosure in which God himself takes the initiative. In Brunner's famous sentence, 'Through God alone can God be known'.[34] This much at least can be said on the positive side.

But there are serious weaknesses in the whole approach. The isolation of biblical revelation and the development of a theological language not subject to philosophical canons of criticism have meant that communication between theologians and philosophers has largely broken down: a sad loss to both. Of course,

34. Emil Brunner, *The Mediator* (London, Lutterworth, 1934), p. 21.

some people are not disturbed by this at all; they consider it inevitable. Is not this the age of specialization, when each man has to stick to his own last if he is to learn anything, and is not the demand for the integration of disciplines a case of trying to put the clock back? This is the intellectual pulse of the modern era. The medieval concept of a unified culture, informed by a comprehensive system of knowledge, appears to have been decisively rejected, and today there is widespread disbelief that such an ideal is possible of attainment.

Obviously this is in large measure true, and scholars in one field have no business to invade the disciplines of others and as amateurs dictate either presuppositions or conclusions; the days of the sovereignty of theology are gone for ever. At the same time, those whose concern is with God as the ultimate reality and ground of everything that is cannot fruitfully conduct their research shut up in an ecclesiastical ivory tower. They need to cross the frontiers and relate what they are saying to the whole range of human knowledge and inquiry. This means, among other things, taking metaphysics seriously and striving to relate theological insights to questions which are essentially metaphysical. The exponents of biblical revelation may provide, as I believe they do, the interpretative clue for a comprehensive, albeit mysterious, view of reality. But revelation, if revelation it is, has to be related to metaphysical questions in metaphysical terms; and attempts to do so have been signally lacking in recent years. To put the matter another way, if the biblical revelation affords a valid insight into the nature and purpose of God, it is not just a shaft of light piercing the darkness of a world which remains as dark as ever; it is a light to lighten the darkness. Conversely, if the theologian is going to venture out of an artificially walled enclosure, he has to be prepared for his own categories of thought and his own use of language to be subjected to the most rigorous criticism from those who do not share his point of view. It is no good objecting that the language of faith is one thing and the language of reason another, with the implication that only the man of faith can understand the language of revelation. There is an overlap which cannot be avoided. As Austin Farrer points out at the beginning of his discussion of *Finite and Infinite*, the whole problem of analogy is implicit in a statement like 'God created the world', and for that matter in all statements which speak of the great acts of God that constitute the Christian revelation.[35] The language used crosses the barriers between a carefully fenced theology and the realm of ordinary discourse. It is the common speech of everyday life applied to unique events; and this is the proper subject for philosophical criticism.

But we must go further. If the investigations of scientists or philosophers actually exclude a distinctively theological interpretation of reality, then the case is lost from the outset. To protest that they are not within the framework of faith is to evade the issue; for their claims purport to undercut the framework of faith in its entirety. It is, therefore, absolutely vital for the Christian apologist to meet the sceptic on his own ground and on his own terms. To put the matter otherwise, unless reality is found to be ultimately mysterious from the philosophical standpoint, there will be no place left for the specifically Christian mystery.

To sum up, we have reached the stage when theology can no longer be profitably pursued in a ghetto of its own, but must be shown to be both intelligible and illuminating to those whose search for truth starts elsewhere. This was the task undertaken by the Fathers of the Church in the early centuries of the Christian era when the Faith had to be expounded in a world dominated by Greek ways of thinking; but each generation, or at least each cultural epoch, poses the same challenge. Many have concluded that it is at the point of man's despair that the meeting takes place, and hence, in so far as Christian theologians have broken out of their ecclesiastical enclave, they have sought to come to terms principally with the Existentialist movement; and not without some success, for the Christian faith does speak to man's helpless-

35. Austin Farrer, *Finite and Infinite* (London, Dacre Press, 1943), p. 2. Cf. the admirable statement on the relationship between Christian theology and philosophical inquiry by John E. Smith in *Reason and God* (New Haven, Yale University Press, 1961), pp. 134-56.

ness. However, the more serious question arises whether this is not a form of whistling in the dark, and whether the affirmations of faith can be validated as grounded in the very structure of things. It is just at this point that the challenge of empiricism has to be faced. Unless a thorough-going empirical analysis of the total range of man's experience discloses a dimension to which the Christian faith is manifestly relevant and illuminating, the latter is bound in the end to be dismissed as fanciful imagination.

Let there be no misunderstanding. The questions I have raised in this chapter about the radical reductionist empiricism of much modern philosophy have not been intended as criticism of empiricism as such or as pointing to the conclusion that the empirical foundation for philosophy should be abandoned in favour of *a priori* reasoning. On the contrary, my complaint against many modern empiricists is that they are not empirical enough. So often they set arbitrary limits to human experience and thus themselves exclude mystery *a priori*. It is only when experience is taken into account in its full dimensions that we can have an adequate basis for philosophizing; and it will be my contention in the following chapters that the most rigorous analysis of our experience confronts us with mystery as its depth: mystery that is illuminated, though not dispelled, by the distinctive mystery of the Christian revelation. But before appealing to the Christian mystery, the specifically philosophical task must be undertaken, *and on its own terms*. It is central for my purpose to be clear about this. Our experience must speak for itself without questions being begged in advance. The next four chapters will, therefore, be concerned with a strictly philosophical inquiry, in the endeavour to understand the nature of our common experience for what it is. Whether or not this will uncover the kind of mystery that is in any way illuminated by the Christian revelation remains to be seen.

CHAPTER TWO

THE MYSTERY OF THE SELF

✳

'We are brought to face the mystery of Being most of all', says W. R. Matthews, 'when we attempt to understand ourselves.'[1] This is not where most empiricists begin. Under the influence of the natural sciences, they start with the objective world into which they try to fit the embarrassing fact of the experiencing subject; and the latter, when treated as an object among other objects, becomes distorted in the process, thereby bedevilling all attempts to devise a coherent theory of knowledge. Whatever his subsequent mistakes, I am persuaded that Descartes was right in deciding that the self was the logical point of departure for philosophical inquiry. Following the breakdown of the medieval system, he wanted to find a sure vantage ground from which he could think out afresh the nature of the universe. Is there anything, Descartes asked himself, about which we can be absolutely certain beyond all shadow of doubt? And he believed that he had found it in the thinking subject: '*Cogito ergo sum.*' 'I came to the conclusion', he wrote, 'that I could accept it without scruple as the first principle of the philosophy for which I was seeking.'[2] Surely, he argued, I cannot doubt the existence of myself without contradiction since no statement about myself or anything else for that matter can be made apart from a subject making it. This is the *sine qua non* of all further ratiocination and the basic foundation of human knowledge. Without presupposing this indubitable fact it is impossible to make headway in any direction.

Now many take for granted that Descartes has been torn to

1. W. R. Matthews, *God in Christian Thought and Experience* (London, Nisbet, 1930), p. 261.

2. René Descartes, *Discourse on Method*, Part 4.

shreds by modern philosophers. He has been accused of vitiating philosophical inquiry for three hundred years by making a dichotomy between mind and body, which led his successors to ask all the wrong questions about the universe and which has been exposed as a spurious problem by present-day logical analysis. His fundamental mistake, it has been held, has been responsible for the wastage of innumerable hours of fruitless argument and a mountain of books and papers which must be allowed to collect dust on the shelves if progress is to be made in real understanding. 'If I were asked', wrote William Temple, 'what was the most disastrous moment in the history of Europe I should be strongly tempted to answer that it was that period of leisure when René Descartes, having no claims to meet, remained for a whole day "shut up alone in a stove".'[3] Austin Farrer has added to the strictures by accusing him of intellectual laziness in simply rehashing Aristotle in the light of the mechanistic interpretation of phenomena current amongst the scientists of his day, without really thinking through the fundamental problems raised by these new ideas; the dichotomy of body and mind was the simplest solution to hand. He was, says Farrer, the child of his times, a representative of the way in which his contemporaries were looking at the universe. So far from forging a new path through a radical rethinking of the problems, he simply chose the easiest way out.[4] In short, there seems to be very little left of Descartes when modern philosophers have finished with him.

It should, however, be noted that Descartes himself was not unaware of the difficulties into which his presuppositions had led him. In a letter to the Princess Elizabeth, written in June 1643, he confesses that 'it seems impossible that the human mind should, distinctly and at the same time, conceive the distinctness of body and soul and likewise their union; for so to do, it must conceive them as a single thing while yet conceiving them as two, which is

3. William Temple, *Nature, Man and God* (London, Macmillan, 1934), p. 57. Cf. G. F. Stout, *Mind and Matter* (Cambridge, The University Press, 1931), pp. 152 ff.

4. Austin Farrer, *The Freedom of the Will* (London, Black, 1958), pp. 13 ff.

self-repugnant.'[5] Here was the problem which was to plague philosophers right down to the present day. Nevertheless, impatience with the way Descartes handled it should not blind us to the very important contribution he actually made to constructive thought. Surely he was starting in the right place, in the only place where we can begin with absolute certainty: the reality of the self. We may face all kinds of difficulties when we endeavour to analyse the nature of the human subject and its relation to the world of which it is a part, but, in spite of all arguments to the contrary, I am prepared to maintain that there is an awareness of our own existence which is available to us in a more direct and intimate way than anything else which we claim to apprehend.

Such an assertion as this is frequently challenged by saying that the self is nothing except in relation to its environment, and that we become aware of ourselves through our rapport with the larger world of which we are part.[6] A baby does not begin by being conscious of himself. First he discovers his body, then his surroundings, and only much later does he learn to think of himself. This may be true, but the order in which we become aware of things does not necessarily imply that a greater degree of clarity or certainty attaches to the earlier rather than to the later. We frequently begin with confused ideas of a subject and attain to clarity subsequently. The point is not that we are aware of the self in isolation. Even Descartes never claimed that; he was prepared to concede that at least the awareness of God was implicit in the awareness of ourselves. And we may go further in agreeing with those who insist that the knowledge of the self arises through rapport with an environment the reality of which we are assured of from the very beginning of conscious life. But, when all this

5. *Oeuvres de Descartes*, ed. Charles Adam and Paul Tannery (Paris, Cerf, 1899), Vol. III, p. 693.

6. Cf. F. R. Tennant, *Philosophical Theology* (Cambridge, The University Press, 1956), Vol. I, p. 70; and A. C. Ewing, *The Fundamental Questions of Philosophy* (London, Routledge & Kegan Paul, 1951), p. 94. See also Jean-Paul Sartre for the argument that intersubjectivity is included in the '*Cogito*' in his essay, *L'Existentialisme est un Humanisme* (Paris, Nagel, 1946), p. 64.

has been said, we may still claim that we have an immediate intuition of our existence in the act of apprehending anything else. Our environment is mediated to us through our senses, and we may be reasonably sure that it is not a figment of the imagination; but the self has a special status in that it is the subject of awareness. We cannot treat it over against itself as we can treat anything else. Even if we argue that the self is an idea objectified through the physical processes of the brain, the subject is still there as that to which the idea is objectified. Whatever else in the universe can be more or less plausibly explained as being something other than it appears to be, the 'I' is different: it is irreducibly there at the heart of any statement about anything, not simply as the subject of the sentence, but as the existential being, making thought and discourse possible. This is the importance of Descartes's contribution to philosophical inquiry, a contribution that should in no way be minimized. If we lose sight of his starting-point through impatience with the conclusions he drew from it, we shall be in danger of forsaking the most promising, if not the only, vantage station from which metaphysical thinking can be pursued.

Nevertheless, the fact that Descartes began with the thinking subject appears to land him in the well-nigh insuperable problem of determining the relationship between mind and body, between the conscious subject and the physical mechanism through which he expresses himself. Due to the mechanistic theory of the functioning of the latter, Descartes found himself reserving to the mind all the active functions of the self, thinking, willing, sensation, and so on, with the result that there appeared to be no way of connecting the mind thus defined with the mechanism of the body. 'East is East, and West is West, and never the twain shall meet', said Kipling.[7] But, on Descartes's own showing, mind and body not only meet; they are inextricably connected in the same person, and the functioning of the one is dependent on the functioning of the other, though in his account he separated them so radically that it was impossible to conceive how they could

7. Rudyard Kipling, 'The Ballad of East and West'.

interact. The only way out of the difficulty was to introduce a *deus ex machina* to perform the conjuring trick; and it was left to Malebranche to develop a thorough-going occasionalism as the logic of the Cartesian dichotomy.

But did Descartes present the matter in the right way at all? If he did, we may find ourselves left with a threefold mystery: the nature of the body, the nature of the mind, and the connexion between them. Attempts have not been lacking to elucidate the mystery thus formulated,[8] but the general consensus of opinion, at least amongst modern empiricists, is that the starting-point is altogether the wrong one; radical dualism, it is held, leads to unnecessary mystification, and the nature of persons can be most clearly explicated if we unequivocally reject the Cartesian dichotomy and turn our attention to the observable behaviour of human beings as objectively given.

Now, while I fully agree that this radical dualism will not do and that persons have to be regarded in their organic unity, I am not persuaded that the only possible way of explicating the matter is to concentrate on overt bodily behaviour, with the consequent reduction of human beings to what is publicly observable:[9] a conclusion which seems to me to make nonsense of certain of the most obvious facts in our experience. On the contrary, I believe that it is more fruitful to begin elsewhere, as Descartes did, with our own private self-awareness, accounting for our physical aspect as the outward expression of an ultimately mysterious organizing centre of activity, of which we are directly aware, even though we are incapable of fathoming it. In other words, I propose to start from the other pole of the Cartesian dichotomy, and to see whether the latter can be broken on the basis of a more adequate conception of man as an organism than was available to

8. Cf. Austin Farrer, who, although repudiating Cartesian dualism, continues to use the mind-body language: op. cit., pp. 54, 88, 92 ff. See also H. D. Lewis, 'Mind and Body—Some Observations on Mr Strawson's views', *Proceedings of the Aristotelian Society*, Vol. LXIII (1962-63), pp. 1-22; and his fuller treatment in *The Elusive Mind* (London, Allen and Unwin, 1970).

9. This approach is criticized by D. Long, 'The Philosophical Concept of a Human Body', *The Philosophical Review*, Vol. LXIII (July 1964), pp. 321-37.

Descartes with his view of the body as a mechanism, sharply differentiated from the mind.

At once I shall be suspected of taking a plunge into idealism, asserting the primacy of mind over matter, and pursuing an *a priori* method against which the whole empirical tradition was a justified protest. On the contrary, the starting-point remains empirical, but attention is concentrated on the centre of experience rather than on its periphery, with a view to understanding the embodiment of the *self*, the body being regarded as the expression of an otherwise hidden organic centre. Whether this will enable us to give a more complete account of the data available to us remains to be seen; but first we must consider the alternative: the proposal that, instead of looking inwards upon ourselves, we should consider other people in their objectivity as they present themselves to our senses. If this turns out to ignore or explain away the most obvious factors in our experience, then we shall have strong ground for presuming that, if we agree to reject a rigid dichotomy between mind and body, the approach we have suggested is at least along the right lines.

Leaving aside the most extreme position, still widely adopted amongst experimental psychologists, that human beings are simply very complicated machines,[10] probably the most sophisticated and influential form of the thesis is found in Gilbert Ryle's *The Concept of Mind*,[11] where he argues that Cartesianism depends upon a logical blunder: the use of mind-body language, whereas it is proper to talk only about persons and their behaviour. Accordingly, he sets himself to explode the myth of what he calls 'the ghost in the machine', the theory that there is an inward world of the mind corresponding to the observable world of behaviour. In Ryle's view there is no mysterious, occult process which goes on behind closed doors whereby a person thinks, decides, judges, desires, wills and so on, followed by the transla-

10. Cf. Karl S. Lashley, 'Cerebral Organization and Behaviour', *The Brain and Human Behaviour*, Proceedings of the Association for Research in Nervous and Mental Disease (Baltimore, Williams & Wilkins, 1958), pp. 1-18.
11. Gilbert Ryle, *The Concept of Mind* (London, Hutchinson, 1949).

tion of these so-called mental operations into actual practice; there is but one operation: that of the thinking, deciding, judging, desiring, willing person. Thus the mind-body problem is a category mistake. No such division as Descartes made and others have perpetuated is necessary; it rests on the fundamental error of supposing there are two processes whereas there is actually only one.

The case is argued in great detail and with the charming persuasiveness of one who is telling us that we need concern ourselves no longer with what is after all a bogus problem. What was believed to be complicated and difficult turns out to be delightfully plain and easy; use the right language and the puzzle vanishes. Now there is something wrong here; our questions about the self are not resolved as simply as this. Ryle's position enjoys what plausibility it has in view of the very close connexion between many so-called mental processes and the observable behaviour in which they are given expression, as when my decision to watch a football game instead of going to the library is given effect by bending my steps towards the ground where the match is to be played. But the crucial point at issue is whether the decision can justifiably be resolved into its expression without remainder. Even this most plausible example is open to the objection that we do seem to detect ourselves taking a firm decision before ever we put it into effect. But let that pass, and allow it to be assumed that no real decision is made unless and until it is executed. We are still left with two criticisms which, taken together, appear to be fatal to the whole thesis.

In the first place, Ryle fails to give due weight to the radical distinction between public behaviour and private activity. This becomes most obvious in his discussion of the intellect, where he tries to reduce thinking to the activities of teaching, explaining, arguing, writing, and so on. According to Ryle, thinking is not a different process from the overt behaviour to which he is consistently directing our attention; it is not a parallel process which goes on behind the activity we can observe. To substantiate this he produces two arguments neither of which, so far as I can tell, justifies the position he is advocating.

(a) Ryle says that thinking is the preliminary exploration which leads to the exposition of an argument; it is not the thinking of the argument behind closed doors, but the tentative search for the solution to a problem which is later to be expounded, and between the two there is no correspondence. Are we to look, he asks, 'for the supposed acts of "judging", "having abstract ideas", "inferring" and the rest in the theorist's exploratory, or in his expository operations? Are they supposed to be manifested in his saying things, when he knows what to say, or in his travailings, when he does not yet know what to say, since he is still trying to get this knowledge? When he is exercising acquired facilities, or when he is still in difficulties? When teaching *how* or when learning *how*?'[12] But this is not an accurate psychological account of what normally takes place. While Ryle may have given a reasonably precise description of the method by which he prepares and delivers his lectures, this is not the way in which the lesser lights do their thinking. Dr Joseph Parker, the distinguished minister of the Victorian era, was once asked to criticize the sermon of someone who had only recently begun to preach. 'Young man', he said, 'for the last half-hour you have been trying to get something out of your head instead of something into mine.'[13] In other words, we may still be exploring in our speaking, as well as in our reflection. Conversely, the whole of an argument may be rehearsed with as much clarity in what Ryle calls silent soliloquy as in a carefully delivered lecture. The distinction is not between the activity of exploration and the activity of expression, but between private unobservable ratiocination and public interpretable behaviour.

(b) The second argument is a curious attempt to exhibit private reflection as similar in kind to public exposition, it being merely incidental that the one is done privately and the other

12. Ibid., p. 297.

13. Cf. James Stewart, *Heralds of God* (London, Hodder & Stoughton, 1946), p. 124.

publicly. A so-called mental act, it is alleged, is talking to oneself instead of talking out loud. 'It may be done', says Ryle, 'in silent soliloquy, but it may just as well be done aloud, or in ink. Indeed, we expect to find a thinker's most subtle and most careful arguments, where we expect to find a mathematician's best calculations and demonstrations, namely in what he submits in print for the criticism of his colleagues.'[14] But what is 'talking to oneself' or 'silent soliloquy'? It is not talking and it is not audible to others. The difference between what is public and what is private is a radical one.

Here is the fundamental weakness in Ryle's whole position. If someone were looking over my shoulder at this moment, he would observe me writing this sentence with my pen, and, presuming he were able to read my handwriting, he would learn from my behaviour what I was intending to say. So far Ryle's thesis is relatively plausible: my thinking is discerned by means of what someone else observes. But suppose I am sitting in my chair reflecting on what I should write next; my behaviour gives not the slightest clue to what I am doing. I may be daydreaming, letting my mind wander discursively through a series of associated pictures. On the other hand, I may be thinking about my plans for the next day or the next week or the next year. My observable behaviour would probably be exactly the same whichever were the case, and yet I would be doing something quite different, and the difference would be known only to me.

The activity of thinking constitutes a particularly striking example of the difficulty inherent in Ryle's position, but the same objections may be extended to his account of all experiences which are not necessarily expressed in terms of overt behaviour: feelings of pain and pleasure, and the whole gamut of human emotions which may be more or less successfully concealed; indeed, the very possibility of concealment is a crucial problem for the thesis in question. In this connexion it is interesting to find Ayer reaching the same conclusion when he says: 'However intimate the relation may be between an "inner" experience and

14. Ryle, op. cit., p. 301.

its "outward" expression, it is not necessary that the one should accompany the other. I can behave as if I had thoughts, or sensations, or feelings that I in fact do not have; and I can have thoughts or feelings that I keep entirely to myself. No doubt I could always express them if I chose; perhaps I am always disposed to express them; but this is not to say that my having them consists in nothing more than my being disposed to perform certain actions, or utter certain words.'[15]

The second major criticism of Ryle's position, as Farrer points out,[16] is that he by-passes the neuro-physiological account of thinking, and so avoids the behaviour problem inherent in it; his view may not unfairly be dubbed as pre-scientific, and, incidentally, as failing thereby to give an adequate description of overt action. If we ask what is observable when a person thinks and does not do anything else, we are compelled to say one of two things. At the superficial level we must answer, 'He is simply sitting there with a certain expression on his face which may tell us nothing at all about his intellectual activity.' Alternatively, we may ask the neurologist what he can observe, and he will talk to us about electrical disturbances in the cerebral cortex which can be inferred from experiments with delicate recording instruments. Now this second account bears no resemblance at all to the behaviour which Ryle describes at such length; for electrical disturbances in the brain do not tell us what a person is thinking in any way that is parallel to our understanding of his overt conduct. We are, therefore, faced with a much more complicated problem than Ryle suggests: the relationship between overt behaviour which is partially interpretable, neurological disturbances which of themselves afford no clue to the processes of thought, and human consciousness. In particular, the scientific account of

15. A. J. Ayer, *The Problem of Knowledge* (London, Macmillan, 1956), p. 241. For explicit criticisms of Ryle's thesis, see C. A. Campbell, 'Ryle on the Intellect', reprinted in *Clarity is not Enough*, ed. H. D. Lewis (London, Allen & Unwin, 1963), pp. 278-310; and A. C. Ewing, 'Professor Ryle's Attack on Dualism', in the same symposium, pp. 311-38.

16. Farrer, op. cit., pp. 11 f.

bodily functioning in relation to human consciousness is seen to be the crux of the problem, glossed over by Ryle's preoccupation with observable behaviour.

As we have already observed, the difficulties inherent in Ryle's thesis were clearly recognized by A. J. Ayer in *The Problem of Knowledge*, and in his latest treatment of the concept of a person he attempts to account for the obstinate fact of subjective experiences without falling back into Cartesian dualism or admitting that there is an unobservable subject to whom these experiences belong.[17] He develops his argument against the contention of P. F. Strawson that the concept of a person is primary, such that corporeal characteristics and states of consciousness can concomitantly be ascribed to persons, whether to oneself or to others, the only difference being that what he calls 'P-predicates' (or predicates that refer to persons which we would not refer to bodies *per se*) have the logical oddity of being patent to immediate awareness in the case of ourselves and ascribable on the criterion of observable behaviour to others.[18] Ayer denies the two assertions on which Strawson's case appears to rest: that behavioural criteria are logically adequate for ascribing experiences to other people and that this is a precondition for ascribing them to ourselves. His reason for doing so is basically the same as that which, I argued, proved fatal to Ryle's position: the occurrence of experiences which are not invariably disclosed in any form of observable behaviour. And so Ayer falls back on the much criticized analogy from our own experience to that of others as justification for ascribing experiences to other people, at the same time advancing his own view that experiences are necessarily conditional on the state of a body, the identity of which is the criterion of personal continuity.

Now, although Ayer does not claim to have solved all the problems, he proposes an account of human beings which, superficially at any rate, appears to eliminate the self and thereby to exclude the element of mystery from consideration: a person is a

17. A. J. Ayer, *The Concept of a Person* (London, Macmillan, 1963), pp. 82-128.
18. P. F. Strawson, *Individuals* (London, Methuen, 1959), pp. 87-116.

body to which certain experiences may be ascribed and on the continued existence of which they are dependent. But his proposal is open to three main criticisms. In the first place, Ayer seems to me to have failed altogether to meet the objection to what Strawson calls the 'no-ownership theory'—the view that experiences are not owned by anyone, but are simply contingent on the state of a body. Strawson argues that this theory lacks coherence in that it is impossible for its proponents to avoid the use of personal pronouns in their definitions, thus surreptitiously reintroducing the concept of an owner of an experience other than a particular body. Ayer tries to meet this difficulty,[19] but only at the cost of talking about experiences as if they were physical objects, which is surely an instance of what Ryle elsewhere calls 'a category-mistake'.[20] 'Pure experience', as Tennant once argued so forcibly, 'is a complete abstraction.'[21] We cannot consistently speak about experiences without presupposing an owner, and indeed Ayer himself cannot avoid doing so.[22] The fact is that the grammatical form of the word 'experience' is misleading; it is not an object that can be grasped in its sheer objectivity; it is logically an experienc*ing*; and the verbal form requires a subject not only linguistically, but ontologically.

Second, Ayer's positive thesis, that the continuity of a person is to be equated with the continuity of a body, bristles with difficulties; for the latter, viewed as a collection of cells, never does remain constant. We are told by biochemists that a complete metabolism has taken place by the end of every seven years. Wherein, then, does the identity of a person and his continuity over a lifetime lie if his bodily state is subject to such radical

19. Ayer, *The Concept of a Person*, pp. 116 f.

20. Ryle, op. cit., pp. 16 ff.

21. Cf. Tennant, op. cit., Vol. I, pp. 18 f. See also in this connexion the whole of Chapters II and III (pp. 13-43) and Appendix A (pp. 366-8). A more recent treatment of the same theme is to be found in C. A. Campbell, *On Selfhood and Godhood* (London, Allen & Unwin, 1957), pp. 73-94.

22. Ayer, *The Concept of a Person*, p. 119; cf. his admission in *The Problem of Knowledge* that 'we cannot talk of experiences without implying that they have owners' (p. 224).

change? Ayer would probably reply that there is continuity throughout the whole process of physical development, but the problem in the case of an organism is just what this could mean. An organism can hardly be resolved into the contiguity of discrete physical states. What would these be anyway? And the real question is how I can identify an experience as having been mine when it occurred at a time when the chemical composition of my body was totally different from what it is today. The only way out of the difficulty seems to be to discard the idea of the body as a given entity and to speak of an organism as a centre of activity which is continuously expressing itself in publicly observable ways. This, at any rate, is to stick more closely to the biological data than any kind of crude static physicalism: this is the thesis that I shall try to amplify in the next chapter. For the present, all I want to insist is that the notion of a body as the principle of personal identity is one that is open to grave objection on the ground that the very nature of a living organism appears to preclude the kind of identity that is required. The sole reason for Ayer advancing the theory he does appears to be his lingering attachment to the verification principle and to sense awareness of physical bodies as the paradigm of veridical knowledge. Once that is called in question, the proposal loses all its initial plausibility.

This leads directly to the third objection to Ayer's thesis, and incidentally to Strawson's as well: their refusal to take the deliverances of introspection seriously, with the resultant denial that we have any direct awareness of the self as the organizing centre of our experience.[23] Indeed, Ayer dogmatically asserts that there is no way of identifying the subject of consciousness.[24] Such a paradoxical position is, of course, nothing new. It was enunciated in the eighteenth century by David Hume, who held

23. I see no valid reason for questioning the method of introspection as a way to knowledge about the self. I have nothing to add to what seems to me to be the conclusive discussion of the subject by C. A. Campbell, op. cit., pp. 110 ff. and his summary on p. 157.

24. Ayer, *The Concept of a Person*, pp. 112 f.

that when we turn inwards upon ourselves we find only a bundle of perceptions, each of which may be regarded as distinct, and for which no connecting link may be discovered. 'For my part', says Hume, 'when I enter most intimately into what I call *myself*, I always stumble on some particular perception or other, of heat or cold, light or shade, love or hatred, pain or pleasure. I never can catch *myself* at any time without a perception, and never can observe any thing but the perception. When my perceptions are remov'd for any time, as by sound sleep; so long am I insensible of *myself*, and may truly be said not to exist. And were all my perceptions remov'd by death, and cou'd I neither think, nor feel, nor see, nor love, nor hate after the dissolution of my body, I shou'd be entirely annihilated, nor do I conceive what is farther requisite to make me a perfect non-entity. If any one upon serious and unprejudic'd reflexion, thinks he has a different notion of *himself*, I must confess I can reason no longer with him. All I can allow him is, that he may be in the right as well as I, and we are essentially different in this particular. He may, perhaps, perceive something simple and continu'd, which he calls *himself*; tho' I am certain there is no such principle in me.'[25]

Is this the end of further discussion? Admittedly, it is difficult to argue with anyone who categorically declares he has no awareness of the self when he looks within, and, if that is all there is to be said, then those who give a different psychological account of introspection will simply have to go their own way as long as they cannot reinterpret their experience to accord with that of Hume. There would be no way of arriving at agreement. But Hume, in spite of the confidence with which he dismisses the notion of the self in the passage quoted, finds great difficulty in maintaining his position when he tries to account for the reason we have for mistakenly assuming, as he believes, the identity of the self through a variety of experiences. What holds the perceptions together, when they are initially presumed to be discrete? Hume confesses his perplexity in the appendix to the *Treatise*.

25. David Hume, *A Treatise on Human Nature*, Book I, Part IV, Section VI, ed. L. A. Selby-Bigge (Oxford, Clarendon Press, 1897), p. 252.

'There are two principles', he says, 'which I cannot render consistent; nor is it in my power to renounce either of them, viz. *that all our distinct perceptions are distinct existences*, and *that the mind never perceives any real connexion* among distinct existences', and concludes, 'For my part, I must plead the privilege of a sceptic, and confess, that this difficulty is too hard for my understanding.'[26] But that is not all. Hume is not only perplexed by the factual association of perceptions; he has to bring back the organizing self, which he has denied, for the exposition of his paradoxical theory. 'Identity', he says, 'is nothing really belonging to these different perceptions, and uniting them together; but is merely a quality, which *we* attribute to them, because of the union of their ideas in the *imagination*, when *we reflect* upon them.'[27] The italics are mine to draw attention to the impossibility of getting rid of the attributing, imagining and reflecting subject: a conclusion underlined by the introduction of memory as the ground for being aware of the continuance and extent of the succession of perceptions.[28] As G. F. Stout says, 'The important reservation which mars Hume's consistency is that he assumes memory.'[29] The fact is that no sense can be made of the idea of perception without a perceiving subject; Hume was misled by his phenomenalist premise—that we can be certain of nothing but discrete impressions—without realizing that this made no sense at all apart from something to make the impression and someone or something on which the impression is made. So far from getting down to rock-bottom, Hume began and ended with an abstraction. His account of experience may be likened to the description of a husband and wife as 'the marriage bond'.

Accordingly, we find no serious obstacle to pursuing our inquiry in the views of those who attempt either to reduce the self to that which is amenable to public observation or to follow Hume in his radical phenomenalism. All alike appear to begin in the wrong place, and end up by ignoring or distorting the plain deliverances of introspection. The truth is that it is all too com-

26. Ibid., p. 636.   27. Ibid., p. 260.
28. Ibid., p. 261.   29. Stout, op. cit., p. 28.

mon because of logical or metaphysical presuppositions to explain away the psychological facts. As Tennant said, although in unnecessarily cumbersome language, in the introductory pages of his *Philosophical Theology*, 'When the data have been described without suppression or mutilation, without gratuitous interpretation in terms of supposititious theory framed according to predilection: then, and only then, can we reasonably proceed to consider what implications they contain, and what metaphysical interpretation they may suggest or require.'[30] This is what many philosophers singularly fail to do. Is it the case that we are never aware of ourselves as the subjects of activity? Hume, certainly, said he was not; but surely this was an example of psychological accuracy giving way to preconceived theory On the basis of his conviction that the self was a bundle of perceptions and that nothing could be observed save the impression of an idea, he had no room for the awareness of the self. So he persuaded himself that he had none. But Hume was not empirical enough. When we examine our experience do we not find the self inextricably bound up with what we are considering? Are we not aware of an organizing centre in all activity? Are we aware of anything more directly, more ultimately, than ourselves?[31] Ryle is so nearly right in his refusal to separate the self from its activities. We could at least go this far with him, that our knowledge of the self is restricted to our knowledge of its activities; but then to extrapolate the activities and deny their organizing, motivating centre is to fly in the face of what we know most clearly and to leave us with something like the Cheshire cat's grin without the cat. Of course, the grin is superficially so much simpler than the cat!

We conclude, therefore, that the Cartesian dichotomy cannot be broken by concentrating on the phenomena of bodily behaviour. We are driven to start elsewhere—with the organizing centre of human activity, the self as disclosed to us by the way of introspection. But before proceeding to a positive reconstruction,

30. Tennant, op. cit., Vol. I, p. 3.

31. Cf. Francis Aveling, *Psychological Approach to Reality* (London, University of London Press, 1929), pp. 192 ff.

there is an objection of a completely different kind that has to be met. It is alleged that although the self is rightly understood as the subject of all experience, we are quite unable to scrutinize it. We cannot turn it into an object. All that we can do is to consider dispositions or activities as they have already receded into the past; for, as soon as I say that I am aware of myself being angry, I really mean 'I am now aware of a state of being angry a split second ago': I move on from being angry to the contemplation of it, but 'I' still remains the subject of the experience, not its object, and so on *ad infinitum*. This point has been forcibly made by the German philosopher-theologian, Karl Heim, who has argued at length for the transcendent reality of the ego against any possibility of its being objectified. He quotes with approval the words of Fritz Künkel: 'The Subject . . . is neither the organism nor any part of the inner world . . . The Subject is nothing that can be expressed in words; for then it would be part of the outer world, an object, and no longer a Subject.' 'Even that which we call the inner world is external . . . since the Subject can contrast itself with these feelings and make them the objects of its criticism. The Subject itself is no part of the world. It belongs neither to the mental world nor to the spiritual world, but always stands out over against the whole world with which it is bound up, and without which it cannot exist, an eternally hidden factor (and yet the most real of realities).'[32] When we speak of the self, contends Heim, we are 'passing from the visible content of the world to something which is on the hither side of the whole objective world, far too close for observation.'[33]

This is, indeed, an unequivocal assertion of the reality of the self. As such it provides a welcome contrast to the phenomenalism of Ayer or the bland dismissal of the transcendental ego by Gilbert Ryle, who regards it as a logical blunder arising out of the confusion of first and second order actions and the assumption that a commentary on something can at one and the same time be

32. Karl Heim, *God Transcendent* (London, Nisbet, 1935), p. 107. See Heim's amplification of the same view on the same page.
33. Ibid., p. 152.

a commentary upon itself.[34] The problem of the 'elusive "I"', as Ryle calls it, is not resolved by logical legerdemain;[35] it is an ontological issue, and Karl Heim leaves us in no doubt that, as far as he is concerned, this is so. Furthermore, it is of great importance that we should be reminded that the self cannot be treated as a mere object, sterile and lifeless, amenable to being observed, classified and pigeon-holed once and for all. On the other hand, it is doubtful, as we shall argue at greater length, whether *anything* can be so objectified. If the whole of the universe is dynamic, there is a sense in which everything is subject, exercising its influence on everything else. Thus to contend that the self cannot be the object of thought because it is pure subject would lead in the end to disclaiming the pretence of thinking about anything. Clearly Heim would not be prepared to accept such a conclusion. Indeed, the fact that he can speak about the transcendental self at all means that he has in some sense objectified it by making it the object of meaningful discourse.

To sum up the position we have reached thus far, we may say that there is much of significance that we can discover about the self from an analysis of our psychological experience, provided we bear in mind that our account is incomplete until we reckon with the polarity of subject and object, and that we may expect to find a depth to the self which the consideration of its most characteristic activities cannot plumb. So we proceed with caution, and yet with confidence that some progress can be made.

What, then, can we discover as we turn inwards and try to say what we know about ourselves? What are the principal functions that characterize the ego? I propose to choose six: perception, remembering, capacity for structural integration and creativity (taken together for convenience in presentation), intuition and overt behaviour. Needless to say, other classifications are possible, such as the traditional distinction between the affective, the cognitive and the conative; but I have decided, for the purpose

34. Ryle, op. cit., pp. 195-8.

35. Cf. Ian T. Ramsey, 'The Systematic Elusiveness of "I"', *The Philosophical Quarterly*, Vol. V (July 1955), pp. 193-204.

of the present inquiry, to exclude from consideration passive affection, since my immediate interest is to show how the self has to be understood in terms of spontaneous expenditure of energy, though this is incomplete unless we reckon with its receptivity to influences exerted upon it. As for cognition and conation, they are implicit in varying degree in most, if not all, of the functions selected.

We begin with perception because it is basic to human experience. Although we may be prepared to allow that there are apprehensions, such as those described by the mystics, in which the senses appear to play no part, we have no evidence of anyone developing distinctive human characteristics without the capacity for perception of some kind. Even the blind and deaf Helen Keller was dependent upon the sense of touch. On the whole, empirical philosophers have been principally concerned with the analysis of what is perceived rather than with the percipient subject. The emphasis is, of course, vitally important, and in the next chapter we shall be considering the problems that arise when we try to describe our physical environment. Nevertheless, without prejudging that issue, we can, perhaps, with profit say something about the subjective aspect of perception, given the reality of the self as the premise from which to start.

However we conceive the nature of the physical world, it is plain that the discreteness of the objects of perception constitutes a serious problem for the radical empiricist. We have already noted the difficulties into which Hume gets when he tries to expound consistently his notion of the self as a bundle of separate impressions. The same dilemma arises in giving any account of perceiving our environment. Clearly the datum of which we are aware cannot be restricted to any instantaneous, discrete sensum; countless impressions are made on the senses, and what we are aware of is a composite whole, both coordinated and selective. Take the case of vision. When I say that I see this table in front of me, what am I describing? There is a centre of my visual field to which I am directing my attention, though I am aware of its extension on all sides, shading off on the periphery of what I say that I see out of the corner of my eyes. By changing the focus or by turning my head the perception alters. I do not create what I see, but I do integrate and select what I am looking at. The same is true *mutatis mutandis* of hearing and touch. The vibrations produced by the various instruments of an orchestra are heard as a unity of sound, and the impressions made on the nerve ends of my fingers when I hold a glass tumbler are felt as a rounded surface which, if I am not blind, is coordinated further with what I see when I look at it and what I hear when I knock it against something else. This activity in apprehension led Kant to develop his theory of the transcendental unity of apperception and the categories of thought whereby the subject was enabled to integrate his impressions. Without committing ourselves in any way to Kant's development of his thesis, we must surely allow that he was right in claiming that all perception depends on the contribution of the experiencing subject.

Another way of making the same point is to raise the difficult question of temporal succession. When I am travelling in a railway train and looking out at the countryside, I am aware of fields and hedgerows, houses and cattle passing swiftly before my gaze. I have no instant perception of an isolated cow, not even such as might be captured in a still photograph. The cow's position is constantly changing in relation to me, and it is a sequence of 'cow' set in a sequence of landscape that I observe from the window. This is a series of impressions which I hold together, much as I combine in a unity of movement the rapidly succeeding still pictures shown on the cinema screen. In the first case the subject is moving in relation to the object; in the second the position is reversed; but in both the unity is achieved by the same process of coordination.

The method of perception provides a clue to the enigma of memory, which has proved to be the source of greatest perplexity to those whose attention has been concentrated upon the objective data of experience. Hume admitted, as we have seen, that it was the principal reason for believing in the continuity of the self, and it has been the major stumbling block for those who, in the interests of an extreme empiricism, have sought to exorcize the ghost. Broadly speaking, three main approaches hold the field, approaches which may conveniently be characterized as the 'Acquaintance Theory', the 'Dispositional Theory' and the 'Presumptive Knowledge Theory'.[36]

The first of these was advocated in its most radical form by Samuel Alexander in *Space, Time and Deity*.[37] He held that memory is direct acquaintance with past events on all fours with sense perception, even going so far as to claim that its object 'is as much a physical object as the percept'.[38] In remembering we are enabled to recall past events which we have experienced and apprehend them for what they were, not indirectly through an image, but immediately in themselves. 'The pastness of the object', he says, 'is a datum of experience, directly apprehended. The object is compresent with me *as past*. The act of remembering is the process whereby this object becomes attached to or appropriated by myself . . .'[39] Later he adds that the lapse of time may alter the appearance of what we remember so that it is 'seen through the haze of Time, as things distant in Space are coloured by their remoteness'.[40] Alexander does not, of course, equate perception with memory, though it is clear that in his view the two faculties are closely related. As for the subjective side of the experience, he thinks of remembering as an active desire, a reaching back into the past to recall what has gone, and he distinguishes this appetitive activity from what he calls 'quasi-memory', understood as the retention of something in the mind such as the subject

36. The present state of the discussion is summarized in a recent monograph by W. Von Leyden, entitled *Remembering: A Philosophical Problem* (London, Duckworth, 1961), in which the author is chiefly concerned to contrast and harmonize the views of Gilbert Ryle and Bertrand Russell, described as 'the Past Approach' and 'the Present Approach' respectively. In the course of his review he takes a passing glance at modifications of 'the Direct Acquaintance Theory' which he dismisses in a few sentences; ibid., p. 24.

37. Samuel Alexander, *Space, Time and Deity* (London, Macmillan, 1920), Vol. I, pp. 113 ff.

38. Ibid., p. 114.   39. Ibid., p. 113.

40. Ibid., p. 116.

of a sentence while the sentence is being spoken.[41] The impression left upon the reader is that Alexander regards the sequence of events as somehow existing in itself and accessible to the mind through direct perception of a continuum, and through memory in so far as the continuum has receded into the past beyond the range of the senses and yet has been part of the subject's experience; it is also accessible by anticipation in so far as the shadow of things to come impinges on the threshold of consciousness. The difficulties inherent in such a view bedevil anyone who tries to state it.

The 'Dispositional Theory' is particularly associated with the name of Gilbert Ryle. In brief, he holds that memory is a term standing for two characterizations of behaviour: first, the ability to perform a certain task, and second, the 'not having forgotten' a certain skill. The first is fundamental for Ryle, for he is concerned, as we have seen, to reduce all so-called mental activity to a behaviouristic pattern. He will therefore have nothing of mental images referred to past events, and the recollective process which seems to lend credence to this way of talking is explained in terms of a past experience which is built into our present activity. Thus memory is not a means of knowing; it is a performance which embodies that which has already been learnt.

The third approach has been thoroughly canvassed by Bertrand Russell, who insists that remembering is essentially a present experience which is supposed to give us knowledge of a past to which we have no other access. The problem then becomes one of relating this memory I now have to the event alleged to have happened long ago. Logically there is no way of being sure that anything we say we remember actually did take place, and it is impossible to disprove the bizarre suggestion that the whole world has just come into existence complete with the memories of all its inhabitants. Russell does not really believe this and admits the idea is a silly one, but he toys with it because his view of the self does not allow him to think in terms of anything but discrete experiences. 'The real man', he writes, 'however the police may

41. Ibid., p. 120.

swear to his identity, is really a series of momentary men, each different one from the other, and bound together, not by a numerical identity, but by continuity and certain intrinsic causal laws.'[42] Of course, Russell saves himself from absurdity by the qualification at the end of the sentence, but it is hard to see how 'continuity' and 'causal laws' can ensure the transmission of an experience through a series of discrete individuals, when the essence of the memory situation is that the last in the line affirms that *he* had the original experience. Be that as it may, Russell admits there is no way of demonstrating that occurrences which we remember actually did take place in the past, though all knowledge depends on the reliability of the assumption. These, then, are the two points on which he differs most sharply from the holders of the 'Dispositional Theory': first, memory is a present experience: and second, it provides us with knowledge of the past, albeit assumed knowledge.

Obviously these views can be discussed in considerable detail since all of them bristle with difficulties, but to do so would be to lose sight of the wood for the trees. Suffice it to say that, when Von Leyden in his review of the problem has finished dissecting and comparing the theories of Ryle and Russell, he finds himself baffled, on either account or on both put together, to see how a present experience can be veridically related to one that is past: 'The Past Approach to memory no less than the Present Approach leaves room for doubt: neither can, singly or in conjunction with the other, dispose of the "sense of disconnexion", the logical gap or discontinuity between a present claim to recollect and the past event to which this purports to refer. At the same time, while both approaches, though indispensable, are in the last analysis insufficient as criteria for the correct application of the word "remember", there appears to be no other approach.'[43] But is this really so? As long as we are preoccupied with the data of experience and tacitly assume that the idea of a continuing subject

42. Bertrand Russell, *Mysticism and Logic* (London, Longmans, Green, 1918), p. 129.
43. Von Leyden, op. cit., p. 43.

cannot be taken seriously, there is no escape from Von Leyden's dilemma. But do not the very difficulties of the conclusion to this way of thinking force a reappraisal of its presuppositions? If the past event and the memory of it (used in Alexander's sense of the object of remembering) cannot be held together in themselves, is it not possible that the clue to the puzzle may lie in the coordinating activity of the self?

This has at least the merit of sticking more closely to the deliverances of introspection. We normally take it for granted that the real continuity lies not between an event in the past and a present memory, but in the experiencing subject, who both participated in the original happening and relates it to his present awareness. After all, everyone admits that we never remember anything we have not experienced. We may be entirely convinced from the evidence at our disposal that Wellington defeated Napoleon at the Battle of Waterloo in 1815, but we never claim to remember it except in the sense that we remember the proposition either as something we have heard a teacher enunciate or as something we have arrived at for ourselves through reading history books. Then the memory is not of the Battle of Waterloo, but of subsequent experiences of our own related to learning about it. The continuity of the subject is the *sine qua non* of memory, and we have to say that Hume, Russell, Ayer, and all those who argue like them, are fundamentally mistaken; they make nonsense of memory by questioning its essential condition.

The mystery still remains; it only has a different focus. Instead of trying to join together inseparables by definition, we have to face the extremely puzzling fact that the self is able to reach back into its own past and recall what has already receded beyond immediate experience; but at least this is to state without distortion what we are aware of doing. All the same, we should not expect to resolve the issue by stating it, though it is some gain to state it correctly, if that is what we can legitimately claim to have done. The problem is still there. However, we can begin to elucidate it, in the sense of pointing beyond the bare givenness of the act of remembering, by linking it with what was said about perception. Clearly some affinity may be detected between the two in that perceiving involves holding together in the unity of experience what is given in the specious present. Not only is there a fringe to vision, more or less related to the centre on which attention is focused; there is a time fringe which also varies with the concentration of the percipient. The instantaneous moment is an abstraction which can only be conceptualized. The object of sense experience is temporally extended, shading into the 'just gone' and the 'not yet', and it is impossible to draw the lines of demarcation with any precision. That is because there is a continuity of experience which is dissected only artificially. If this is the case with perception, why should we not understand memory as an extension of the same capacity? Of course, we must be on our guard against pressing the similarity too far. Alexander may be justified in talking of memory as 'appropriated by the self and recognised as my past object',[44] and of remembering as 'a kind of desire . . . unlike expectation, directed backwards',[45] but the latter is admittedly an analogy, and he certainly goes too far when he speaks in the passage quoted above of the appearance of memory 'altered by the lapse of Time, seen through the haze of Time, as things distant in Space are coloured by their remoteness.'[46] It is not just like perception in that there is lacking a directness of sensible awareness, which is replaced by the faculty of imaging.[47] Seeing Jones and remembering what Jones looks like when he is far away are two quite different experiences. Nevertheless, however dissimilar, they are not entirely discontinuous. At the fringes

44. Alexander, op. cit., pp. 117-18.

45. Ibid., p. 118.   46. Ibid., p. 116.

47. Ryle is surely wrong when he argues that images are not fundamental to the function of remembering. He regards 'knowing how' as basic, and tries to explain away memory images in the same behaviouristic terms as 'knowing that'. But we are aware of memory images, and these are not the same as past experiences. It is much more plausible to account for habit as due to the discarding of conscious images through practice than it is to start the other way round. When driving a motor car is second nature to us, we can still recall, if we wish, the steps by which we learnt to handle the controls, and this can be done through a series of mental pictures.

of perception we catch ourselves making use of incipient images, and the shading of one into the other is a fascinating subject for further study. At all events, the holding together of past and present is a basic feature of human consciousness, and in all probability, *mutatis mutandis*, for other forms of life as well.

The same thesis may be extended to our capacities for structural integration and creativity. By the former I mean the ability to piece together various elements of our experience into an ordered whole; by the latter, the production of something new as a result of such activity. An example of structural integration is the assembling of an argument. Once the topic has been settled, the work of selection and coordination begins. Memories of books, articles and conversations are brought into play, with the result that, after a great deal of intellectual effort, the form of the argument begins to take shape. We start with a confused jumble of ideas, most of which have to be discarded as irrelevant; we end up with a systematized train of thought ready to be expressed in speech or writing. The final polish may come in the actual communication of the argument, and certain adjustments may be made to it in response to the audience or because of the exigencies of the moment. But this should not lead us, as it does Ryle, to identify the construction of an argument with its delivery; it is psychologically questionable whether even the alterations made in the course of communication are to be understood in this way; they are more plausibly accounted for as shortened forms of preparatory work. At any rate, this seems to me to be as accurate a description as I can give of what I have done in the foregoing pages. Every sentence has been thought out before it has been written on paper, and where words have been crossed out and changes made, the new pattern has in every case preceded its execution.

All structural integration may be deemed to be creative; and so it is in the sense that something new supervenes in consequence of the energy that has been expended. Even a bad argument, loosely constructed and full of logical blunders, may be highly novel! Yet we generally reserve the notion of creativity for those works of singular originality which are not simply to be explained as the rearrangement of ideas culled from several different sources, but are infused with some insight or fresh idea which is peculiarly the author's own. The dividing line between plagiarism and originality is extremely difficult to draw since the most novel production draws upon funded experience, gleaned over the course of time from interplay with other people. Nevertheless, when due allowance has been made for this, the poet, the painter, the musician, the sculptor, and artists of all kinds, if they deserve the name, exhibit a quality in their work which is inadequately described in terms of the arrangement of the materials at their disposal. Certainly there is an element of ordering even in the most impressionistic paintings and the most discordant cacophonies, for they are at least contrived and are dependent upon the assembling of colours and the juxtaposition of sounds. But these works in particular display a feature common to all art: the spontaneous creativity of the self, the welling up of some new idea, some novel expression, which has its origin not in the environment, though this provides the raw stuff on which the artist depends, but in the mysterious centre of energy which he knows to be uniquely himself. Both structural integration and creative activity direct our attention to the same source we found necessary to explain perception and memory.

The picture is beginning to take shape, and will be filled out when we come to deal with overt behaviour. But, before doing so, we should briefly notice another function of the self implicit in all the other activities we have so far considered. This is the capacity for intuition, for apprehending in a unified act the coherence of what is put together in mental construction, and for penetrating beyond the superficial appearance to deeper levels of reality. Without such a faculty neither perception, nor memory, nor intellectual integration, nor creativity would be possible, though it is so closely bound up with all of them that some may hesitate to treat it separately. What, for instance, could we mean by perception if we were to extrapolate from it the ability to discern the wholeness of whatever is selected from the given? I do not for a moment wish to pretend otherwise. Coordination and intuition are aspects of the same activity inextricably related to one another. And yet there is some virtue in focusing attention on the cognitive aspect of all these activities because this helps us to see that they are not separate faculties bound together by the self, but expressions of the self in its coordinating expenditure of energy. Moreover, the intuitive aspect of all these activities illuminates their essential character.

Some more precise definition is required to elucidate the rather vague and general statements made in the foregoing paragraph. What is meant by saying that intuition is the apprehension of coherence and the capacity to penetrate beyond the superficial appearance to deeper levels of reality? To answer the first part of the question, we may conveniently refer to A. C. Ewing's discussion of 'The "A Priori" and the Empirical',[48] where he argues that knowledge is available to us which cannot possibly depend on sense experience: 'The laws of logic must be known *a priori* or not at all. They certainly are not a matter for empirical observation, and the function of logical argument is just to give us conclusions which we have not discovered by observation.'[49] Later he continues: 'Inference is impossible unless we have the idea of logically necessary connexion between the premises from which we start in our inference and the conclusion we reach, and this idea is clearly quite different from any which could be given in sense-experience.'[50] Now Ewing is careful to guard himself against the criticism that he is appealing to the theory of innate ideas which was so vigorously repudiated by John Locke. Nor will he have it that what is innate is the faculty to form ideas. On the contrary, he holds that, while logical connexion, causation, substance and values are not perceived by the senses, they are apprehended as given in and through introspection and sense experience. The use of the phrase '*a priori*' is therefore somewhat misleading in this context. All that is required is the recognition of our capacity to apprehend what is given and yet not sensible.

48. Ewing, op. cit., pp. 26 ff.
49. Ibid., p. 28.   50. Ibid., p. 43.

Thus the concept of sight or vision is extended to something quite different: we may call it insight if we like, provided we are clear that the mode of apprehension is *sui generis*, and that is why another word altogether, such as intuition, is more appropriate. Needless to say, I am not committing myself at this stage to Ewing's catalogue of the objects of intuition, and, in particular, I should hesitate considerably about the category of substance. All I am concerned to do here is to acknowledge that we have the ability to apprehend the coherence of what we hold together in perception, memory, structural integration and creativity.

The critical reader will at once detect an ambiguity in what has been claimed, an ambiguity familiar to all students of Immanuel Kant. Is the coherence of which we speak given to us or is it the product of our own construction? Is it the form of presentation or the form of apprehension? Which are we proposing as the object of intuition? But the alternatives are not as clear-cut as this. I have not argued that the self reads into the given what is not there. My contention has been that the self is capable of holding diverse elements together in the unity of experience, but that does not mean that they are of themselves discrete. We need the concept of integration to explain both the range and selectiveness of subjective activity, but we may equally affirm that our capacity to do this without complete distortion is grounded in the interconnectedness of the data. We never see everything and see it whole. Our apprehension is at best partial and to that degree abstract, but it is apprehension none the less. Thus intuition is insight into the real connectedness of what we in varying measure hold together.

But intuition is more than the apprehension of coherence. I have also described it as penetration beyond the superficial appearances to deeper levels of reality. What does this mean? An example may make the matter plain. Imagine four people playing bridge at a seaside hotel. At a certain point in the game the one who is dummy may get up from the table and walk across to the window which commands a splendid view of the sea with the sun setting on the distant horizon. He may do no more than merely notice something that seems quite ordinary and familiar. 'Ah, a sunset!' he may say to himself, and go back to the cards. Alternatively, he may be captivated by the sight and exclaim to his companions, 'What a magnificent sunset! You simply must come over and look.' But suppose he is an artist; the sunset may make such an appeal that he may forget all about the game and rush off to find his canvas and paints, breaking up the party to the consternation of his partner and their opponents. There is another possibility still. Let us imagine that he had just lost his wife and that life had tumbled in, no longer making any sense at all, and suppose that he was so downcast and dispirited that some people in the hotel had invited him to play bridge to take his mind off his troubles. Then at the moment in question he walks across to the window and something in the view over the ocean arrests his attention. Begging to be excused, he leaves the hotel for a point on the cliff where he can be completely alone and look out to sea. There, as he stands by himself and gazes at the distant horizon, he is overwhelmed by the sense of the presence of God, and a deep peace possesses his heart. In all four cases the phenomenon is the same, but what is seen in it is entirely different.

Many people would try to account for such levels of apprehension in purely subjective terms. The sunset is simply a sunset; the variation lies in the different attitudes described. But this is to explain away a common factor in human experience all too easily. We say of someone 'He had a remarkable insight into that man's character', and we are not describing simply a subjective attitude; we mean that he really did see something in the other man which the superficial observer was almost bound to overlook. St Luke tells us that when Jesus was crucified at Golgotha 'the people stood beholding' (Luke 23:35). Presumably they were watching just another Roman execution. When it was all over, the centurion is reported to have exclaimed, 'Certainly this was a righteous man' (Luke 23:47).[51] But the apostle Paul went much further: 'God forbid that I should glory, save in the cross of our

51. Matt. 27:54 reads 'Truly this was the Son of God', but the variant makes no difference to the point at issue.

Lord Jesus Christ, by whom the world is crucified unto me, and I unto the world' (Gal. 6:14). I do not press at this point the validity of the deepest level of insight either in the case of the sunset or the Crucifixion; it is sufficient to note that the claim to intuition in depth can be carried this far. What I do urge is that all events have a dimension of depth which is open to penetration, and when anyone remains at the superficial level, we normally recognize that not only is this a defect in him, but a defect which shows that reality is to that degree opaque to him.

Finally, we need to give some account of overt behaviour, under which is subsumed all the observable activity which Ryle describes in *The Concept of Mind* and to which he tries, as we have seen, to accommodate what have commonly been assumed to be mental processes. So far the activities of the self which we have enumerated have been essentially private, inaccessible to the outside observer, known and analysed through the capacity we have for introspection. Clearly this is the case with perception, memory, structural integration and intuition as long as these are our own uncommunicated experiences; but I have argued that the same is true (*pace* Ryle) of creativity. While the latter is generally expressed in works of art open to the public view, they have their *fons et origo* in the unperceived imagining of which we know ourselves to be capable, as when we devise the plot of a novel we never write. In this case there is an incipient creation which is entirely private to us. But when all this has been allowed for, the fact remains that, as far as the unsophisticated majority is concerned, activity is chiefly channelled in observable behaviour, and, with the necessary qualifications, the same is true of those who are given to reflective pursuits. This activity may be classified under four headings: deliberate, habitual, instinctive and reactive; though the lines should not be drawn too sharply and there is obviously a considerable measure of overlap in the categories named.

Deliberate acts are characterized by a pattern of organization directed towards a chosen end. I decide that I want to go to Washington to see the Lincoln Memorial. If I am living in another city this means making arrangements to be away a sufficient length of time for the trip, packing a bag with the necessary articles for a brief stay, booking a hotel, buying a railway or plane ticket, ordering a cab to take me to the station or airport, and so on. These subsidiary actions are themselves made possible by the coordination of a series of movements, involving walking, picking up the telephone, talking. and so on, all of which are undertaken with the end in view; and, in turn, these movements are dependent on muscular coordination which is both habitual and instinctive in the senses to be explained below. In other words, for the fulfilment of any purpose, consciously conceived, there must be a whole hierarchy of coordinated activity which I both initiate and carry into effect. Here we may concede a point to Ryle, while continuing to differ from him in his denial of any activity not part of the behavioural pattern. He is surely right, as we have already noted, when he argues that the decision to do something cannot be separated from the doing of it without landing in an infinite regress of decisions or choices. Moreover, no means could be found of connecting the supposed decision with the effecting of it if the one were held to be separable from the other.[52] But this does not mean that the self cannot hold an end in view in the light of which decisions, in the sense of deliberate actions, are made; and it is extraordinary that Ryle should ignore this plain psychological fact. The only explanation for his doing so is his preoccupation with a theory and his determination to make everything fit in with it. Deliberate behaviour, then, is activity coordinated to an end in view.

The more developed a person's capacities are, the more dependent he is on habit. Indeed, life as we know it would be impossible if we had to direct every movement we make; we should get scarcely anything done. At the same time habits are formed through the constant practice of skills which initially have to be patiently acquired. We learn to drive a motor car by paying close attention to the different movements necessary for securing the desired result. First we learn what to do with the steering-

52. Ryle, op. cit., pp. 62 ff.

wheel, the gear-shift, the clutch, the brake and the accelerator, and then how to coordinate our movements in relation to all of them. When we take our driving test we may still have to concentrate on certain aspects of the operation which we have not yet mastered with complete confidence, but afterwards we handle the car without thinking about the details of what we are doing. Habit is, as it were, the 'shorthand' performance of purposive activity.

The third classification has been described as instinctive, the word being chosen to denote that kind of behaviour which has never been the subject of conscious design, and yet can be thought of only as coordinated towards a certain end. The digestive process is a good example. We have never been conscious of the detailed functioning of the intestinal organs, which are open to inspection by the surgeon, but completely hidden from the patient and entirely beyond his control. Again, when we cut a finger, we do not decide that the wound shall heal; still less do we summon up the process of tissue-building or become conscious, even if we pay the closest attention, of the physiological functioning which restores the finger to health. Such coordinated activity may be paralleled in the animal kingdom, illustrated in the impressive examples, such as those of the diadem spider and the cuckoo, adduced by C. E. Raven in the second series of his Gifford Lectures;[53] and it is reflected in the botanical field as well.

At this point the question may well be asked whether we have not come back full circle to the mind-body problem in our talk of physiological processes ordered towards a certain end. This is a conclusion I wish to resist, on the ground that it is more fruitful to consider the self without remainder as an organizing centre of energy, partly conscious and partly unconscious, what we call the body being its unconscious expression. The elucidation of this highly problematical concept depends to a large extent on the view we take of the nature of the organic in general. The only point I wish to make here is that physiological functioning is an

53. C. E. Raven, *Natural Religion and Christian Theology* (Cambridge, The University Press, 1953), Vol. II, pp. 135-9.

inalienable part of the coordinating activity of the self. Amputate a limb, and it becomes something different, no longer my arm or my leg, but an object which has to be accounted for in terms of itself.

Fourth, all behaviour is to some extent reactive; that is to say, nothing takes place in a vacuum; everything is, in varying degrees, conditioned by its environment, and this is all the more plain if the contention to be advanced later can be sustained: that the whole universe is most appropriately described in terms of centres of energy, acting and reacting on one another. When I do anything, such as moving the book on the table in front of me, I meet with a measure of resistance to which my own output of energy has to be adjusted; and this interplay of forces is such a universal feature of human experience that we take it for granted, scarcely bothering to note it at all except in moments of philosophical reflection. Such reactive output of energy is itself coordinated with instinctive, habitual and deliberate behaviour, which in all its forms displays the same pattern of organization as the private activities of perception, remembering, structural integration and creativity. But we are still left with the bewildering mystery of the ego, the coordinating centre, the well-spring of all human vitality. Here is the real enigma.[54]

One thing appears to be clear. We cannot be content with any kind of Cartesian solution. Not only is the dichotomy of mind and body the wrong way of stating the case, since the body is to be conceived as the way in which the self is actively expressed, but the formula, '*Cogito ergo sum*', is needlessly restrictive and excessively intellectualist. John Macmurray seems to be nearer the

54. No mention has been made in this analysis of the psychological categories of the subconscious and the unconscious. That is because I believe the fourfold classification of behaviour as deliberate, habitual, instinctive and reactive to be a more accurate way of describing the empirical data and less open to the charge of confusing the issue with unnecessary mythology. This does not mean that the psychologist, who uses these categories for the explanation of certain kinds of behaviour, is not contributing to our knowledge of human motivation. Indeed, it is another way of emphasizing the metaphysical mystery of the self.

truth when he contends that the fundamental fact about the self is not that it thinks, but that it acts.[55] And this has virtually been the conclusion to which our survey of the deliverances of introspection has led us. Nevertheless, analysing the activities of the self simply makes us increasingly aware of the deepening mystery of what we are trying to understand. We can say a good deal about these activities, both private and public, and we have seen reason to believe that the former are more fundamental than the latter; but the coordinating centre, the essential self, remains sheer mystery, the depth of what we encounter as we turn in upon ourselves. We can only declare that it exists, irreducible to anything but itself in its individuality. Further than that we cannot go, at least by the way of introspection.

55. John Macmurray, *The Self as Agent* (London, Faber, 1957). Cf. Stuart Hampshire, *Thought and Action* (London, Chatto & Windus, 1959).

CHAPTER THREE

THE HUMAN ENVIRONMENT

In the last chapter we saw some of the difficulties which arise when the attempt is made to understand the self in terms of the mind-body relationship. The Cartesian dichotomy, which provides the framework of reference, posits two entities irreconcilable with one another. That is why we undertook to explore the self as a unity given from the start, and, by turning inwards upon our own experience, we reached the conclusion that the self is an organizing centre of activity, profoundly mysterious, and yet capable of being detected through its dynamic expressions. At the same time the account was obviously far from complete in that, for the purpose of the discussion, the self was artificially separated from its environment. We cannot get the picture in perspective without considering the world of other selves and living creatures, as well as organic and inorganic matter, which is our matrix and in rapport with which we have our being.

Unless we are very careful, we shall find ourselves caught once more in the meshes of the Cartesian dilemma. For the question is almost instinctively framed in such a way as to suggest that mind is set over against matter: an extension of the mind-body dualism to the whole universe, and exemplified in the idealist-realist controversy. If the argument of the previous chapter was along the right lines, then this is the magnification of a fundamental error, though it is one that has dominated the history of Western philosophy for more than three hundred years, and has become so much part and parcel of our thinking that it is very difficult to discard it in the interests of a new perspective.

My conviction is that this may be achieved by centring our attention on biology rather than on physics, taking our cue from what has been called the philosophy of organism. There is nothing very novel about this. A rough family tree may be traced from Aristotle, through Leibniz, Lotze, Ward, Stout, and down to the metaphysical system of Alfred North Whitehead and his highly original modern interpreter, Charles Hartshorne. I do not mean to suggest that the progeny would always recognize their parents, at any rate to the extent of invariably agreeing with them! The names mentioned are chosen to illustrate an approach to philosophical problems which is outside the main stream of the mind-matter, idealist-realist controversy, and takes with full seriousness the idea of centres of organized energy. These thinkers have been noted for the construction of massive metaphysical systems, which, because of their range and comprehensiveness, have not surprisingly failed to convince the critically minded. Such a bold intellectual adventure as Whitehead's *Process and Reality*, no less than Leibniz's *Monadology*, is speculative to the point of being incredible, especially to those steeped in the empirical tradition. One of the most widely held convictions today is that it is impossible in the nature of the case to construct a comprehensive metaphysical system, though it is refreshing to turn from some of the trivialities of linguistic analysis to the magnificent sweep of Whitehead's thought. At all events, my purpose is much more modest. Taking the general standpoint of those who might, though in some cases anachronistically, be called the philosophers of organism, I want to move outwards from the self and try to see, on an empirical basis, what can be learnt about man's environment. This is not to be understood as implying a *petitio principii*. I have merely indicated in advance the broad conclusion to which I believe such a procedure leads.

The previous chapter ended with the definition of the self as an organizing centre of activity, defying ultimate description, but inescapably open to critical introspection. Some have toyed with the idea that it is theoretically possible to stop there and maintain that the self is the universe, everything else originating in its imagination. The difficulty of sustaining this position is obvious in view of the exigencies of practical living. The theory can only be entertained as long as unexpressed thought is held to take precedence over all other activity, and indeed to engulf it, which is clearly not the case. When Dr Samuel Johnson claimed to have refuted Berkeleyan idealism by kicking a stone, he may not have answered Berkeley in his belief that for anything to exist it has to be perceived or even that all sensations are private to the percipient, but he did indicate the way in which he for his part was aware of the existence of an environment independent of himself; the resistance of the stone to his foot was but an example of the resistance everyone encounters in all forms of self-initiated activity.[1]

The importance of Dr Johnson's impatient experiment was his appeal to the sense of touch rather than to that of sight. If he had claimed to refute Berkeley because he had seen the stone, what he said would not have been very significant; for vision is notoriously deceptive; the stone might simply have been an hallucination. But in appealing to touch, he was on stronger ground because he selected an obvious example of something fundamental to human experience: the awareness of meeting resistance which originates in our environment and for which we cannot conceivably hold ourselves responsible. If anyone is inclined to reply that this is still a private sensation beyond which we are not entitled to argue, we need not dispute the contention that it is private, but we shall have to insist that the sensation is one of meeting with resistance, which by definition has its origin apart from us. If we try to walk through a brick wall, we cannot do it because there is something that stops us. Practical experience sets the bounds of theory.

John Macmurray is, therefore, undoubtedly right when he claims that empirical philosophers have often been misled by assuming that sight is fundamental to sense perception and the principal clue to the nature of the external world.[2] As I shall argue in more detail later, vision, though biologically useful and aesthetically satisfying, is often a stumbling-block to genuine

1. Cf. H. F. Hallett, 'Dr Johnson's Refutation of Bishop Berkeley', *Mind*, Vol. LVI (April 1947), pp. 132-47.
2. John Macmurray, *The Self as Agent*, pp. 111-13.

knowledge, suggesting that reality has always to be pictured if it is to be apprehended. Macmurray holds that touch is basic to sense experience, and that vision in depth simply gives us a clue to what we would feel if we were in a position to handle the objects in question. However that may be, the fact remains that touch does make us aware of resistance which prescribes our movements and curbs our initiative.

This resistance is first encountered in infancy as a limited field of pressures exerted upon us by the people and things in our environment. Gradually, with the growth of our powers and the increasing range of our activities, we become conscious of a larger world to which we have to adjust and which simply cannot be moulded to our own will. Watch a small child trying to fit a square peg into a series of round holes. Sooner or later he is likely to discover that he cannot do it and burst into tears in sheer frustration. This is a step in the process of learning that his surroundings are not completely tractable to his purposes. And at a very early age the senses of sight, sound and smell begin to be integrated with touch to give us a workable knowledge of the way in which to adapt to the exigencies of our circumstances. We adjust more easily to things than to persons because the latter are far less stable and predictable in their behaviour.

But it is with the world of persons that we may profitably start from the metaphysical point of view. The scientist naturally begins from the other end—with the inorganic, which is more amenable to controlled experiment and classification, as well as being the matrix of all forms of life. Philosophical inquiry, on the other hand, being directed towards understanding the essential nature of things, proceeds from the centre outwards: from self-awareness to other persons, to the animal kingdom in its developed and primitive forms, and so to the organic and finally the inorganic realms.

The objection may be raised that such a procedure is untenable in view of modern developments in astro-physics. Has not the Copernican revolution been carried beyond any bounds that the pioneers could have conceived, and have not cosmologists, compelled to measure distances in light years, rendered ridiculous any claim to understand the universe in terms of man, a transitory phenomenon on a speck of astral dust? It is easy to become mesmerized by questions like these and to lose our sense of proportion. After all, it is man who puts the questions and in reference to whom the problems arise. An objective standpoint from which the human perspective has been eliminated is in the nature of the case impossible. This is the main theme of Michael Polanyi's trenchant criticism of the dogma of scientific objectivity. 'We must inevitably see the universe', he says, 'from a centre lying within ourselves and speak about it in terms of a human language shaped by the exigencies of human intercourse. Any attempt rigorously to eliminate our human perspective from our picture of the world must lead to absurdity.'[3] The fact is that, so far as we know, man is the only creature in the universe capable of asking ultimate questions, and we must give up all attempts to apprehend anything, even about cosmology, unless we are prepared to accord unique significance to the human inquirer. In principle, the difficulties are by no means new. The Hebrew prophet of the Babylonian exile declared that 'the nations are as a drop of a bucket, and are counted as the small dust of the balance: behold, he taketh up the isles as a very little thing' (Isa. 40:15). And the Psalmist exclaimed, 'When I consider thy heavens, the work of thy fingers, the moon and the stars, which thou hast ordained; what is man, that thou art mindful of him? And the son of man, that thou visitest him?' (Ps. 8:3-4) But he answered his own question: 'For thou hast made him a little lower than the angels, and hast crowned him with glory and honour. Thou madest him to have dominion over the works of thy hands; thou hast put all things under his feet' (Ps. 8:5-6). However vast the universe, it is man who knows it to be so, and it is at least possible that in him is the clue to what he claims to apprehend.

We start, then, with ourselves, and move outwards to the environment with which we are surrounded, beginning with other

3. Michael Polanyi, *Personal Knowledge* (London, Routledge & Kegan Paul, 1958), p. 3.

people who confront us as organized centres of conscious life similar to our own. We find them resistant to us not primarily through physical obstruction, but through the exercise of deliberate purpose, the general nature of which we can comprehend because we know that our own activities are likewise directed towards the achievement of certain ends. The whole of our environment, organic and inorganic, is at different levels and in varying measure resistant to our designs, but it is in inter-personal encounter that we meet our equals. Of course, there are wide differences between individuals in intellectual capacity, resourcefulness, cunning and physical strength. But these are differences within the same field of reference. Men are *matched* with one another in their ability to pursue a preconceived purpose, and it is this planned activity which we meet as resistance in the execution of our designs. The burglar faces physical opposition on the part of the watchdog, who is governed by a capacity to respond to his movements as long as he is perceived through the canine senses. The dog's master is an opponent of an entirely different calibre. He is able to devise schemes to counteract anything a *hypothetical* night prowler might attempt to do; he can arrange a complicated system of bolts, bars and alarm bells, and, if he is so minded to take such precautions, he can set all kinds of traps for the unfortunate housebreaker.

This is not simply to be accounted as an extension of the animal powers of cunning and anticipation; it is the supervention of conscious purpose upon those instinctive abilities which human beings share with other forms of life. Consider a game of chess. A dog's reaction to my arrangement of pieces on the board could only be to knock them over; but in the case of a human opponent, I have to reckon with a calculated series of manœuvres, adapted at every stage to whatever I do. If I am to beat him, I have to do so by anticipating his thoughts.

It is no part of my concern to exaggerate the differences between human beings and animals. On the contrary, I hold very strongly to the continuity of powers through evolutionary development. But the emergence of the novel can hardly be gain-

said. Man is an intelligent animal, but more. A dog is an organization of cells, but more. A living cell consists of chemical com-
ponents, but more. The lines of demarcation are notoriously difficult
to draw in the process of biological evolution, and the emergence
of the novel, just because there is no complete discontinuity with
the past, is hard to detect until it is firmly established in some
advanced form. From the objective standpoint of the scientific
observer, the anthropoid ape and primitive man are not far apart;
and even human beings who are our contemporaries can sink to
the animal level, illustrated in the description of the commander
of the infamous Nazi concentration camp as 'the beast of Belsen'.
But when full allowance has been made for the element of similarity, we know that there is a distinction of a radical kind between
the sort of resistance we encounter from an animal and what we
anticipate from a man.

It is at this point that the behaviourist theory is seen to be hope-
lessly wide of the mark. The distinctive feature of human resistance in personal encounter is not observable conduct, but hidden
thinking to which we are given clues by means of another's overt
activities, though it is primarily accessible through imagination.
On what grounds is such a use of the imagination to be justified?
It can only be because I know directly what it is to be myself and
to plan a certain course of action. Therefore, by projection, I can
begin to understand another person's thoughts and anticipate
what he will do. The theoretical objection that I merely observe
his conduct and cannot possibly know anything else about him,
not even that he bears any similarity to myself, is implausible to
the point of being silly.[4] It can be advanced only on the assumption that we know nothing save discrete phenomena directly
presented to the senses. But we are not aware of ourselves in this

4. Even John Wisdom, who is so impressed by the logical difficulty of the
claim to know other minds, concludes that we do in fact sometimes know what
is in the mind of another: see *Other Minds* (Oxford, Blackwell, 1952), p. 235.
And Ayer, as we have noted in the previous chapter, has recently argued for
the reinstatement of the argument from analogy: see *The Concept of a Person*,
pp. 104-11. Cf. also Stuart Hampshire, 'The Analogy of Feeling', *Mind*, Vol.
LXI (January 1952), pp. 1-12.

way, and, and, as we have already argued, our self-knowledge is direct and immediate in a fashion nothing else is. To give an entirely different account of other human beings when we observe them behaving in the same way as we are conscious of doing is to stretch the bounds of credulity beyond reason.

The behaviourist will, of course, reply that I have been unfair and that he does not draw a distinction between the observer and those whom he observes. All alike are to be accounted for in terms of their behaviour. He simply interprets the self in the light of his account of other people. My reply is that this is the wrong way round, and leads to the neglect of the most obvious psychological facts, open to anyone who gives himself to introspection. So far from behaviourism offering a plausible account of the self in the light of other human beings, it ignores the plain truth about other human beings by failing to start with a rigorous scrutiny of the self.

We are, then, aware of a peculiar kind of resistance in our encounter with other people, a resistance which is imaginatively interpretable in the light of our own conscious processes. We know what we are up against in so far as we know ourselves. But that is not the whole story. While in broad principle we can understand what it is to be another person, we have no direct access to him in his individuality. Observation and imagination carry us as far as we can go, but that is not a very long way. H. D. Lewis is surely right in criticizing the I-Thou terminology which has been much in vogue in recent years, because it suggests that there is an unmediated, direct awareness of other persons in our encounter with them.[5] We are faced with an impenetrable barrier if we try to understand another human being in his essential individuality. Just because he is not reducible to observable behaviour and because he is only imaginable after analogy with ourselves, he is bound to be inaccessible to complete analysis. For the distinctive characteristic of our own self-aware-

5. H. D. Lewis, 'God and Mystery' in *Prospect for Metaphysics* (London, Allen & Unwin, 1961), pp. 208-17. Cf. also his discussion of 'Encounter and Immediacy' in *Our Experience of God* (London, Allen & Unwin, 1959), pp. 280-95.

ness, in the light of which we can imaginatively conceive other people, is the privacy of what we know. The successes of psychologists should not mislead us. It is true that a great deal can be learnt from observable behaviour, including what a patient says about himself and his attitudes, and this may not be understood by the person in question. But that does not mean that everything is known about him in this way. What he does not reveal is just inaccessible. Nobody can get inside another person and experience his feelings and think his thoughts. Nobody knows what it is to be someone else subjectively.

Herein lies a major handicap for psychology, and to a lesser extent for all the social sciences. Their exponents properly follow the scientific method of experiment and classification, and therefore look for similarities in what they observe. But this becomes an increasingly unsatisfactory approach as we ascend the biological scale of evolution. Even at the molecular level in physics, distinctions have to be drawn about the behaviour of electrons, and laws can be formulated only on a statistical basis. But for practical purposes there is sufficient similarity between objects at the inorganic and organic levels to make classification serviceable. Nobody bothers to talk about the individuality of an acorn or an oak leaf even though they are separable from all other acorns or oak leaves; their differences are unimportant for the naturalist. Individuality becomes more marked in the animal kingdom, particularly in its higher forms. Fido is not replaceable by Jock as a household pet with no sense of loss. In so far as he is Fido, he is not just a dog. But with the interior life of human beings we reach a stage of individuality at which classification becomes positively misleading except at a level of admitted generalization. And this is what makes the deliverances of some psychologists and sociologists so problematic. They are inclined to forget or ignore the limitations placed upon their own research in comparison with their colleagues in other scientific fields.[6]

6. We may go even further. The unwillingness of many modern psychologists and sociologists to admit the limitations of their disciplines is due not merely to an over-facile attitude to the subject-matter of their investigations.

We meet, then, in our encounter with other human beings, an increasing number of unique centres of resistance, impinging upon us and requiring adjustment on our part in proportion to the closeness and frequency with which we come into contact with them. This experience is a day-to-day occurrence as far as the members of our families, our friends, and our business and professional associates are concerned. In widening circles the same is true of a host of other people with whom we have but slight and passing acquaintance. They all resist us, not in the sense of deliberately opposing our plans, though this is sometimes the case, but in the sense of pursuing their own objectives with which we have to come to terms in view of the fact that, far from being isolated individuals, we live together in society. The problems of community arise from this bewildering proliferation of independent and often conflicting purposes, which impatient politicians and administrators would sometimes like to ignore. The question before us today is whether man's developed individuality, expressed in nationalism and the demand for social and economic advancement, is so explosive as to lead to the total disintegration of the human race and the destruction of its earthly habitation. Or is there a cohesive, reconciling centre of activity at the heart of the universe which will bring the evolutionary process to a climax? This will concern us later. For the moment I am simply interested in describing the human situation for what it is in itself: a vast complex of unique, interacting centres of energy, posing the possibility of inevitable and catastrophic conflict.

As I have already indicated, man's encounter with dynamic resistance is by no means restricted to his relationship with other human beings. He is no less aware of it in the case of animals, even

---

The question of their own *power* is often at issue. The demand that human beings should be subject to control in the same way that scientists in other fields seek to subdue material things and make technological use of them is one of the most disturbing aspects of the growing influence of psychologists and sociologists in the contemporary world. To insist that men should be treated as things is not just a mistake; it is demonic.

though, generally speaking, they are incapable of thwarting his purpose if he is sufficiently determined. All the same, their resistance can be formidable, as many a burglar has discovered to his cost. When a dog bars the entrance to a house, the intruder is faced with an obstacle of an entirely different order from the window he has so painstakingly forced: one that can respond to his movements and manœuvre in defence. Two courses of action are open to him: he can try to overpower the dog by sheer brute strength or to outwit the animal by one means or another. Whichever he chooses to do, he will be in no doubt about there being something actively resisting his purpose.

It is commonly said that what differentiates human beings from animals is that the former are capable of abstract thought whereas the latter function through instinct. But this is just a way of stating the limits of our knowledge and indicating the ultimate mystery with which we are confronted. If we find ourselves baffled by our inability to comprehend ourselves, and can understand other people only by analogy from our imperfect insight into our own natures, how much more difficult is it to conceive what an animal really is from within! From our observation of its behaviour and from our experience of actual encounter, we are none the less driven to admit that it displays the characteristics of spontaneous energy, however limited in range, that we find to be basic to ourselves and all other human beings.

But we may go further. Man's home is a planet teeming with life. While this is a statement of the obvious, many people find it hard to adjust their thinking to the facts. So steeped have we become in nineteenth-century materialism that we tend to take for granted that everything in our environment has to be explained in terms of lifeless, inert stuff. In spite of the abandonment of this concept on the part of physicists and the increasing problems involved in defining the inorganic, many scientists, as well as ordinary laymen, persist in talking of the organic world as if it were an awkward phenomenon to be explained away as something else rather than to be taken for what it clearly is. This is to resort to the strange device of reducing the relatively known to the relatively unknown. An example of such an approach is found in an article by J. J. C. Smart in which he declares, 'It looks today as though the ultimate laws of nature are those of physics. The laws of chemistry are in principle explicable in terms of the quantum theory of the chemical bond, though to be sure it would be optimistic to carry out such explanations in detail in any but the simplest cases. In biology, I should be prepared to argue, there are no true laws at all. There are generalizations of natural history and explanations of these natural history generalizations in terms of physics and chemistry . . . much as in radio engineering the study of wiring diagrams stands to the theory of electricity.'[7] While this quotation represents a widely held view, it is surely as far from the truth as anything can be. The objection to it is not merely that the higher and more complex is said to be explained in terms of the lower and simpler: an objection which was relevant from the standpoint of biology *vis-à-vis* nineteenth-century materialism; the real difficulty is the proposal to reduce the known to the unknown. As long as the physicist was confident about the nature of matter, it was theoretically possible to regard this as the substratum on which the superstructure of living organisms could be erected. Undermine the foundations, and what happens to the superstructure? I hasten to add that I do not intend to imply that the physicist thinks he is not investigating anything! All I am saying is that the inherent nature of the inorganic is found to be profoundly elusive, and it is much more plausible to suggest that we shall begin to understand the nature of the inorganic in the light of the organic, the unknown in the light of the known, rather than vice versa.

At any rate there are not wanting voices amongst the scientists, and particularly amongst those given to philosophical reflection, who reject out of hand any explanation of the multitudinous forms of life inhabiting our planet in terms of physical and chemical processes alone. Mention has only to be made of Michael Polanyi and Pierre Teilhard de Chardin, both of whom from somewhat different standpoints argue for an internal principle of

7. J. J. C. Smart, 'Colours', *Philosophy*, Vol. XXXVI (April-July 1961), p. 130.

organization in the whole process of evolution as well as in every living thing. After criticizing the neo-Darwinian theory of successive, accidental hereditary changes leading to better equipped variants, Polanyi states his own view as follows: 'I shall regard living beings as instances of morphological types and of operational principles subordinated to a centre of individuality and shall affirm at the same time that no types, no operational principles and no individualities can ever be defined in terms of physics and chemistry.'[8] At the same time he acknowledges that physical and chemical conditions, themselves random or accidental, must be such as to provide an opportunity for life to originate. His conclusion is that 'evolution, like life itself, will then be said to have been *originated* by the *action* of an ordering principle, an action *released* by random fluctuations and *sustained* by fortunate environmental conditions.'[9] Teilhard de Chardin sees the history of the earth as a process of what he calls 'guided groping', the upward urge of everything to achieve higher forms of life. He holds that this has resulted in innumerable dead-ends like the extinct reptilian branch of dinosaurs, pterosaurs, ichthyosaurs and many other such monsters, or the whole of the insect world, which he considers to have become stereotyped and incapable of further development through precision of behaviour, epitomized in the habits of ants and bees.[10] He believes that the goal of the entire process is the appearance of man and his spiritual maturity in community with his fellows.

Of course, a great many biologists would reject this approach as a resurgence of vitalism to be dismissed because the theoretical presuppositions are not amenable to scientific verification.[11] But it is questionable whether the alternative theory of natural selection has any more claim to be empirically founded.[12] The fact is

8. Polanyi, op. cit., p. 383.   9. Ibid., p. 384.

10. Pierre Teilhard de Chardin, *The Phenomenon of Man* (London, Collins, 1959), particularly pp. 153-5.

11. Cf. T. A. Goudge, *The Ascent of Life* (London, Allen & Unwin, 1961), pp. 81 f.

12. Cf. Goudge's admission that the process of natural selection cannot be observed; ibid., p. 96.

that perception, as we shall see later, implies going beyond the activity of sensing and cannot be reduced without remainder to it; and it is confusion on this point, particularly in the implicit rejection of any metaphysical account of perception, that vitiates many expositions of neo-Darwinianism. In any case, we may ask, is 'natural selection' an explanatory principle at all? We may accept it as a *description* of the way in which life has evolved, but it requires supplementing with some such theory as vitalism if any metaphysical explanation of the process is to be given. Vitalism and natural selection are not really alternatives on the same level; the one belongs to metaphysics and the other to scientific description. However that may be, it is not germane to my immediate purpose to discuss any of these views in detail nor to become involved at this stage in their ultimate implications. Sufficient for the moment is to note that some biologists are convinced that, whatever random characteristics may mark the pathway of evolution, there is some kind of ordering principle in every living thing, and it is difficult to resist the conclusion that, if they are right, this is analogous to the dynamic centre of activity which we have found to be essential for the understanding of human beings.

Once this has been granted, we are able to give an account of our environment, both organic and inorganic, which accords much more closely with our experience than the theory that life is a peculiar phenomenon that has occurred on an essentially lifeless planet. If living organisms are differentiated centres of energy, does it not make sense to interpret the entire universe on the same principle? When we pause to reflect, we are no less aware of resistance in what we normally call our natural environment than we are in our encounter with human beings and animals. The degree of active resistance is doubtless very much less, but that does not entitle us to suppose it is non-existent. On the contrary, when the explorer fights his way through the tangled undergrowth of the jungle, the trees, the thickets, the foliage and the creepers are not just there until the erosions of the elements wear them down or they are destroyed by some external agency; they are in a constant state of change, of growth and decay, originating from their own internal nature. They constitute an active obstacle, though their response to environmental factors is much more stereotyped and far slower than even the more primitive animal organisms. That is why we are inclined to ignore the essential aspect of similarity. The perspective is changed once we view the processes of sustenance and growth through the medium of an accelerated moving picture. The subject has been dealt with at length by Karl Heim who argues that the growth of flowers seen through the time lens is reminiscent of the respiratory movements of human beings, adding: 'If we film with the same chronological foreshortening a creeper climbing up a wall and then over on to a pole into which it can sink its roots, we cannot resist the impression that this plant is moving like a man who stretches out his arms into the void, trembling, seeking and groping, and then, when he has at last found the hold he so intensely longs for, grasps it for all he is worth, as a drowning man grasps a rescuing plank and lies clinging to it with immense relief.'[13]

Some people will regard the whole thesis I have propounded as an extravagant example of the pathetic fallacy. Is it not a serious mistake to read our own experiences into animal and plant life, whatever qualifications we find it necessary to make? There is some substance to the objection; for it is possible to exaggerate and indulge in flights of fancy. But, provided we are careful to stick to the data of experience, appealing to the phenomena as they present themselves to us, it is difficult to avoid a dynamic account of the whole organic realm. Nevertheless, the organizing principle, the dynamic centre of energy as we have called it, is almost completely opaque to us. We can declare it to be there; we cannot experience it for what it is. Although the Self is an irreducible 'that', we have direct acquaintance with it through introspection; but we have no such immediate acquaintance with other selves, as we have already seen, and still less with animals and plants. If Teilhard de Chardin is right in suggesting that there

13. Karl Heim, *Christian Faith and Natural Science* (London, SCM Press, 1953), pp. 88 f.

is a 'within' and a 'without' of everything,[14] then the 'within' becomes progressively more hidden the further we get from close comparison with our own experience. 'We cannot', says Heim, 'understand the language of flowers or crystals and we cannot interpret the inner world which perhaps lies hidden behind it, even though we may endeavour with poetic imagination to project our human inner world into these entirely alien beings.'[15] All the same, the observational data justify us in predicating an inner principle of organization animating and bringing to fulfilment every individual centre of organic life. The blade of grass under my feet, the rose-bush I prune, the tree I lop, all respond to me in a very limited way, but after a fashion analogous to the resistance I encounter from the most intelligent human beings.

This brings us to the most primitive and all-pervasive substratum of existence—what has traditionally been called 'matter'. Here individuality is most difficult to detect. Indeed, some argue that it is impossible to distinguish between one thing and another except for purely practical purposes,[16] though it is hard to see how such a radical division can be drawn between the organic and inorganic worlds without landing in a dualism which the theory of evolution in particular seems to preclude. Nevertheless, individuality at the suborganic level is far from easy to pin down. The early Greek atomists believed that the universe consisted of minute particles having solidity and extension, albeit exceedingly small. Out of these tiny bricks everything was thought to be constructed, their differentiae being due to the multitudinous variety of ways in which the basic constituents were related to one another. These atomic particles were held to be in a constant state of movement and perpetually colliding with one another, thus producing the phenomenon of change. How this movement originated was left unexplained by Leucippus and Democritus,

14 Teilhard de Chardin, op. cit., *passim*; cf. Karl Heim, op. cit., p. 91.

15. Ibid., p. 97. Cf. Charles Hartshorne, 'The Social Structure of the Experience', *Philosophy*, Vol. XXXVI (April-July 1961), p. 102.

16. Cf. W. R. Sorley, *Moral Values and the Idea of God* (Cambridge, The University Press, 1930), pp. 220, 226.

though the later Epicureans maintained that all atoms moved downwards in virtue of their weight: a sort of primitive gravitation theory.[17] Centuries later, the image of colliding atoms was wedded to Newton's theory of magnetic forces, and this provided the background for the development of a thorough-going materialist philosophy.

All this has changed with the abandonment of the notion of the atomic brick and the substitution of dynamic categories for talking about the ultimate constituents of the physical world. No longer do physicists claim to know what matter is. They merely discuss its behaviour in terms of differential equations, and when symbolic pictures like particles and waves are pressed into use to reduce the formulae to common-sense language, they turn out to be grossly misleading. Take, for instance, what is called the principle of complementarity, enunciated by Niels Bohr as a result of experiments with the transmission and diffraction of light. He showed that it was impossible to determine both the position and momentum of an 'atomic object'.[18] Light appears to have both particle and wave-like characteristics, and yet it cannot be conceived in terms of one or the other. As Lord Cherwell once said, the principle of complementarity 'seems a confession of failure rather than an explanation.'[19] The fact is that, while a great deal is known about molecular behaviour and while scientists like David Bohm have speculated on possible future discoveries in sub-molecular structure,[20] the nature of what matter is in itself proves wholly elusive. Its behaviour can be described and pre-

17. Cf. F. C. Copleston, *A History of Philosophy* (London, Burns & Oates, 1946), Vol. I, p. 73.

18. Cf. Philipp Frank, *Philosophy of Science* (Englewood Cliffs, N.J., Prentice-Hall, 1957), pp. 207 ff.

19. See Viscount Samuel, *Essay in Physics* (Oxford, Blackwell, 1951), p. 43. For further discussion of his views, see 'A Criticism of Present-Day Metaphysics', *Philosophy*, Vol. XXVII (January 1952), pp. 51-7; and *A Threefold Cord. Philosophy, Science, Religion, A Discussion Between Viscount Samuel and Professor Herbert Dingle* (London, Allen & Unwin, 1961).

20. David Bohm, *Causality and Chance in Modern Physics* (London, Routledge & Kegan Paul, 1957), pp. 137-40.

dicted, but what it actually is remains hidden, apparently as un-knowable as Kant's thing-in-itself.

Viscount Samuel has wrestled with this problem in his *Essay in Physics*, where he suggests that energy is the ultimate constituent of what we call matter. This energy may be quiescent or active, and in one state or the other is a physical continuum. Thus the idea of an ether, which was at one time supposed to be the medium through which atoms acted and reacted on one another, is replaced by the concept of energy, constantly being quickened to activity from a quiescent state by contiguous energy already active and becoming quiescent. Viscount Samuel argues that this account of physical interaction gets rid of the idea of the constant creation of matter[21] and of action at a distance which many scientists have declared to be impossible.[22]

Now this discussion is important in so far as it makes quite explicit the radical change that has taken place in the realm of physics during the course of this century and unambiguous-ly declares that henceforth matter, like everything else in the universe, has to be regarded in terms of energy. Nevertheless, there is one particular difficulty in the thesis which Viscount Samuel recognizes himself. If quiescent energy is brought into a state of activity by that which is already active, how did the process ever get started? This is not simply the ultimate mystery of the existence of everything, as Lord Samuel suggests;[23] it is a peculiar difficulty of the theory in question. For, granted the existence of energy, why should it be thought that its quiescent state is altered by active energy which, according to the theory, must surely have been itself quiescent in order to become active? This merely adds to the mystery of existence without explaining anything.

But, leaving this on one side, no one should be deluded into thinking that Viscount Samuel, or anyone else, has solved the metaphysical mystery of matter by redefining it as energy, be-

21. As in Fred Hoyle, *The Nature of the Universe* (Oxford, Blackwell, 1960), p. 112. On this, cf. Viscount Samuel, op. cit., pp. 63 f.

22. Ibid., pp. 37 f.   23. Ibid., p. 52.

cause to speak of matter in these terms invites the question with which we have become increasingly familiar—'Energy of what?' Surely the word, though grammatically a noun, is logically a verbal form; it is in the category of doing, seeing, etc. We can speak of something energizing something else when we are speaking of a relation of interaction, but the activity itself presupposes a subject. Energy may describe the characteristic behaviour of things, but what 'things' are is left entirely unexplained. It is the equivalent of calling the constituents of reality X, X being unknown.[24] In the end, Viscount Samuel's attempt to give objective status to the findings of modern physics proves elusive, as the appended letter of Albert Einstein makes plain.[25]

Thus, wherever we turn, we encounter multitudinous expressions of energy resistant in varying degree to our own activities. In the case of the primitive and all-pervasive substratum of matter, we find it much more difficult to discriminate between individual entities than at any other level and we are far less aware of any 'come-back'. Indeed, on first impressions we take it for granted that matter is completely inert and passive in relation to us. It is only when we reflect on the phenomenon of resistance in the light of modern physical theories of atomic structure that we begin to see the kinship of the inorganic to the organic. Instead of drawing a clear-cut, radical distinction between mind and matter or the living and the inanimate, we are likely to be much nearer the truth in conceiving the universe as a hierarchy of energy, with individuation becoming increasingly marked the higher in the scale we go.

Clearly this raises the problem of what is meant by a centre of energy or activity, and how we are to understand the principle of individuation. One way of dealing with the question is to return to the concept of substance as it was developed in classical philosophy from Aristotle onwards, particularly by St Thomas

24. As Karl Heim concluded: 'Energy itself, which calls forth these manifestations and produces these mobile fields of force, has become no less invisible and unobjectifiable than the Ego or the Spirit.' *God Transcendent*, p. 41.

25. Samuel, op. cit., pp. 137 ff.

Aquinas and the medieval scholastics. Apart from those Catholic scholars who have sought to reinterpret the basic teaching of St Thomas against the background of the contemporary philosophical climate, the idea has for a long time been at a discount, simply regarded as a piece of metaphysical lumber with which we can profitably dispense. Hume has been the accepted authority, with modern empiricists building on the sceptical foundation which he laid down. But, in doing so, like their Scottish mentor, they have entirely failed to account for the continuity of anything, and we have already seen the difficulties inherent in any view which reduces the self to a bundle of impressions without anything or anyone on which such impressions are made. Why, then, reject the idea of substance? Are we not bound to return to this or something very like it to make sense of our experience?

Much water has flowed beneath the bridge since the medieval period, and we have to recognize that the influence of John Locke, not St Thomas Aquinas, has been the major factor in the development of the empirical tradition. When modern philosophers reject the notion of substance, they are generally thinking of the theory associated with the father of British empiricism, who regarded substance as having solidity and extension, and as the physical substratum characterized by the primary qualities. This has been the main target of criticism. The difficulty of separating primary and secondary qualities is notorious, and, after Hume, many believed there was no need to posit an unknowable basis for sensory experience: physical objects are just what they appear to be. But whatever initial plausibility Locke's theory may have had was dealt a death blow when modern physics abandoned the imagery of the solid, self-sustaining, atomic brick as the ultimate constituent of matter. How, then, could substance be conceived? The new language of electron, nucleus, proton and neutron, when understood pictorially, was seen to be inadequate to the point of being misleading, and such words, as we have seen, came to be used as symbols for the unknown which could only be described in terms of its observed effects. This, in turn, led to the suggestion that the universe basically consists of 'point-events': a confession of metaphysical bankruptcy, since a point is a mathematical abstraction and an event the Cheshire cat's grin without the cat unless it is an expression of something. No wonder that many philosophers gave up the problem and came to rest in some form of phenomenalism.

But the Thomist, as distinct from the Lockean, theory of substance is not to be dismissed as easily as this. While the scholastics took for granted a view of matter that owed much to the speculations of Greek atomists such as Leucippus and Democritus, their notion of substance was much subtler and more intellectualized than any crude conception of a solid brick which served as the substratum of appearances. A substance for them is a mode of being, an object in its essential individuation and continuity. It is that in virtue of which it persists through change; and this cannot be pictured; it can be grasped only by the intellect. As Father D'Arcy says, 'It should be noted that substance belongs to the order of intelligible reality and not primarily to the sensible order; it is a *noeton* or noumenal real.'[26] The importance of this point can hardly be overstressed. We are bedevilled in our thinking by our inveterate tendency to visualize everything and we are inclined to suspect the reality of anything that cannot be imaged. Of course, if we pause to reflect, we shall see how this denigrates the whole of our experience. But that would be to digress. The significant thing to notice in connexion with the problem on which we are engaged is that St Thomas believed that substance, and indeed the whole realm of metaphysics, could be apprehended, but not pictured.

In further explication of his notion of substance as a mode of being, St Thomas takes over from Aristotle two sets of contrasting concepts; form and matter, act and potency. Form is that which gives to any substance the character it has and renders it intelligible, while matter is the stuff which is the principle of individuation. Thus without the form of a table we could not

26. M. C. D'Arcy, *St Thomas Aquinas* (Dublin, Clonmore & Reynolds, 1953), p. 90.

know anything to be a table at all, while the embodiment of form in matter explains how there can be many different tables. The second contrast is introduced to account for change. Act is the expression of a mode of being: that which it is at any time and place; while potency is what it may become. Thus an acorn is an acorn in act, but potentially an oak-tree. This distinction between act and potency at first glance suggests the possibility of finding in the philosophy of St Thomas a way of giving full weight to the dynamic character of reality as we encounter it in experience; and, indeed, some modern Thomists have sought to reinterpret the Angelic Doctor in the light of dynamic categories.[27] But the marriage is an artificial one. While St Thomas had to account for the fact of change, his fundamental concepts were static, and the contrast between act and potency was closely connected with his other distinction between essence and existence.[28] Moreover, his view of substance was inherently wedded to the Greek idea of informed matter. This is the point at which the Thomist theory of individuation breaks down and proves wholly inadequate as a metaphysical basis for the multitudinous and variegated expressions of energy which characterize reality as we experience it. For St Thomas, as we have seen, matter is the principle of individuation, but as such is unintelligible stuff; only the universal form is of any significance, and therefore, on his theory, no room is left for the inherent distinctiveness of the individual. This might not appear to constitute any very great difficulty at the level of the inanimate world, but the higher in the scale we go, the more marked is the uniqueness of individuality, and in human beings it is inescapable. But if matter is the principle of individuation, and if, following Aristotle, the soul is the form of the body, how is the uniqueness of the soul to be established? According to Father D'Arcy, there is no evidence that St Thomas ever really recog-

27. Ibid., pp, 202 f. Cf. D. J. B. Hawkins, 'Towards the Restoration of Metaphysics' in Prospect for Metaphysics, ed. I. T. Ramsey, p. 115: 'Being becomes more like an ultimate subject beyond all subjects, and things are determinate variants of the fundamental energy of being.'
28. D'Arcy, op. cit., p. 83.

nized the problem,[29] and, if he had, he would have been driven to insist that it is the body which confers individuality on the soul. However that may be, Greek thought in general began with the universal and found the particular somewhat of an embarrassment, whereas a thorough-going analysis of experience reveals that the particular is the primary datum. The problem is not how the One has become differentiated, but how the many are held together and what each existent *is* in its essential individuality.

It is interesting to find this judgement echoed in certain neo-Thomist circles. D. J. B. Hawkins, for example, argues for a straightforward empirical approach in which 'the primary object of the metaphysician, as it is the primary object of thought in general, is the real in the sense of the existent singular',[30] and he holds that St Thomas was prevented from reaching this conclusion partly by the semi-Platonic Aristotelian theory of knowledge which he inherited and partly by his untimely death at an early age.[31] At all events, whatever the difficulties in comprehending the particular within the Aristotelian-Thomist framework of thought, it is immense gain to recognize that this is where the crux of the metaphysical problem lies.

A completely different approach to the whole question is suggested by that great seventeenth-century thinker, Gottfried Wilhelm Leibniz. Although there is certainly no one today who would be prepared to accept his metaphysical system as a whole, his basic idea of the monad as a centre of activity and the fundamental constituent of everything has helped to shape the thought of all those subsequent philosophers who have been dissatisfied with static concepts as a means of understanding and interpreting reality. Leibniz was a genius, not only in the penetration of his thinking, but in the extraordinary range of his competence. Besides being a metaphysician and logician, he was a theologian, mathematician, scientist and political theorist. It is therefore not surprising that such a fertile mind should have produced so many pregnant ideas, and we can learn almost as much from what we

29. Ibid., p. 111.   30. Hawkins, op. cit., p. 119.   31. Ibid., p. 118.

find unacceptable or even incredible in what he says as from those of his views which are more likely to commend themselves to us; for he raises the problems inherent in any pluralistic account of the universe, and his least plausible solutions are instructive in compelling us to think out the difficulties afresh.

It is no part of my purpose to attempt a comprehensive survey of the Leibnizian system; that can be found elsewhere.[32] I simply want to select certain features of his thought which seem to me to be particularly instructive for anyone exploring a dynamic approach to metaphysics. For this purpose by far the most important theme is the monadology itself. Leibniz cannot, of course, claim complete originality for this thesis since it was at least adumbrated in a great deal of Greek thought. Aristotle, for instance, believed that 'Spirit' penetrated everything,[33] giving to it life and energy, and 'the Pythagoreans spoke of an ἄπειρον πνεῦμα encompassing the universe, which the world breathes in (ἀναπνεῖ), or of "one πνεῦμα pervading the whole universe like a ψυχή, which also unites us with other living things".'[34] But Leibniz went a great deal further in his individuation of energy and virtual reduction of everything to it. His monadology, though it had affinities with past theories, represented an entirely new approach, and in many respects foreshadowed the outlook of twentieth-century physicists. Certainly Leibniz had no sympathy with Descartes and his dualism of mind and matter. 'It was one of the primary errors of the Cartesians', he wrote in a letter to a correspondent, 'that they conceived extension as something primitive and absolute and as what constitutes substance.'[35] He totally rejected the notion of substance as

32. See, for example, Ruth Lydia Saw, *Leibniz* (Harmondsworth, Penguin, 1954); C. A. van Peursen, *Leibniz* (London, Faber, 1969); and Bertrand Russell, *A Critical Exposition of the Philosophy of Leibniz* (London, Allen & Unwin, 1906).

33. Πνεῦμα διὰ παντὸς διήκει — 394b. 10f.

34. C. H. Dodd, *The Fourth Gospel* (Cambridge, The University Press, 1953), p. 213.

35. Leibniz in a letter to de Volder, *Die philosophischen Schriften von G. W. Leibniz*, trans. C. J. Gerhardt (Berlin, Weidmannsche, 1879), Vol. II, pp. 233-4.

defined in terms of solidity and extension, and replaced it with the idea of nucleated centres of energy, each mirroring the universe from its own point of view. The monads, as he called them, were simple, indivisible, and therefore not spatially extended; they were thought to be metaphysical points, distinguished from both mathematical and physical points,[36] and containing within themselves the seeds of their development and the power to change from one state to another.[37] These extensionless centres of activity constituted the core of Leibniz's metaphysical theory. Second, the monads were given a virtually personal connotation, and we are left with the impression that Leibniz derived the idea of their essential nature from his own self-awareness. For example, he wrote to Queen Charlotte: 'As I conceived that other beings may also have the right to say "I" or that it could be said for them, it is through this that I conceive what is called substance in general.'[38] Third, these quasi-personal centres of energy were thought to be self-contained and without any power to influence one another. Because of their supposed unalterability and internal origination of activity, Leibniz described them as having 'no windows by which anything could come in or go out',[39] and therefore without any capacity for interaction. Hence God was introduced as the cohesive force to hold everything together, to arrange for mutual adaptation in the development of all monads, and to overcome

36. 'Physical points are only indivisible in appearance; mathematical points are exact, but they are merely modalities; only metaphysical points or those of substance (constituted by forms or souls) are exact and real, and without them there would be nothing real, for without true unities there would not be multiplicity.' Gerhardt, op. cit. (1880), Vol. IV, p. 483. For an important discussion of Leibniz's theory of individuation, cf. Ivor Leclerc, 'Individuals', *Philosophy*, Vol. XXXVIII (January 1963), pp. 20-39, though his discussion becomes obscure when he treats of the relations between constituent monads. However, this is the heart of the problem for any pluralistic philosophy.

37. This capacity for development Leibniz called 'appetition'; see *Monadology*, Section 15.

38. 'On the Supersensible Element in Knowledge and on the Immaterial in Nature', Gerhardt, op. cit., Vol. VI (1885), p. 493.

39. *Monadology*, Section 7.

what would otherwise have been their isolation and disruptive tendency. Thus the doctrine of 'the pre-established harmony' was a necessary consequence of the theory that each monad constituted a world unto itself. Fourth, unlike the indistinguishable atoms of Leucippus and Democritus, the monads were held to differ from one another in the point of view which they occupied and in the degree of 'perception' which each happened to possess. Since they were indistinguishable in terms of spatial location and since the logical principle of the identity of indiscernibles made some method of differentiation necessary, Leibniz had to find a way of securing the uniqueness of each centre of energy. He believed that he had done so in the notion of perspective by which every monad, consciously or unconsciously, perceived or reflected the universe from a particular point of view.[40] Finally, Leibniz maintained that physical objects and living things consisted of 'colonies of monads', the constituent members of which reflected one another in varying degree. In addition, animals and human beings were characterized by the possession of a dominant monad—a soul in the case of the former and a spirit in the case of the latter—which more completely reflected the monads composing the body, and presumably gave such distinctive individuality to all living creatures as they happened to enjoy.

From this brief and selective summary of Leibniz's thought it will immediately be obvious that the major difficulty it presents is the complete failure to allow for any interaction between the monads. For the moment I leave this on one side[41] in order to draw attention to the importance of Leibniz's insistence upon the principle of individuation in terms of centres of energy. The use

40. It is obvious that one of the principal obscurities in the Leibnizian system is the concept of space. How can you have a point of view which is not spatially located? Leibniz might possibly have replied that he conceived of 'metaphysical space' in terms of relation, not extension. But this requires a great deal of amplification and clarification. On the difficulties inherent in this position, see P. F. Strawson, *Individuals* (London, Methuen, 1964), pp. 117-34.

41. The subject of interaction and the concept of colonies of monads are left for discussion until the next chapter.

of the phrase carries with it three significant implications. First, like the Thomist idea of substance, a centre of energy cannot be pictured. It can only be intellectually apprehended, and therefore all pictorial imagery is likely to be more misleading than helpful in elucidating what it is. Second, it draws our attention, particularly when used in the plural, to the radical character of individuation. When I say that I am aware of myself, I mean that, however necessary it is to give an account of my connectedness with my environment, I know that 'I' am radically differentiated from all other selves and from everything in the world around me. This is not an ephemeral illusion; it is the very bedrock of all I claim to know. Similarly, my encounter with other people and with the myriad variations of living things and inanimate objects in the world around me convinces me that the individuality I am aware of in myself is a fundamental characteristic of everyone and everything else. In other words, the real is divided, but not to infinity. The latter is a purely abstract concept which precludes determination. Thus the phrase 'centre of energy' may be used to denote the individuality of everyone and everything that is. Third, it conveys better than any other expression the consciousness we have of what I can best describe as the integration of energy for the achievement of a determinate result. 'Take away active tendency', says G. F. Stout, 'and the unity of any process is lost. It dissolves into a multiplicity of successive and simultaneous parts each existentially independent of the others and of everything else.'[42] The idea of a centre of energy, though most readily applicable to the Self, is by analogy used of every other individuation of being to express that which holds it together in continuity of activity, rendering it determinate and distinguishable.

This way of looking at reality has markedly influenced the thinking of certain modern philosophers. James Ward is a notable case in point. Starting from an uncompromising empiricist position, Ward argued that we are confronted with the interaction of myriad centres of individuality, each bearing some analogy to the

42. G. F. Stout, *Mind and Matter* (Cambridge, The University Press, 1931), p. 300.

human mind. This was why he rejected the common differentiation between mental and physical, holding that physical phenomena are the products of incipient minds, ossified by habitual repetition, and in this connexion he made great play with the scholastic distinction between *natura naturans* and *natura naturata*.[43]

Stout has subjected Ward's view to severe criticism in his treatment of what he calls 'the Activity Factor',[44] because of what he considers to be its false individualism. Speaking of monadists in general and Ward in particular, he says: 'They assume that because the individual's activity is his own, it must belong to him, not as a member of a whole within which he has his own distinctive place, but separately and independently.'[45] In so far as this is so, Stout is clearly justified in his criticism, but that does not really touch the substance of Ward's position. He may have developed it without due attention to and emphasis on the connectedness of everyone and everything (though he was by no means unaware of the problem),[46] but the importance of his contribution lay in his insistence on the fact of individuation and his definition of it in dynamic terms. Stout himself gets into much more serious difficulties when he defines activity as a character of process which may be more or less partial. His account of continuity makes it very hard to see how one thing can be separated from another, and how any process, and therefore any activity, could be partial. He claims that his object is to avoid the discrete particulars of Hume and he accuses Ward of resurrecting Hume in a new guise. But in all this he tends to lose touch with individuality, as indeed did Lotze when he virtually abandoned monadism in favour of modes or phases of an all-embracing mind,[47] and that is to start out on a road which leads progressively

43. James Ward, *The Realm of Ends* (Cambridge, The University Press, 1911), p. 72 *et passim*.

44. Stout, op. cit., pp. 283-307.   45. Ibid., p. 293.

46. Cf. his concept of 'intersubjective intercourse' in *Psychological Principles* (Cambridge, The University Press, 1918), *passim*.

47. 'Every single thing and event can only be thought of as an activity, constant or transitory, of the one Existence, its reality and substance as the mode of being and substance of this one Existence, its nature and form as a consistent

away from the data of experience. We have to take individuality seriously and face the problem of connectedness in the light of it.

Perhaps the most imaginative attempt to deal with the question of the one and the many in contemporary metaphysics is that of the American philosopher, Charles Hartshorne, whose writings have hardly been given the attention they deserve either inside or outside his own country. Following his mentor, the late A. N. Whitehead, Hartshorne has developed a unified view of the universe which nevertheless leaves room for the widest variety of individual particulars. This he calls 'organic monism'.[48] Rejecting all forms of traditional dualism, Hartshorne holds that the concept of organism enables us to account not only for human and animal life, but also for the whole of our natural environment. He starts, as we have done, from man's experience of his own spontaneity and sense of purpose, coupling with this the notion of feeling, and unashamedly attributes the same characteristics with necessary qualifications to everything else that exhibits teleological features.

He faces the obvious anomaly of maintaining that something like a mountain is an organic unity by drawing a distinction between the more complex forms of organism, such as human beings and animals, and simple forms, such as cells and molecules, which may be related to one another in different ways. Thus a complex organism, such as a man, consists of a multitude of cellular organisms, each with its own internal dynamic structure subordinated to the whole; whereas physical objects and plants, as well as primitive types of animals, are simply collections of organisms without any organic life of their own: they exhibit operative unity in their component parts rather than in their

---

phase in the unfolding of the same.' Hermann Lotze, *Metaphysic* (Oxford, Clarendon, 1887), Vol. I, p. 184.

48. Cf. Charles Hartshorne, 'A World of Organisms' in *The Logic of Perfection* (Lasalle, Ill., Open Court, 1962), pp. 191-215. The preceding and following essays, entitled 'Freedom Requires Indeterminism and Universal Causality' and 'Mind, Matter and Freedom' respectively, also repay careful study in this connexion.

wholeness. 'There are', says Hartshorne, '. . . certain many-celled animals without brains—such as some of the lower worms—which seem not in any pronounced fashion to act as wholes, and often not to feel what is happening in their various parts. But this may only mean that while the various cells, which do act as wholes, may for all we know, have feelings, there is probably no feeling which is felt by the whole animal. A similar interpretation is applicable to the many-celled plants. Each of the cells of a tree has more functional unity than the whole tree. As Whitehead puts it, "a tree is a democracy". An animal, at least a vertebrate animal, is not a democracy; for its cells are strongly subordinated to the whole animal acting as a unit—its feelings, desires, perhaps thoughts and purposes. A man's mind is king over his cells. Plants, and some low animals, may have no such master-minds ruling over their cells. Yet each cell has a functional unity, and may have its own master-mind ruling over the molecules composing it.'[49] Nevertheless, on Hartshorne's view, a macrocosm, though not itself an organism, may still contribute to a larger organic whole; and he commits himself to the conclusion that God is the all-inclusive organism for whom everyone and everything in their relative individuality have value. Thus 'organic monism . . . includes within itself a limited or relative dualism. The assertion is not that all wholes are purposive or organic; but that, first, all well-unified wholes are organic, and second, that all wholes whatever both involve and are involved in organic wholes.'[50]

Whatever one may think of the speculative conclusion to which Hartshorne's argument leads him, at the level of what may be called 'descriptive metaphysics' he does seem to stick closely to the experienced data. The occupational danger of the philosopher has so often proved to be a tendency to explain away the obvious in the interests of some tidy theory. This must be avoided at all costs. The particular merit of Hartshorne's work is that he insists

49. Charles Hartshorne, *Reality as Social Process* (Glencoe, Ill., Free Press, 1953), p. 35.
50. Hartshorne, *The Logic of Perfection*, p. 192.

on man's ineradicable awareness of purposeful spontaneity as he reflects upon his experience both of himself and also of his environment in its bewildering variety. At the same time, the case is not overstated by arguing that some supreme design determines the details of everything that happens. His account leaves ample room for the random character of events as well as for the order which is no less a feature of the universe.

When all this has been said, we still remain baffled as we try to comprehend the nature of what we have called centres of energy. Hartshorne takes us some of the way in explaining the organic form in which such centres are related to and differentiated from one another, but this is to describe their behaviour rather than to penetrate to what they essentially are. That is the mystery which is utterly beyond us: the mystery of the particular in itself.

To sum up, whatever obscurity attaches to the concept of centres of energy, it does at least deliver us from the unsatisfactory dualism between mind and matter which has been the bane of philosophers for so many years. No longer are we compelled to do our thinking within the strait-jacket of the idealist-realist controversy and decide whether we are to settle for the primacy of the mental or the material. Ever since Descartes the history of philosophy has been dominated by questions put in a form in which they were incapable of answers: for, if mind and matter are defined in such a way as to make their interrelationship inconceivable, it is necessary either to say that this is just brute fact or to explain one in terms of the other, with the resultant distortion of the plain facts of experience.[51]

51. For an attempted synthesis between realism and idealism, see W. M. Urban, *Beyond Realism and Idealism* (London, Allen & Unwin, 1949). Urban holds that both standpoints enshrine truth that cannot possibly be ignored: the mind-dependence of everything known and its antecedence to human thought; and he maintains that both are necessary *life forms* of the human reason (ibid., p. 25). But when we ask what the synthesis amounts to in positive terms, we are left completely puzzled; for all that Urban appears to say is that idealists and realists are both right. Put the two opposing positions together and affirm them as a unity. The mind contributes something, but not everything, to its object; the latter is partly, but not wholly, determined in the act of knowing.

Doubtless some people will be tempted to retort that the pluralism in which we seem to have landed is intellectually far more puzzling and simply multiplies the problems. My reply to this is to appeal once again to the empirical evidence which, I maintain, requires the kind of account I have tried to give. That is where we must start, and it is my contention that the mind-matter dichotomy is no longer self-evident. To continue to use it as an explanatory principle is to force facts to fit into a pattern of thought which was relevant only so long as a pre-twentieth-century materialism held the field. Further, I believe that a pluralistic description of the empirical data not only accords with the facts, but also provides a much more fruitful starting-point from which to pursue metaphysical inquiry and see the way in which some seemingly intractable philosophical problems may begin to be resolved.

In the second place, this different approach does enable us to take with full seriousness the revolution in the scientific outlook that has occurred since the end of the nineteenth century. The discovery of nuclear fission and the hitherto unimagined sources of energy available to man have opened up a new philosophical perspective, hidden from those who believed that mind, in its active origination, stood over against inert, lifeless matter, to which it was entirely alien. The old notion of the atom as a tiny solid brick has given place, as we have seen, to the dynamically conceived electrical charge, symbolized by electrons, neutrons and protons, and what was a relatively stable picture of the natural world has been replaced by the idea of everything being in a state of teeming activity. Moreover, the life sciences have now to be recognized in their own right and not simply as branches of physics and chemistry. The twentieth century has seen the growing importance of the study of biology with its various subdivisions, and more recently the younger disciplines of psychology and sociology have been competing for a place within the scientific field. The time has long since passed when the subjects recognized for teaching and research at the university level could be divided into the natural sciences and the humanities. A third area of study—the social sciences—has come to be accepted and is rapidly claiming equality of status with the other two. Anyone who has participated in lengthy discussions on curriculum policy is also aware of the ambiguity attaching to some of the subjects concerned. How is psychology to be classified? Is it a pure science, or one of the social sciences, or is it more akin to philosophy and should it be termed one of the humanities? All this represents a significant change of emphasis. Moreover, the close links between the life sciences and organic chemistry, taken in conjunction with the abandonment of static concepts in physics, means that all the old landmarks have disappeared. If any one broad area of scientific investigation is now pivotal, a strong case can be made out for biology.

Perhaps the most important advantage of all which this dynamic perspective affords is that the problem of knowledge can be investigated from a fresh point of view. Instead of conceiving the philosopher as standing on some Olympian height, viewing the universe objectively, we have to face the situation existentially in interaction with our environment. Human knowledge is then seen to be no complete conspectus of the world in which we live, but a partial viewpoint which cannot be abstracted from the inter-relationship in which man stands to everything else. That is where empiricism and existentialism meet in disclosing the inescapable dimension of metaphysical mystery.

CHAPTER FOUR

THE PRINCIPLE OF INTERACTION

By confining ourselves to the analysis of our experience in terms of individual centres of energy, we have as yet left unexplored the way in which they are related to one another. We cannot be satisfied with discrete particulars without reverting to Hume and the problems which he has bequeathed to modern empiricists. On the other hand, if, like Lotze and Stout, we concentrate on the unity of active process, we are in danger of falling into the opposite error of losing touch with the data of experience and landing in some form of pantheism or panpsychism.

To return to Leibniz. As we saw in the last chapter, the principal weakness of his system was his failure to allow for any interaction between the monads. Once these had been described as windowless and containing within themselves the whole process of their development, the only way in which they could be connected was through a divine miracle, involving a complicated account of an interrelated system of mirrorings or reflections, completely baffling to the imagination. But the thesis is strained to the limit when we realize that the monads are said to 'perceive' one another, not in the normally understood sense of the active apprehension of an object, but as a reflection which is neither active nor passive in relation to the environment. An activity which is self-contained and affects nothing else seems far removed from our common experience of initiating changes and encountering resistance in everything we try to do. The hardest pill of all to swallow is the theory of physical objects and living things as 'colonies of monads' when the latter have been defined in such a way as to preclude anything but an artificial connexion. And the whole case is given away by the introduction of 'dominant monads' which cannot dominate in any accepted sense of the word.

Of course, the pre-established harmony is Leibniz's answer to all these difficulties: a divine miracle to overcome what would otherwise be a chaotic pluralism in flagrant contradiction to our everyday experience. But why did Leibniz resort to such a device? Why did he not admit the possibility of interaction and forsake the dogma of the windowless monad? We do not have to look far to find the reason. Leibniz was a rationalist, not an empiricist. He began with logic rather than with experience, and his belief that analytic propositions were the only valid ones determined all his thinking. He argued from the premise that the logical subject contains all its logical predicates to the monad as the metaphysical subject containing all its metaphysical predicates, and that was why he held it to be windowless, without the need or possibility of interaction. 'In saying that the individual notion of Adam', he wrote, 'involves all that will ever happen to him, I mean nothing else but what all philosophers mean when they say that the predicate is in the subject of a true proposition.'[1] A clearer statement of his fundamental assumptions could scarcely be required.

The dependence of Leibniz on logic for his metaphysical theories was the main theme of Bertrand Russell's critical exposition of his works, and the conclusion was supported through the publication not long afterwards by Louis Couturat of a collection of hitherto neglected manuscripts.[2] But it is not necessary to follow Russell in his dismissal of the Leibnizian metaphysic as virtually worthless or to suppose that its author is of real interest only as a mathematician and logician. Certainly Leibniz himself believed that he had reached important metaphysical conclusions, and these, however derived, were central to his thinking. The conception of monads as centres of activity and the theory of

1. Leibniz, 'Remarques sur la lettre de M. Arnaud', Gerhardt, op. cit., Vol. II, p. 43.

2. Cf. Bertrand Russell, *The Philosophy of Leibniz* (London, Allen & Unwin, 1937), Preface to Second Edition, pp. v-vi.

colonies hierarchically ordered constitute a most fruitful basis from which to explore metaphysical problems, provided we allow full weight to the principle of interaction. If only Leibniz had started with experience instead of with logical premises, he might well have reached a monadology free from the most obvious difficulties which characterize his system. As it is, his views challenge us to think again about the nature of interaction and to see whether a pluralism which allows for centres of energy affecting and being affected by one another enables us to give a more satisfactory account of our common experience than is possible on any other basis.

We have already noted that the idea of interaction arises through the experience of resistance which we encounter everywhere in the world around us. If it be the case that the primary datum for metaphysics is our awareness of ourselves as initiating activity and meeting with all kinds of obstruction to which we have to adjust, and if we are entitled to conclude that this is strong presumptive evidence in favour of the belief that we are surrounded with analogous centres of activity ranged in a hierarchical structure, then we may expect to find in the principle of interaction a clue to the way in which everything is held together without individuality being absorbed in a unified whole. Even if in the end we are compelled to acknowledge that the coherence of the universe is an ultimate metaphysical mystery, beyond the capacity of finite man to comprehend, we shall not be surprised to discover that some of our philosophical enigmas begin to be illuminated in the light of the principle of interaction, provided that the latter is well grounded. Indications that we are on the right road are given to us when certain long-standing problems are seen to admit of a constructive approach when tackled on this basis.

The first of these is causality. Here we are faced with a highly anomalous situation. The scientist, as well as the ordinary layman, proceeds on the assumption that everything has a cause, meaning thereby that every event is to be explained by its antecedents which are believed in some way to bring it into effect. This notion has seemed so obscure and so full of difficulties to many philosophers that the idea of causation has been virtually abandoned to be replaced by the concept of regularity and statistical laws of probability which are held to be sufficient for scientific purposes. But the question arises whether the philosophical critique has not in fact parted company with common sense and has also undermined the whole basis of scientific investigation.

Let us begin with the views of the average intelligent person, untrained in philosophical disputes. If he is asked what he means by saying that one thing causes another, he will probably reply that force is exerted by x on y to make it behave in the way it does. Invited to illustrate his general statement he might cite the case of a billiards-player potting the red ball into a pocket. He would describe the action of aiming the cue at the white ball to make it hit the red one at such a speed and at such an angle that the latter would roll gently into the opening at the corner of the table. In other words, the player causes the cue to cause the white ball to cause the red ball to fall into the pocket. Admittedly, the description isolates a chain of events from its context, and he would go on to tell us that a ramification of causes would have to be adduced to explain why the table and the balls and the player were in that particular position at that given moment, and, before he knew where he was, he would be involved in an intricate tangle of events extending far beyond the room and the building in which the game was being played.

Now the initial problem that presents itself in the above account is to explain the action of the billiards-player. Is he the first link in a chain of events directly traceable to his own origination, or is his action caused by something else? Is his aiming of the cue explicable in precisely the same terms as the effect on the red ball by the impact of the white? Some philosophers and scientists have supposed the latter to be the case, and this, broadly speaking, is what has come to be known as the theory of determinism.

Three serious difficulties face those who opt for this conclusion. In the first place, they are landed with the dilemma of positing either an infinite regress or an uncaused cause within the process.[3] To suppose an infinite regress is to court the objection that the chain of determinate existents cannot be extended to anything that is not itself determinate. Infinity is a conceptual term, useful in mathematical calculations, but inapplicable to the world of existence. Theoretically you can conceive an infinite number, but to go beyond a given series of actual events is simply to assume more actual events, and sooner or later you have to settle for a first link in the chain. If the alternative is preferred and one or more uncaused causes are posited, then the question arises why there should not be others. What, in fact, becomes of the determinist position once an exception has been allowed to the rule? In any case, the myriad varieties of phenomena make belief in one finite uncaused cause well nigh incredible; for how on this basis are differences to be explained? If the uncaused causes are many, the game has clearly been given away.

Second, the protagonists of a determinist theory have to reckon with David Hume. According to him there is obviously no logical necessity that one event should succeed another, and any factual connexion proves to be elusive. All that we are justified in saying is that x habitually follows y, but the idea that x 'produces' y or is related to y other than by contiguity and precedence is a mental fiction. 'We have no other notion of cause and effect', says Hume, 'but that of certain objects, which have been *always conjoined* together, and which in all past instances have been found inseparable. We cannot penetrate into the reason of the conjunction ... the objects require a union in the imagination.'[4] And his view is further emphasized later when he writes: 'The efficacy or energy of causes is neither placed in the causes themselves, nor in the Deity, nor in the concurrence of these two principles; but belongs

3. The cosmological argument for the dependence of everything on God argues *beyond* the finite process of determinate events to their ultimate metaphysical ground. Whatever the merits or demerits of this line of reasoning, it is quite different from the theory under consideration, which involves an infinite regress or an uncaused cause *within* the natural process.

4. David Hume, *A Treatise of Human Nature*, Vol. I, Part iii, Section 6.

entirely to the soul, which considers the union of two or more objects in all past instances. It is here that the real power of causes is placed, along with their connexion and necessity.'[5] In fairness to Hume it should be said that he seems to imply elsewhere that there is more in the idea of cause and effect than passages like those quoted allow. For example, in the last of the rules by which to judge of causes and effects he says that 'an object, which exists for any time in its full perfection without any effect, is not the sole cause of that effect, but *requires to be assisted by some other principle, which may forward its influence and operation.*'[6] All the same Hume's critique of the idea of causality represents his real position, and, as we have seen, it has come to exercise increasing influence amongst scientists and philosophers. As a result, the belief is now widely accepted that the notion of causality is confusing and better dropped in favour of laws of statistical probability.

The third and by far the most serious difficulty in the determinist case is man's experience of freedom. Whatever the theorist may say, we find it well nigh impossible to believe that every action is inescapable because we are compelled to do one thing rather than another. The writing of this particular sentence at this particular time is something I could have avoided. I could have gone to bed and left the next stage of composition until the following morning. I could have torn up my manuscript and started all over again. I could have abandoned the attempt to write anything at all! Of course there are antecedent conditions which make any activity possible. I had to have pen and paper, a chair to sit on, and a table at which to write, while a host of other factors have entered into the situation, far too numerous to mention. Furthermore, the physiologist and the psychologist may be able to detail many features of my physical and mental constitution without which I could not engage in philosophizing at all. But when every condition, known and unknown, has been allowed for, they remain conditions and do not determine my

5. Ibid., Book I, Part iii, Section 14.
6. Ibid., Book I, Part iii, Section 15 (italics mine). This may be yet another instance of Hume's common sense getting the better of his theorizing.

action. The irreducible element of initiation is something of which I am immediately aware and of which I am as certain as I am of anything. If I am told that my sense of freedom is illusory and that if I were to know of all the factors involved I should see that I am compelled to act as I do, I remain completely unconvinced. For one thing, I want to make sure that the theoretical objector is not confusing condition with determinant; for another, I wish to know why he should try to explain away the obvious by the unknown. It is hard to resist the conclusion that the determinist view of human initiative is dictated by an *a priori* desire to have a tidy intellectual dogma, whatever the empirical data. The fundamental weakness in the determinist's case is that he finds it impossible to take his theory seriously when it comes to the practical test. He does not say, 'I cannot help what I am doing and therefore I will let myself be carried along like a cork on the water'. That would mean objectifying himself and treating himself just like a cork without being able to get rid of the subjective 'I'; for even such a hypothetical attitude would involve a decision which would be inalienably his own. Living, for human beings at least, carries with it the exercise of freedom, and a theory, however ingeniously argued, which runs counter to universal practical experience is profoundly suspect.

What, then, is the alternative? Was Hume right, and is the idea of causality to be interpreted in terms of statistical generalization? This seems to be the prevailing view, though it is often presented in terminology which is bound to lead to muddled thinking. Attention has already been drawn to the confusion between conditions and determinants. If the Humean hypothesis is accepted, both these words should be abandoned because mere succession, however regular, of itself implies no other kind of connexion between two or more events. It cannot be claimed that one thing *must* precede another either as a prerequisite in the sense of providing the necessary circumstances in which a given occurrence may take place or as exerting a compulsion which brings about some change. Discrete happenings are just unconnected. If this appears too paradoxical, then the conclusion should be drawn that there is something wrong with the premise. To adhere to a theory and attempt to save it from absurdity by importing concepts which are implicitly denied is to be landed in the most obvious contradiction. Again, both scientists and philosophers are prone to talk about 'causal laws' when they mean statistical generalizations, suggesting sometimes to themselves and more frequently to their audience that these are principles of explanation which account for certain events following others. It cannot be too emphatically stated that a 'causal law' which is simply a shorthand summary of observed regularities explains nothing and makes nothing happen. It is purely descriptive, and to avoid confusion it would be better if the phrase were dropped altogether as long as the hypothesis is being advocated.

Once the theory has been reduced to its essence and stripped of all question-begging terminology, it appears highly implausible and in flat contradiction to a great deal of our experience. The regularity of successive occurrences inevitably suggests that there is some connexion between them, and this can only be ignored by those who insist on adhering to the dogma that the sensually observable alone has the status of reality and can be the object of knowledge; as connexion cannot be sensed in this way, we know nothing about it. Later I shall argue that this is a wholly mistaken theory of knowledge. At the moment I simply want to emphasize the oddness of the conclusion to which it leads. The concept of a discrete occurrence is full of difficulty. For practical purposes we can distinguish between a forest fire in Canada and a blazing barn in Brazil because they are far away from one another, but the distinction becomes harder when the blazing barn is in the middle of the forest fire. Hume was right in seeing that contiguity is a principal factor in suggesting the idea of causality, but the absence of contiguity alone served to make his theory at all plausible; and in the last resort everything is contiguous with something else. This apart, it is impossible to give any convincing account of a sequence of events on the assumption that they can be separated from one another and merely happen to follow in the order in which they do. Take the writing of this paragraph. It does not just happen that I have pen and paper, whereas a blade of grass and a stone slab would equally suffice. Nor does a random collection of words appear on the white surface whereas smudges might equally well be the result of putting pen to paper. If it is objected that I have missed the point, that nothing so ridiculous as this is being suggested, and that there are regularities of sequence on which we can all depend, I want to know why this is so, particularly since irregularities of sequence are common experience. If there is no connexion between one event and another, why should not anything follow anything else? Even if the regularity theory is thought to be adequate for the purposes of physical science because it sticks to the empirical evidence, it does not begin to cover the unique and complex events of history, such as wars and economic depressions, which do not simply occur, but are invariably explained in terms of their antecedents.[7] The data of experience require us to find something more than mere sequence in the connexion of events.

The ordinary man in the street assumes that one thing makes another happen by the exercise of force upon it, and, in spite of the arguments of Hume and his successors, this common-sense view enshrines an aspect of the truth which we are not entitled to explain away. If we follow the course of a river, it seems obvious that the logs and driftwood carried downstream are inevitably moved by the onward rush of the water. It is nonsense to suggest that they regularly happen to go with the current and that there is no reason why they should not float in the opposite direction! But what is this force which we commonly attribute to physical objects? Is not the language we use frankly anthropomorphic? Are not words like 'making', 'compulsion', 'driving', 'shifting'— even 'force' itself—derived from our experience of initiating change in our environment? Are we justified in using them of inanimate objects? And, if we are not, Hume must be right after all.

This is really the crux of the matter. Hume's hypothesis depends on ignoring the basic factor in man's experience of initiat-

7. Cf. A. C. Ewing, *The Fundamental Questions of Philosophy*, p. 161.

ing change and encountering resistance, which enables him to interpret what is happening in his environment when one thing interacts with another. As long as we leave on one side our direct experience of causation, which Whitehead has protested cannot be explained away,[8] or refuse to recognize analogous activity in organic and inorganic matter, then statistical generalization may appear to be as far as we can go. But the usefulness of the method for purposes of classification and prediction should not blind us to the fact that it is not a principle of explanation and ultimately depends on another principle to make sense of our everyday experience.

The view of the universe as consisting of interacting centres of energy enables us to do justice to all the empirical data without having recourse to ignoring or explaining away any of the facts. First, we can take with full seriousness man's awareness of his own freedom in spontaneous initiation, extending this with the necessary qualifications to all living creatures, and even to inorganic matter. To many it will seem highly paradoxical to claim that inorganic matter has the power of spontaneous initiation, but, at the risk of tedious repetition, let me emphasize that this is due to our being accustomed to regard it as inert stuff and to our failure to adapt our thinking to the dynamic categories of modern physics. Of course, spontaneity at this level is of a very restricted kind and manifestations are stereotyped to a degree that leaves the impression of inactivity. But the vast difference between a lump of rock and a human being should not lead us to deny *any* spontaneity at all to the former, especially when there are so many gradations in between.

Second, the experience of initiating a course of action involves overcoming resistance and making other things, and sometimes other people, instrumental to our purposes. Here is the element of truth in the determinist case. While resistance is encountered in

8. Cf. A. N. Whitehead, *Process and Reality* (New York, Social Science Book Store, 1929), pp. 255-79. It is also interesting to note that G. R. G. Mure argues that we cannot grasp causation in science 'save as volition with something left out'; *Retreat from Truth* (Oxford, Blackwell, 1958), p. 40.

everything we try to do, it is not absolute; otherwise nothing could ever be done at all. We have power to make our environment pliable, though the extent to which we can do so is settled by the degree of spontaneity with which we have to deal. For instance, a man is far less malleable than a tool since the purpose of one individual may be set over against the purpose of another in matching conflict. Nevertheless the weaker have always been subject to domination by the stronger, and in modern times the techniques of tyranny and exploitation have markedly increased. Even those who preen themselves most on their freedom are often the victims of social pressures too subtly exercised for them to notice. All the same, a man is never completely at the disposal of his fellows as long as he can say 'No', and even when this elemental freedom has been removed by brain-washing or the deterioration of personality, he still has to be reckoned with as he then is; he cannot be treated as if he were something else. Equally we cannot do anything that we like with an inanimate object; we have to adapt ourselves to what it is. I can take up my pen at will and use it to write whatever I want, but I cannot make it serve as a conducting agent for electricity, or tie a knot with it as if it were a piece of string. Everything, to use a phrase of Tillich's, has its own power of being.[9] It has the capacity to be itself and to become what it may be in its own distinctive individuality. But it is not isolated, and, because of this as well as because of its inherently dynamic character, it acts upon other centres of energy and in turn is acted upon by them. Thus everyone and everything from man downwards are what they are in virtue of their own intrinsic nature and the influence exerted upon them by their total environment. The lower we descend in the scale of evolution, the lesser the spontaneity and the greater the plasticity. Thus the determinist case accounts for our experience at least to this extent: one thing is, within limits, made to be what it is and to do what it does by the action of other agents upon it.

Third, this interplay of spontaneity and determinism should

9. This is the basic theme of Tillich's *Love, Power and Justice* (London, Oxford University Press, 1954).

not be conceived purely in terms of external relations. Indeed, radical externality would preclude interaction altogether, and at every level causality has to be interpreted after the figure of interpenetration: an explanatory principle most evidently applicable to the influence which human beings exert on one another. In a growingly intimate marriage husband and wife contribute to the development of one another's personalities almost to the point of what might be called living in and through one another, though remaining distinct individuals and therefore externally distinguishable. But, while relative externality characterizes a great many relationships, we have not covered all the facts unless we recognize what may be called the hierarchy of instrumentalism or the absorption of some centres of energy by others. The human organism is the most obvious example we can take. The cellular structure of the body may be described without undue extravagance as a complex empire in which each unit is made to serve the purposes of the whole while having a life of its own.[10] Leibniz so nearly saw this with his theory of the dominant monad, and was only prevented from working out the full implications of this pregnant idea because of his logical premises which led him to deny the possibility of interaction. As a result, this significant insight was left as an unintegrated appendage to his thought. But, given the reality of interaction, his colonies of monads, together with the principles of the hierarchy of domination, constitute one of the most important contributions to our understanding of the nature of man, and for that matter of all complex existents.

Fourth, we are able to go beyond statistical generalizations in accounting for the regularity of occurrences. If everything that happens owes its origin to spontaneous initiation, while the range

10. Cf. the way this is worked out by Hartshorne: *supra*, pp. 97f. While we can attribute to human beings and to the higher forms of animal life a hierarchical structure within which more primitive centres of activity are subordinated to an instrumental role, we should be careful not to press the point too far to include the organic and inorganic realms at large where spontaneity is more diffuse and stereotyped, less subject to organic instrumentality.

of possible activity is in most cases strictly circumscribed by the intrinsic limitations of a given centre of energy and by its interaction with other centres similarly circumscribed, it is not surprising that we should find regular sequences and patterns of events. If no such limitations existed and anything could do anything, the universe would be chaotic. But it is essential to my thesis that spontaneity is restricted even in the case of man where the element of randomness, and therefore unpredictability is most marked. By how much more do not restrictions apply down the scale of evolution, so that physical objects present the illusory appearance of being completely inert, their habitual behaviour being construed as ruling out of court the possibility that they are dynamic in any way at all? One of the major errors frequently made in discussions of determinism and chance is the assumption that the contrast is between that which is absolutely fixed and dependent and that which is absolutely random. The truth is that nothing conforms to either extreme, and this, with gradations of capacity for spontaneous initiation, enables us to understand why there should be the regular and apparently fixed patterns of behaviour which are an obvious empirical fact.

Thus causality may be conceived as operating in three different ways. The first of these may be designated as 'dominant' where one individual centre of energy is virtually absorbed into another, and, while having functions of its own, has those functions completely subordinated to the whole of which it is a part. This is the most close-knit example of causality that we know and is characteristic of organic structure as such. Here the interaction is continuous rather than sporadic and is integrated into the life of a distinct individual. The word 'instrumental' may conveniently be reserved for a different kind of causality which is more occasional and does not involve the absorption of the more pliable into the controlling centre of energy. This is exemplified by the use of tools which for short periods become an extension of the human body, though they can be dropped and later put to the use of someone else. A third type of causality has to be distinguished from the other two where interaction takes place in such a way as to affect the nature of whoever or whatever is involved without complete or even partial domination. This is generally the case in the interrelationship of persons and whenever equals meet. Causality therefore denotes different levels of interaction.

We turn now to perception, the other major philosophical problem on which fresh light may be shed by the principle of interaction. Since the days of the early British empiricists the difficulties in accounting for sense perception have become increasingly acute, and the gap has merely widened as a result of twentieth-century scientific developments. Now instead of the well-known distinction between primary and secondary qualities —the former characterizing the objects themselves and the latter sensations produced in us by the objects[11]—we are faced with the much sharper dichotomy between a world of electrical charges symbolized in mathematical formulae and the world of common sense objects which we all believe we see and touch. To complicate matters further, there is the physiologist's account of the way in which our nervous system is stimulated by light and sound waves with the result that the brain is activated and we see, hear, feel and smell. How is this to be reconciled with the firmly held conviction that we can perceive and describe in terms of our perceptions a world that is external to our own bodies? Finally, the phenomena of sense perception themselves present us with a bewildering array of difficulties. We have to reckon with the undoubted facts of perspective, distortion and hallucination, which appear to make everything we perceive dependent upon some bodily state of our own. On reflection, the whole world of com-

11. The distinction is to be traced to John Locke, though it has been argued that he held secondary qualities to be powers in the object, and not sensations in the percipient. See Reginald Jackson, 'Locke's Distinction between Primary and Secondary Qualities', in *Mind*, Vol. XXXVIII (January 1929), pp. 56-76. Actually Locke is not altogether clear at this point. He says that they 'are nothing in the objects themselves, but powers to produce various sensations in us by their primary qualities'. *An Essay Concerning Human Understanding*, Book II, Chapter 8, Section 10. But if the agency in the object is the primary qualities, it is difficult to see how the secondary qualities can *be* the powers in the object when they have already been denied objective status.

mon sense seems to disappear in a mirage, though such radical scepticism ill accords with the practical exigencies of daily
life.

To deal with these difficulties the theory of sense data was
introduced, and for a time virtually held the field. In essence it is
the view that whatever we claim to perceive is presented to us
exactly in the form we perceive it. Thus, when I say that I see a
house in the distance and walk towards it, the different perspec-
tives are all given objectively; they exist independently of my
observation of them. Clearly the sense data of modern empiricism
are the direct descendants of the ideas of John Locke, the mental
representations of physical objects, with the important qualification that they are no longer conceived as originating in the mind,
but as somehow existing in independence of it.

The difficulties inherent in this position have been widely
canvassed and are now well enough known.[12] Accordingly, the
tendency amongst modern empiricists has been to abandon the
theory of sense data and resort to some form of naïve realism, in
which physical objects are perceived for what they are—perspective, distortion and error being explained as due to differences
in the technique of the percipient.[13] But, in spite of all attempts to
get round the problems,[14] the stubborn fact remains that, as Ayer
points out, there is an apparently unbridgeable gap between things
as they are and things as they appear to be.[15]

Unless we are prepared to be complete sceptics about the
possibility of knowing anything, a different approach seems to be
demanded by the facts: one that gives full weight to the deliverances of the physicist and the physiologist and at the same
time accounts for the phenomena of sense experience. This, I

12. Cf. R. J. Hirst, *The Problems of Perception* (London, Allen & Unwin,
1959), pp. 26-73.

13. Cf. Gilbert Ryle, 'Sensation' in *Contemporary British Philosophy*, ed. H. D.
Lewis (London, Allen & Unwin, 1956), pp. 427-43.

14. e.g., R. W. Sellars, 'Direct, Referential Realism', *Dialogue*, Vol. II
(September 1963), pp. 135-43; and my comment in *Dialogue*, Vol. II (March
1964).

15. A. J. Ayer, *The Problem of Knowledge*, p. 124.

suggest, is provided by the application of the principle of interaction, according to which knowledge arises through the interaction of centres of energy whereby the human subject becomes
progressively aware of the nature of his environment as it impinges upon him. In other words, knowledge grows out of the
evolution of what William Temple called 'the process of adjustment between organism and environment', and 'is indeed an extension of that process'.[16] On this view the phenomena of sense
experience arise out of the interaction of subject and object, and
tell us how things work rather than what things essentially are.
Thus we are not driven to suppose that physical objects are just
what we observe them to be nor to assume the existence of
myriads of sense data or sensibilia corresponding to everything
that has been or could be observed. The book in front of me is
not actually covered with a green binding, as at first I take for
granted, nor is it a collection of green sense data. The greenness is
neither 'in my mind' nor 'out there' on the surface of the book. It
arises through the interplay of a trans-sensational, metaphysically
conceived, centre of energy which in conjunction with other
centres of energy stimulates the metaphysical 'me' to see what is
green. If we want to retain the terminology of sense data or
sensa, we should understand that they have no objective existence
of themselves. They are events, arising out of the interaction of
subject and object, clues to the nature of reality emerging in a
purely relational context and making a trans-sensational, metaphysical account of reality inevitable.

Obviously this view entails a precise delimitation of the role of
sentience or sensation in the acquisition of knowledge. Much confusion has resulted from the loose interchange of words in this
connexion: apprehension, perception and sense experience frequently being used as if they denoted the same activity. On the
contrary, sentience is to be differentiated from both perception
and apprehension, the former being the direct act of comprehension through sense experience and the latter being reserved for

16. William Temple, *Nature, Man and God* (London, Macmillan, 1934),
p. 128.

intellectual intuition based upon reflection. Thus sentience is to be discerned within the framework of these embracing activities. Its function, as Kemp Smith so powerfully argued, is biological rather than cognitive: basically it is a practical tool whereby organisms have been able to adjust to their environment; and only sophisticated reflection has led to its being elevated to a medium of knowledge.[17] The result of this has been to put more strain upon sentience than it can possibly bear; at least this is true if sentience is defined as the stimulation of the physical organism by impulses external to it. As long as we stop there, sentience cannot possibly *be* perception, which involves holding together in an act of comprehension the immediately given and that which lies beyond it. Judgement is implicit in any description of what is perceived, and surely that means it is impossible to explicate perception in terms merely denoting sense data presented to the observer.[18] I can distinguish, if I try hard enough, between the process of visually sensing a red pencil and perceiving it to be such, though ordinarily I never bother to do so; but the physical and physiological process does not cover what I mean when I say that I see or perceive it.[19] Once we recognize that perception invariably goes beyond mere sentience, we are bound to assign to the latter a different role from the knowledge by direct acquaintance so often attributed to it. Perhaps we may say that sentience provides clues to the nature of things in virtue of the fact that it is the means whereby we learn how things work. In this respect it is parallel to the activities in which the self is expressed, and by which we come to know ourselves. In my view, then, sentience is basically pragmatic and we have to transcend it if we are to

17. Cf. Norman Kemp Smith, *Prolegomena to an Idealist Theory of Knowledge* (London, Macmillan, 1924), pp. 13, 32 f.

18. Cf. C. A. Campbell, *On Selfhood and Godhood*, pp. 36-72. I am completely unconvinced by R. J. Hirst's attempt to refute this position; op. cit., pp. 219-45. See my article 'Perception and Judgment', *Dialogue*, Vol. II (June 1963), pp. 65-74.

19. Cf. G. E. Moore's distinction between seeing and knowing in *Some Main Problems of Philosophy* (London, Allen & Unwin, 1953), pp. 50 f., 183.

know anything about the nature of the universe in which we live. Perception is a form of knowledge just because it is trans-sensational.

This general standpoint has certain clear advantages. In the first place, we are able to give full weight to the physical and physiological factors which have proved so embarrassing to many philosophers. Once the trans-sensational character of perception has been granted, there is no reason why we should not accord genuine significance to the theories of physicists who describe the world in terms of what cannot possibly be sensed. The use of words like 'wave', 'particle', 'electron', etc., may not be adequate to denote the mystery with which the physicist is confronted. Indeed, his insistence that he is speaking symbolically, particularly when he resorts to mathematical formulae, simply indicates how mysterious the object of his investigations actually is. Yet he does use language which is trans-sensational and within limits conveys a genuine apprehension of the physical world. He may not, as Jacques Maritain points out, plumb the nature of things, and he may only attain to the real in its measurable aspects,[20] but none the less the physicist is making a genuine contribution towards understanding reality in trans-sensational terms. Similarly, the conclusions of the neurologist fall into their proper place. If the phenomena of perception are caused by a chain of events ending in the stimulation of the cerebral cortex, we are faced with insoluble problems if we try to insist that the resultant visual image, to take the most obvious example, *is* the object 'out there'. But, on the theory I am advancing, these images are the products of interaction in which the whole physiological process plays an essential part.

In the second place, the view outlined enables us to account for the phenomena of perspective, distortion, hallucination and dreaming without positing a vast number of sense data of which the mind may become aware. Here we may take sides with common sense which supposes that these phenomena are explicable

20 Jacques Maritain, *The Degrees of Knowledge* (London, Bles, 1959), pp. 196 f.

in terms of the relationship of the subject to the object concerned. When I approach a house in the distance, its appearance changes as I get nearer, but I do not suppose that I am seeing a number of different houses. I take it for granted that the visual phenomena differ because of my relative position to the object in question. The same is true of distortion. The double image of the letters on my pad when I press my finger on my eye is accounted for by an interference in the physiological functioning of the optical nerves. Hallucinations and dreams are more difficult to explain, because, by definition, there is nothing outside me which actually exists as I suppose it to do when I am suffering from delusions or experiencing adventures in my sleep. But, generally speaking, we recognize that these appearances are caused by some agency acting upon us, though it is not the thing we suppose it to be. The consumption of alcohol may affect my brain so that I see pink elephants; the direct stimulation of the cerebral cortex by an electric shock may induce feelings that are indistinguishable from those caused by the sensation of external objects; the falling of bedclothes to the ground may induce imagery of the Arctic region! In each case the sensation as such, which in most instances gives rise to visual imagery, is the result of the interaction of something with the human organism.[21]

If this is the case with abnormal phenomena, there is no reason why we should not extend the same principle of explanation to the normal as well. As I have already maintained, what appears to be the green surface of the book cover in front of me is not 'out there', but is the result of interaction between the external object and the apprehending subject; it provides one of the clues to the nature of the object through its uniform interaction with the

21. The difficulty, of course, has to be faced as to the explanation of those sensations, sometimes giving rise to visual imagery, which are produced by changes in the metabolism of the body without any external agency being involved. It is by no means certain that an external agency can in every case be excluded, but, even if it could be, the principle of interaction operates *within* the organism, especially in so complicated a hierarchy of centres of energy as constitutes the human being.

subject, 'me'—uniform not only in my continuing experience, but also in the coherence of my experience with that of others in relation to the same object. What I see as the green surface enables me to know one way in which the object works in relation to persons. We are not committed thereby to assume that every human being has exactly similar sensations, nor *a fortiori* that other living organisms sense what human beings do. All that I am concerned to point out is that, given a degree of uniformity in the perceiving organisms, the interaction with any object will naturally give rise to similar phenomena, making communication possible within a single frame of reference. A human being cannot really communicate with an animal, not merely because the animal does not possess the power of speech, but also because the mode of sentience is so different. Thus this broad approach not only has the advantage, already noted, of giving full value to physical and physiological theories; it also enables us to avoid the invention of a host of wild sense data to account for all abnormalities in sense perception, with the resultant difficulty of defining the normal. Granted the premise of a metaphysical subject and a metaphysical object, phenomena of all kinds become more or less reliable clues to the nature of the objects in question. No radical distinction has to be made between normal and abnormal sense data, a distinction impossible to sustain.

This leads directly to the third advantage inherent in the view I have been advocating: we are delivered from the tyranny of vision. Some surprise may be felt at the use of a rather provocative expression, and yet I have used it deliberately. For most people, as we have already noted, the sense of sight has come to represent the most reliable medium for apprehending the world of reality, the senses of hearing, touch and smell being relegated to a subsidiary role; and few have questioned the justification for this assumption. Thus it has been tacitly assumed that the pictorial image is the most accurate way of denoting the real. G. K. Chesterton epitomized this very common fallacy in lines he inscribed in a child's picture-book:

Stand up and keep your childishness:
Read all the pedants' screeds and strictures;
But don't believe in anything
That can't be told in coloured pictures.[22]

Such an injunction, if quoted outside its original context, is hardly to be taken seriously. Most of the philosophical problems we encounter in the theory of perception are in the realm of vision where we are constantly being misled; and those who have been deprived of this sense, the blind from birth or early infancy generally show a remarkable capacity for apprehending the world around them, in many cases being far more perceptive than sighted people. Helen Keller, for example, bereft of sight and hearing from her earliest years, achieved an insight into the nature of things, principally through the sense of touch, which far exceeded that of the majority of those who possess these faculties and have come to depend on them in a way that has often blinded them to any dimension of reality other than the readily visible. 'I did not understand anything', she writes in her autobiography, 'unless I touched it.'[23] Again, the great Japanese social reformer, Toyohiko Kagawa, is reported to have said: 'I am forced to feel that, having so largely lost my eyesight, the power to see has extended into every part and parcel of my person.'[24] It is striking how little attention philosophers have paid to the implications of testimonies such as these. The trouble is that we have increasingly come to take sight for granted as the principal clue to the nature of the world around us, and the influence of television has simply accentuated this tendency for a great many children and young people in particular. We may well wonder how far the baneful effects of an extending use of the visual medium may lead to a serious reduction in man's capacity for penetrative apprehension. It is not without point to quote the exultant cry of the blind ploughman:

22. Cf. A. G. Gardiner, *Prophets, Priests and Kings* (London, Dent, 1917), p. 336.
23. Helen Keller, *The Story of My Life* (New York, Doubleday, 1955), p. 40.
24. William Axling, *Kagawa* (London, SCM Press, 1932), p. 154.

God, who took away mine eyes
That my soul might see!

The growing use of the visual media of communication has merely built on our inveterate habit of trying to picture what we are thinking about, though our use of words should long ago have convinced us of the impossibility of pictorial representation being in the least adequate for purposes of denotation.[25] The further knowledge extends, the less pictorially representational becomes our symbolism, and it is a mistake to describe this as increasingly abstract, if we mean thereby that it is somehow less denotational than visual imagery. That is why I am prepared to contend that the language of mathematical physics is denotationally more accurate than the picture language derived from the sense of vision, and it explains why visual models like 'waves' and 'particles' prove inadequate and contradictory in the long run. We should not be in the least surprised that experiments concerning the transmission of light should show that the latter cannot *be* anything visually representable.

Fourth, we avoid the difficulty of trying to distinguish between bodily sensations and sense data without landing in Berkeleyan idealism. It is obvious that the initial plausibility of Berkeley's thesis lies in the difficulty of distinguishing purely subjective feelings from the awareness of so-called 'secondary qualities'. Pleasure and pain are states peculiar to the experient and cannot be projected into agencies external to the body of the organism in which they arise. But what about heat and cold? Does not our awareness of temperature depend just as much on our bodily state as pleasure and pain? And once this has been granted, where do we stop? Are there any secondary qualities which are not reducible to subjective feelings? Such considerations led Berkeley to his famous principle: '*esse est percipi*'.

Some people have supposed that they could get round the difficulty by drawing a distinction between the adverbial and the adjectival. Kemp Smith, for example, argues that 'We can speak

25. Cf. Ewing, op. cit., pp. 37, 105, 216 f.

of the self (or mind) as pleased or pained or angry, but not as sweet or loud or red. These latter qualities are contemplated, and though in the process they may awaken a subjective reaction, and so be appreciated, they are in themselves genuinely "objective" existence.'[26] But what does 'objective' mean in this context? In the light of Kemp Smith's disclaimer that any satisfactory account of sense experience can be given without allowing for physiological processes, sweetness, loudness and redness cannot without qualification inhere in physical objects; they must be objective in a different way: as that of which we are aware distinguished from the act of awareness. But in that case why exclude from the same category the feelings of being pleased or pained or angry? They are equally objective when cognized; the only difference being that they are primarily states of the human organism, whereas the awareness of sweetness, loudness and redness occurs through the interaction of the organism with objects in its environment.

No problem of the kind Kemp Smith faces presents itself if we take the principle of interaction seriously. Sentience will then be response to the stimulation of the organism, and perception our awareness of feelings, sounds, tastes, smells and visual images in relation to the larger context in which they arise. If anyone remains perplexed that the self *qua* organism should be the subject of sentience *and* knowledge in all its degrees including perception, the fact has to be faced that this is universally the case, however hard to explain. There might have been no such creature as man with the capacity for knowledge, and then there would have been no problem with no one to raise it! But man has emerged above the sentient level and finds himself capable of apprehending the processes of sentience. He transcends sensation in apprehending it.

Finally, and most important of all, we may recognize that reality cannot be reduced to the observable when the latter is restricted to the sentient. This has been more or less explicit in all the conclusions I have drawn, but the point is so essential that it merits special emphasis. The trouble about much modern philo-

26. Kemp Smith, op. cit., p. 69.

sophy is that the ontological issue is avoided altogether, or in so far as it is faced, the assumption is generally made that the senses give us the only direct awareness we have of the real world. Certainly this is so in circles where the analytic method is regarded as the norm. But that is to mistake the function of sentience altogether, and the error is only compounded when sight is assumed to be the gateway to knowledge *par excellence*. Knowledge is trans-sensational.

This conclusion is greatly strengthened if the evidence for extra-sensory perception is admitted as valid. Research in this field is still in its infancy, and the experiments of Rhine and his associates in the United States and Soal and Bateman in the United Kingdom have as yet done little more than establish a non-random element in the ability of selected subjects to guess correctly the symbols on cards hidden from their view. Some are inclined to the conclusion that the results to date have been trivial to the point of insignificance. Nevertheless, the limited range of objects alleged to be perceived in this way, the incidence of error, and the variation in the performance of those concerned should not be surprising in view of the fact that human beings normally depend on the five senses for perceiving the world around them,[27] and extra-sensory perception, if it is a fact, can hardly be far developed even in the most sensitive subjects. We have already noted the extraordinary way in which the sense of touch may be enhanced through the deprivation of sight and hearing. We may reasonably wonder what are the latent powers in human beings over and beyond the well-tried media whereby we acquire knowledge of the world around us. Certainly the evidence for extra-sensory perception should not be arbitrarily dismissed in the light of any preconceived theory; it is much too impressive

27. It should, of course, be noted that modern psychologists find it necessary to multiply the number of senses in order to classify more precisely the phenomena with which they have to deal; cf., for example, Wolfgang von Buddenbrock, *The Senses* (Ann Arbor, The University of Michigan Press, 1958), pp. 54 ff., though these refinements of analysis do not materially affect the subject under discussion.

for that.[28] At the very least it lends some support to the view I have put forward, though my argument as a whole in no way depends upon such evidence. It stands or falls without it.

If my contention has been correct that all knowledge is trans-sensational, then the real world is immeasurably enlarged for our imagination. We need no longer find difficulty in talking about God or personality or values because they cannot be pictured or even sensed. Reality as such cannot be apprehended in this manner, because knowledge inevitably crosses the boundaries of sentience. In other words, while sentience plays its part in providing clues to the way in which the universe works, reality can only be apprehended, however partially and dimly, by thought; and intuition, the capacity for intellectual insight, is recognized as being the apex of human achievement. I do not for a moment want to minimize the practical value of sentience for the purpose of living, nor for acquainting us with the functioning of our environment as interacting with us in countless ways. But there its importance ceases. We have to transcend sentience to come to grips with the universe as it really is. If this is challenged as metaphysical obscurantism, I can only invite the critic to consider himself. He will find that he cannot describe himself in terms of sentience, and yet he is more certainly aware of himself than of anything else. But, of course, he is on the threshold of sheer mystery, a mystery that confronts him everywhere as he contemplates the innumerable centres of activity that comprise this astonishing universe.

Our review of the problems of causality and perception may therefore be held to strengthen our belief that an account of the universe in terms of interacting centres of energy does enable us to make some sense of certain aspects of our experience which would otherwise be completely baffling. We begin to see how we can allow for the connectedness of everything without explaining

28. Cf. S. G. Soal and F. Bateman, *Modern Experiments in Telepathy* (London, Faber, 1954). For a conspectus of differing conclusions regarding these experiments, see *Science* (Washington, D.C., January 1956), 123, 3184, 9-19.

away the fact of individuation. We are also afforded an approach to the problem of knowledge which does not limit us to the phenomenal and at the same time does not make any extravagant claim for a complete conspectus of reality. But although this may be illuminating to a degree, it only serves to underline the mysterious nature of reality in itself. We may begin to grasp the way in which individual centres of energy interact with one another and account thereby for certain common phenomena, but the *being* of everything, including ourselves, remains unfathomable, and all the fundamental 'why' questions remain unanswered: Why is there anything at all? Why is there individuation? Why is there spontaneity? Why does not interaction result in complete chaos and destruction? The last question simply deepens the mystery uncovered in the preceding chapters. Of course, it is possible to say that these questions should never be asked because they are unanswerable; but that is merely another way of admitting the mystery of which we ourselves are part.

CHAPTER FIVE

THE EXPERIENCE OF VALUE

So far nothing has been said about the range of human experience which is commonly called the appreciation of value: the belief that there are certain 'things'—objects, activities, dispositions or feelings—which are of ultimate worth, to be esteemed and (or) attained for their own sake. At the outset, we need to distinguish between so-called values which are really means to an end and those which are ends in themselves. The chisel used by the sculptor may be said to be valuable for carving the stone, and without it there would certainly be no finished product; but it is only of value in being instrumental to something else which is prized for its own sake. Men and women set before themselves all kinds of goals, such as the acquisition of wealth and the achievement of social status, which, on examination, often turn out to be means to some end, much more difficult to define, like pleasure or happiness. Accordingly, the distinction has to be drawn between intrinsic and extrinsic values: the former designating whatever is esteemed of worth for its own sake, and the latter whatever is contributory to the value of something else, though not regarded as of value in itself. For the sake of clarity, it is probably best to restrict the word to those things which are prized as ends in themselves, and in this sense we shall be discussing 'values' in the present chapter.[1]

1. C. I. Lewis introduces a further refinement in his discussion of intrinsic and extrinsic values. Holding that nothing is, strictly speaking, valuable except as experienced, he regards objects, like works of art, as extrinsically valuable in that, although differentiated from other things which are instrumental to whatever is prized for its own sake, they in turn are contributory to an experience. Therefore, he proposes to say that such objects have inherent

The conventional classification of values is in three categories: truth, beauty and goodness. The second and third of these may be readily distinguished from one another by reference to aesthetic and moral appreciation respectively: from the unsophisticated standpoint, beauty is generally taken to be a quality or pattern inherent in things which gives profound satisfaction to the contemplative mind, while goodness is a disposition of the human being which issues in actions deemed to be worthy of praise. But truth as a category of value is often left ill-defined. The trouble is . that the word is used in a variety of senses. Sometimes it stands for reality; sometimes for the coherence of an intellectual system; sometimes for the alleged correspondence between propositions and that which they are intended to denote; sometimes as a function of propositions of practical use in talking about the whole range of experience. In what sense may truth be designated a value or an end in itself of ultimate worth? Without getting involved here in a discussion of the complex problems raised by these differences of definition, we may perhaps say that the general intention of those who designate truth as a value is to draw attention to the intrinsic worth of acquiring knowledge. It is not morally better or aesthetically more satisfactory to know something than to be ignorant of it. Otherwise this third category of value could be reduced to one or both of the other two. In the familiar trilogy the claim is implicit that knowledge is valuable for its own sake. And this seems to be an ultimate, irreducible to anything else, and intractable to the question 'Why?' As such, I am prepared to argue that truth is the paradigm of all values, bringing us once again face to face with mystery.

This is to anticipate, and certainly runs counter to the widespread view amongst modern philosophers that to speak of values in any absolute or ultimate sense is to create a bogus mystery

rather than intrinsic value. But this is to prejudge the question whether anything can be termed valuable except an experience, and, for the purpose of initial definition it is sufficient to distinguish between what is an end in itself and what is a means to an end. Cf. C. I. Lewis, *An Analysis of Knowledge and Valuation* (La Salle, Ill., Open Court, 1946), pp. 382 ff.

which can be shown to rest on the perpetration of a series of logical 'howlers'. Those who argue in this way may conveniently be classified as reductionists in that, whatever their differences, they are agreed in reducing values to something else. But before considering the adequacy of these theories, we should first review the general position against which they are a protest, and try to understand the reasons why so many contemporary thinkers have found it unsatisfactory.

There is at least a prima facie case for regarding values as objective in the sense that they are taken to be characteristics of objects, activities and dispositions which are discoverable by man, and in no way the products of his imagination. This is probably what most people instinctively believe who are unversed in philosophical controversies and take for granted the obvious meaning of everyday language. Some assertions are true; others are false. One man is good; another man is bad. This thing is beautiful; that is ugly. To accept the relativist and subjectivist views of many modern philosophers would involve for most sensitive people a revolution in attitude: a revolution, incidentally, which the proponents of these views for the most part do not seem to have undergone in fact, whatever their theories may happen to be.

For English-speaking people and Europeans in general, the assumption that values are objective is doubtless rooted in the heritage of Graeco-Roman culture and the tradition of Western Christendom, in which Plato's theory of ideas has played an influential part. The classical exposition of the thesis is found in *The Republic*, where a hierarchy of eternal, self-subsisting forms, culminating in the idea of the good, is held to be the explanation of the physical world, the constituents of which derive whatever intelligibility and reality they have from participation in their eternal patterns. Matter is informed by the ideas, and the resultant individuation and characterization of things is relatively intelligible. But those who aspire to knowledge of reality as it is must apprehend the self-subsistent forms, and the height of wisdom is to apprehend the idea of the good.[2]

2. Plato, *The Republic*, 506B—509C.

With the intricacies of Platonic exegesis we need not here be concerned. Scholars continue to dispute whether the idea of the good is Plato's concept of God, or whether, as the *Timaeus* suggests, all the forms, and the idea of the good in particular, are self-subsisting entities which the 'Demiurge' or heavenly craftsman imposes on pliable matter.[3] For our purpose it is sufficient to observe that the idea of the good constituted an objective standard of moral and intellectual value, the touchstone by which the apprehension of reality and moral excellence was to be measured. In the development of Western thought the Platonic tradition, reinterpreted by Aristotle, has been fused with the Stoic-Roman concept of natural law and the Hebrew-Christian belief in divine revelation. The Stoics held that the universe was governed by immutable laws, accessible to human reason, and the good man was one who ordered his life in conformity with them. They were not of his making, but constituted the very structure of reality, disaster being the lot of anyone who disobeyed them. This concept was given concrete expression in Roman law and was the foundation of the '*Pax Romana*'. However, the embodiment of what were taken to be immutable laws in the decrees of an imperial power inevitably meant their compromise, and the conflict of Rome first with the Jews and later with the Christian Church was focused in the clash between what was believed to be the law of God and the usurpation of the divine prerogative by the Roman authorities. Hence there emerged the idea of a moral law originating in the divine will by which the relative laws of emperors and kings were to be judged. This was the medieval pattern. The Platonic conception of the supremacy of the intellect had given place to the moral law with its religious sanctions, and knowledge was prized as the way to God and the apprehension of his purpose. As for beauty, it began to be valued as a means of expressing religious truth. Thus the trilogy of values was guaranteed by divine revelation and was rooted and grounded in belief in God.

There are several reasons why this objective account of value

3. Plato, *Timaeus*, 27C—69A.

has come under increasing criticism from the beginning of the Enlightenment down to the present day. First of all, the break-up of Christendom and the growth of rationalism have led many to question the self-evidence of belief in God, and this has had a direct bearing on the supposed validity of objective ethical standards in particular. Although Kant attempted to base these on reason, and, contrary to the superficial impression of many, refused to ground them in the will of God,[4] the fact remains that one way of substantiating objective standards of conduct is to maintain that they are divine decrees. Just as no one has any difficulty in recognizing the relative objectivity of the laws on the statute book in that they represent the accumulated legislation of successive governments, so the commandments of God, if such they be, must be regarded as entirely independent of man's fluctuating desires, binding upon him in all circumstances. Awkward questions still remain. We may seem to have made absolute standards of goodness and obligation dependent upon an arbitrary divine will instead of acknowledging that God is himself required by the nature of his being to exemplify such standards which are absolute in themselves.[5] But to pursue this controversy further would be to digress from the matter in hand. The point I am making is that, whatever objections may be raised from the standpoint of ethical absolutism, belief that moral standards are grounded in the will of God is one way of presenting an intelligible case for their objectivity. Reject the fundamental premise, and the case for objectivity is to that extent weakened or, many would probably prefer to say, restricted. The only course then open is to try to substantiate ethical standards in their own right.

This brings us to the second difficulty which has impressed itself with increasing force upon philosophers in the last few decades. If there are absolute values, where and how are they to be dis-

4. Cf. D. M. MacKinnon, *A Study in Ethical Theory* (London, Black, 1957), pp. 99 ff.
5. Cf. A. C. Ewing, 'The Autonomy of Ethics' in *Prospect for Metaphysics*, ed. I. T. Ramsey (London, Allen & Unwin, 1961), pp. 33-49.

cerned and defined? They seem to be singularly elusive, and the more we think about them, the more shadowy and abstract they appear to be. Is beauty a quality like redness? Is goodness a characteristic of things or people or activities, and what kind of a characteristic is it? And what is truth anyway? Redness is discernible to vision, hardness to touch, and so on. How do we apprehend values? Again, if 'the right', 'the good', 'the beautiful', 'the true' are to be defined as *sui generis* and somehow self-subsistent, or if we talk about standards and principles as absolute, can we make this intelligible without falling back on Plato's theory of ideas? And who today believes in the existence of ideas in the Platonic sense? To do so would seem to be nothing more than to hypostatize an abstraction. This difficulty, which assumes so large a place in the thinking of many of our contemporaries, is echoed by A. C. Ewing in his most recent book on moral philosophy. Though critical of subjectivism and anxious to establish the objective validity of ethical judgements, he confesses that, like the great majority of his colleagues, he has either 'failed to find on inspection the simple non-natural quality of good', or at least has been very doubtful whether he has found it.[6]

The third, and probably the chief, reason why so many modern philosophers have rejected an objectivist theory of value is the widespread disagreement that is prevalent regarding principles and standards. To some extent this has always been obvious in the field of aesthetics, but, as long as the Church was the dominant force in the Western world, at least the façade of uniformity was preserved in the realm of ethics. All this has gone, and though the funded heritage of centuries takes a long time to disappear, instanced in the continuing belief that the Christian ethic can survive the abandonment of the Christian faith, the anarchy in moral values in Europe and North America becomes increasingly apparent. If it is hidden from many by the popular and largely empty battle cries of 'democracy' and 'freedom', it lies only just beneath the surface, plain for the critical investigator to discern.

6. A. C. Ewing, *Second Thoughts in Moral Philosophy* (London, Routledge & Kegan Paul, 1959), p. 54.

Indeed, one wonders whether some of those philosophers who have adopted a frankly subjectivist view of ethics on the basis of a theoretical recognition of this disparity in standards have really faced the full implications of their beliefs in practice.[7] The philosopher's study may easily turn out to be an ivory tower. However that may be, it remains true that the spread of knowledge in the fields of anthropology and sociology has posed serious problems for the ethical theorist. The facts have to be faced, and, although disagreements between one generation and another, between one social group and another, can be exaggerated and misunderstood, the differences between races, nations and tribes, as well as between individuals within them, are deep and far-reaching, however inconvenient that may be for those inclined to an objectivist position.

These are the main reasons why the theory of an objective standard of values, valid for men at all times and in all places, is now largely at a discount, in spite of voices raised here and there in protest. Truth is regarded as a highly problematical concept; in aesthetics relativism is virtually taken for granted, and in ethics philosophers like Prichard, Ross and Moore, who have defended some kind of objective standard, are now generally regarded as back numbers, superseded by those who have seen that the whole attempt to substantiate values as *sui generis* has rested on a prodigious logical mistake. They are to be explained away, as we shall see later, either in terms of something else or by showing that a proper analysis of the language used explodes the bubble.

Superficially, at any rate, the case against objective standards seems easiest to make out as far as aesthetics is concerned, since it is notoriously difficult to pin down any common characteristic which gives value to the wide variety of objects men designate as beautiful. What is common to the Wye Valley at Symonds Yat, the snow-capped Matterhorn, Helen of Troy, the Parthenon, Salisbury Cathedral, the Venus of Milo, the Mona Lisa, Keats' 'Ode to a Nightingale' and Beethoven's 'Moonlight' Sonata? Quite apart from the difficulty of finding any common charac-

7. Ibid., p. 57.

teristic in such a catalogue, the choice of examples almost inevitably gives rise to controversy. Whilst it would be hard to find
anyone prepared to argue for the ugliness of any of these things,
another man's selection of what he counted outstandingly
beautiful would almost certainly be different. Many poets might
be rated far above Keats, and the choice of the particular musical
work might well be deemed lacking in taste. But once we leave
the realms of the relatively uncontroversial, disagreement becomes
violent. What are we to say about the turbulent sea, the sky-
scraper, experimental poetry, surrealist art and cacophonous music?
Are they beautiful? Or are we reduced to saying that 'one man's
meat is another man's poison', and ending up with the cliché that
'beauty is in the eye of the beholder'?

Considerations such as these have led many to conclude that
aesthetic value is to be defined in terms of the pleasure or satisfaction derived from the contemplation or enjoyment of nature
and artistic creation. We are mistaken in supposing that it is a
quality inhering in objects and artefacts; it is a feeling induced in
us; and since feelings vary from person to person, depending on
the constitution of a given individual, there can be no absolute
standards. The best we can do is to reach certain generalizations
on the basis of statistical observation. Because of broad similarities between members of particular social groups, there is
likely to be some measure of agreement about what gives
pleasure, and therefore beauty is a relative term—relative to the
common experience of those who share the same social milieu.
Differences in standards amongst those who belong to the same
society are to be explained as due to individual predilections.

The difficulty about such a conclusion is that it savours far too
much of a conjuring feat that has not come off! A vanishing trick
has been performed which has left the rabbit still in the hat, to
reverse the usual order of manipulation. We are entitled to press
the argument and ask whether it is really being maintained that
whatever pleases me is beautiful and whatever displeases me is
ugly, and that the relative merits of what we normally believe to
be the objects in which we delight are to be explained away in

terms of the relative strength or weakness of the pleasures we enjoy. The logic of this is to argue that a Beethoven sonata, for example, is exquisitely beautiful one day, moderately beautiful another, and verging on the ugly another, if we have become tired by repetition. Anyone may toy with such a theory if he likes, but he had better realize that he is flying in the face of common sense. It is stretching credulity too far to be told that a teenager's pleasure in listening to the latest popular song is comparable to the sensitive music critic's delight in Bach's Brandenburg Concertos. And yet, in so far as excitement of emotion is the test of pleasure, the teenager may derive more from the Beatles than the critic from a performance of the New York Philharmonic Orchestra. And the *reductio ad absurdum* is seen in the variation of response in each to the same piece of music.

At once the objection may be raised that this is to pillory the crudest type of reductionism in the field of aesthetics. Modern philosophers who have a penchant towards what may be called an 'Ooh-Bah' account of value are in the main dissatisfied with any theory of beauty which does not allow for some standards of discrimination. A good example of this may be found in A. C. Graham's discussion of aesthetics, where he proposes no less than seven 'necessary standards' for judging a work of art.[8] In the preceding treatment of 'morals'[9] he makes it quite clear that his basic position, whatever the disclaimers to the contrary, is relativist: the good is what I and other people happen to want, and a given action is right in so far as in a particular situation it promotes what may perhaps be called 'the community of ends'. But it is interesting to find that he, like so many other relativists in ethics, is much more uneasy when he comes to treat the subject of aesthetics; for it is often the case that in circles where objective moral standards have been rejected, there is the most vigorous controversy about questions of aesthetic taste. The measure of Graham's difficulty is brought out in the concluding paragraph

8. A. C. Graham, *The Problem of Value* (London, Hutchinson, 1961), pp. 93-138.

9. Ibid., pp. 41-84.

of his discussion, where he argues that anyone 'is right in assuming that a work classed as literature is good or bad in itself, however much critics disagree over it. The mistake is to suppose that this way of talking implies the presence in the work of an aesthetic quality which the imperceptive fail to see. The point is not that the value is in the work, but that the standards by which it is approved are necessary.'[10] But what is meant by saying that certain standards of criticism are 'necessary'? The only sense I can give to the word in this context is 'generally agreed', but, if that is intended, why not say so? In any case, on Graham's showing, what is the basis for accepting such standards other than individual or collective taste? And then we are back to the arguments against crude reductionism. The fact that 'necessary standards' have to be introduced into artistic criticism suggests that the basic problem of value is more intractable than Graham would like to believe.

A far more thorough and persuasive attempt to dispense with the idea of beauty as a quality or characteristic of things in themselves and to account for it in terms of subjective feeling was made by E. F. Carritt, who devoted much of his attention to the study of aesthetics.[11] Following Croce,[12] he holds that beauty is an expression of feeling and that any such expression is beautiful. Thus the artist has an experience of beauty in expressing his feelings on canvas, the sculptor by doing likewise in stone, the poet in words, and the musician in sounds; while those who look and listen may have the same experience through the artistic creation evoking a

10. Ibid., pp. 137 f.

11. Cf. *What is Beauty?* (Oxford, Clarendon, 1932); *The Theory of Beauty* (London, Methuen, 1962); *An Introduction to Aesthetics* (London, Hutchinson's University Library, 1949).

12. Though Carritt differs from Croce in one important respect, i.e. the Italian philosopher's identification of intuition with expression. For Croce, we can intuit only what is already a feeling of our own. Thus whatever is intuited is a form of our own self-expression. Carritt, on the other hand, allows for the discovery of genuine expressions of artistic emotion which may be apprehended as such prior to awakening in us the appropriate emotional response. See *The Theory of Beauty*, pp. 124-48, 196 f.

similar expression of feeling in them. 'That of which we are aware . . . is not thereby beautiful; it only becomes so when it is contemplated without practical interest, without scientific abstraction, and without existential judgement, *as* the pure expression of emotion.'[13] Again, 'each of us has an aesthetic experience in face of a sensible object (which he then calls beautiful), whether it be perceived, remembered or imagined, when it expresses to him feelings of which by his nature and past history he is capable . . . consequently there is nothing in itself beautiful; one thing may be expressive to one man, and another to another. But as a great deal of human nature is common to all men, and a good deal to both men and women, and as a good deal of culture is common to all who share a civilization and a great deal to those who share an education, we meet with much actual agreement.'[14] Thus aesthetic experience is to be equated with empathy.

Now one of the curious things about Carritt's discussion of this subject is that, while he appears satisfied with subjectivism in aesthetics, he is very uneasy about its applicability to ethics. 'To deny the objectivity of duty and goodness', he says, 'is moral scepticism; the aesthetic experience is in no way abated by the reflection that it depends less upon the nature of objects than upon the significance they have for our interpretation.'[15] This dichotomy in the theory of value, as we may call it, is certainly very odd, and reflects Graham's position in reverse. One would have thought that if objectivity is inescapable in the one realm, it is also likely to be inescapable in the other. Nevertheless, Carritt does maintain a subjectivist theory of aesthetics, which is open to at least four main criticisms.

In the first place, like most other philosophers who have written on the subject, he concentrates almost exclusively on the creative arts to the neglect of man's appreciation of beauty in nature. This is merely touched on in a brief and unconvincing passage at the end of *The Theory of Beauty* where he suggests that natural beauty is to be interpreted as the expression of God, and our evaluation

13. Ibid., p. 197.
14. Carritt, *An Introduction to Aesthetics*, p. 38.   15. Ibid., p. 40.

of it as an expression of feeling analogous to that awakened in us through the contemplation of a work of art.[16] If pressed, this implies the crudest type of anthropomorphism which Carritt would surely not be prepared to defend. We are left wondering what he really thinks about the subject, and how far a thorough discussion of natural beauty would have affected his whole thesis. At least we know where we are with Samuel Alexander who argues at length that as beauty in art is due to the constructive imagination of the artist, so natural beauty is discovered through the selective ordering of the human mind.[17]

A major objection to nearly all modern works on aesthetics, including Alexander's, is that they assume the appreciation of art to be fundamental, and, in so far as they deal with nature at all, they try to fit it into a theory which has already been worked out on a frankly subjectivist basis. The plausibility of their conclusions very largely turns on the ordering of their treatment, and Carritt's thesis in particular depends upon starting with the arts. Of course, it is possible to argue that this is the logical procedure, and that man's experience of beauty in nature is derivative from his capacity for imaginative artistic expression. After all, there have been times when what is now commonly taken to be beautiful in nature has been actually abhorred. For example, in his autobiography, Sir George Trevelyan cites the case of a certain Mr Burt, the roadmaker for General Wade in the early eighteenth century, who, contrasting the mountains of Scotland with Richmond Hill, asked: 'Of what use can be such monstrous excrescences?'[18] But this may simply illustrate the roadmaker's practical frustration and insensitivity to what was really magnificent. Although it may be true, as Trevelyan suggests, that through the rise of modern industrialism mountains have come to speak to men of the unchanging in a changing world, this does

16. Carritt, *The Theory of Beauty*, pp. 198-200.

17. S. Alexander, *Beauty and Other Forms of Value* (London, Macmillan, 1933), p. 30.

18. G. M. Trevelyan, *An Autobiography and Other Essays* (London, Longmans, 1949), p. 99.

not imply that mountain scenery is not inherently beautiful for those who have eyes to see. After all, most people would be ready to admit that they can be educated to appreciate music and art which at first seemed to be a meaningless jangle and jumble to their uninitiated ear and eye. The same may well be the case with natural beauty. At any rate, no comprehensive theory of aesthetics can afford to leave this aspect of human experience out of account, and it is at least arguable that it is basic to aesthetic appreciation. Surely there are far more people sensitive to the beauty in nature than to the fine arts and music, and, generally speaking, do we not have to be educated to the latter on the basis of the former? The point is a debatable one, but the onus of proof appears to me to lie with those who maintain that artistic creation is more fundamental than the discovery of beauty in nature, and suspicion of special pleading in the interests of a theory is aroused when our experience of natural beauty is either ignored or relegated to a subsidiary role.

The second criticism that may be directed against Carritt's position is that, in giving an exclusively emotional account of aesthetic experience, he fails to allow for the place of the intellect both in the creation and appreciation of artistic works. No doubt this is in part due to the modern reaction against didactic and representational theories of art, and a willingness to take seriously the insistence, particularly of painters, that they are expressing what they feel: something that cannot be articulated in rationally apprehensible terms. All of this may be readily accepted. A painting, a symphony, a poem are quite different from a logical argument or a description of some set of empirical observations. All are expressed in a publicly available medium, but the former are primarily expressions of feeling while the latter are expressions of more or less clarified thought. Nevertheless, art is a medium of communication even though the expression of emotion may predominate, and the artist often apprehends reality with quite remarkable penetration, enabling others to share his insight through his own particular mode of creativity. Undue preoccupation with non-representational painting should not blind us to the way in which great portraits or landscapes may introduce us to a fresh and illuminating view of their subjects. Again, how many would not gratefully acknowledge the deeper insight into the central themes of the Christian faith they owe to the music of Bach's 'St Matthew' Passion and Mass in B minor? The suggestion is not that we should reject Carritt's analysis in favour of a didactic theory of art. I am simply urging that some allowance should be made for the place of the intellect in artistic expression and for intellectual apprehension in aesthetic appreciation. In so far as this is conceded, a purely subjectivist view of beauty is likely to seem less plausible; for attention is then directed away from the emotional experience of the viewer or the listener to that which he sees or hears.

Third, and closely connected with the point just made, Carritt's thesis is open to the objection that he uses the word 'expression' in a misleadingly ambiguous way, which results in discounting the embodied beauty of a work of art in favour of a purely emotional experience. As we have already seen, he is entirely justified in stressing that artistic creation is an expression of feeling. But when he goes on to talk of the *appreciation* of a work of art as an expression of feeling, he is obviously using 'expression' in a different and very odd sense; for, unlike the artist's expression of his feeling in a particular medium, the expression of feeling in appreciation appears to be a private emotional reaction. Carritt would want to qualify this by saying that our feelings are expressed in the work of the artist, and without that work there would be no aesthetic experience. To quote his own words: 'a man has a genuine aesthetic experience when he finds a sensuous image immediately expressive or significant . . . of his own feelings, desires, emotions, moods.'[19] But to find a sensuous image is very different from expressing oneself in it as the artist does. To use the same word to convey two quite different activities, and then to build a theory of beauty on their identity under cover of the one word, looks like a feat of legerdemain, even though it be un-

19. Carritt, *An Introduction to Aesthetics*, p. 36.

intentional. The result of the confusion is that Carritt, on the basis of an appeal to the artist's account of what he is doing, constructs a theory of aesthetic appreciation which directs attention away from the embodiment of feeling in the work of art to the feeling of the appreciating subject. Thus it appears plausible to hold that beauty is not a characteristic of the object, but is reducible to subjective emotion.

Fourth, and more serious, on Carritt's showing there is no real basis for discrimination between one expression of feeling and another. This is abundantly clear from his remark that reading Croce had convinced him 'that the *expression* of *any* feeling is beautiful',[20] followed by the general statement that 'in the history of aesthetic we may discover a growing consensus of emphasis on the doctrine that all beauty is the expression of what may be generally called emotion, and that all such expression is beautiful.'[21] If that is really the consensus of opinion amongst aesthetic philosophers, then it surely exhibits the bankruptcy of their theories; for there are all kinds of expressions of feeling that most people would consider ugly. When a small child is given a box of paints, a brush, and a sheet of paper, he may produce something interesting to his parents or teacher, but they would hardly be serious in calling it beautiful. And little Willie in certain moods is as capable of expressing his feelings as Michelangelo! Or what more intense and abandoned expression of feeling can we imagine than that of the heart-throb singer and his frequently ecstatic audience? 'Beatlemania', as it has been called, would have to be classified as an outstanding expression of beauty if Carritt's words are to be taken at their face value. If a theory implies this kind of absurdity, there must be something wrong with it. Nor are we rescued from the predicament by Alexander's suggestion that an objective standard may be found in the approval of the group rather than the individual—a view which, according to the quotation cited above, Carritt seems to share. When we ask where we are to find the group whose standard may be taken as definitive, we are told that it consists of 'those whom beauty

20. Carritt, *The Theory of Beauty*, p. 196.   21. Ibid., p. 201.

satisfies in their aesthetic impulse or sentiment'.[22] But unless one can clearly designate what it is towards which the aesthetic impulse is directed, we cannot designate the group in question. In the last resort Alexander's standard is subjective, and is none the less so by making a group rather than the individual the touchstone. The adolescent Beatle fans are as much a group as the most eminent collection of art critics. However awkward it may be, a purely subjectivist theory of aesthetics can logically allow no room for a standard of comparative values, and this makes nonsense of all criticism besides flying in the face of common sense.

Nevertheless, the difficulties in an objectivist view remain. Is it in the least plausible to talk of beauty in the abstract or to suppose that it is a quality inherent in nature or artistic creations? What is the common denominator in virtue of which we call such diverse things beautiful? And where are we to find an objective standard of criticism?

Our perplexity is simply enhanced when we turn to the subject of ethics; for reductionism in this realm is even more unsatisfactory than in the field of aesthetics, and yet the alternative appears to be so highly vulnerable. The attempt to explain away what are believed to be ultimate moral values has, broadly speaking, taken two forms. The first may be described as utilitarianism, by which I intend to denote all those theories which have sought to explain the concepts of right and good (in the ethical sense of that word) in terms of the promotion of self-interest, pleasure, happiness or human welfare. At first this appears to be a promising approach. There is a superficial plausibility about saying that what we pretend to ourselves are moral actions inspired by a sense of duty are really dictated by enlightened self-interest; and if this turns out to be insufficient to cover all the facts, we have recourse to the rubric of 'the greatest happiness of the greatest number', the formula by which Jeremy Bentham and John Stuart Mill claimed to have settled the issue in the nineteenth century. The story of the demolition of this position has often been told, and is to be found

22. Alexander, op. cit., p. 176.

in any of the books dealing with the history of ethical theory.[23] In spite of ingenious attempts to rescue it, the most subtle of which was probably that of the late Professor Henry Sidgwick,[24] utilitarianism stands condemned simply because it does not account for all the data. There are many actions we believe to be our duty, such as self-sacrifice for something we consider to be right, which cannot possibly be brought into conformity with the utilitarian principle. The plausibility of the theory turns on the fact that we frequently do feel obligated to promote the happiness of ourselves and other people, but the idea of duty cannot be reduced to the particular end in view. The promotion of happiness is one amongst a number of prima facie obligations, and the ideas of right and good prove on careful reflection to be much more complex than the utilitarians thought them to be. Even John Stuart Mill found that he was unable to remain entirely satisfied with the general form of the theory he had espoused. He could not bring himself to believe that a man of genius, like Socrates, should be sacrificed for the promotion of the public welfare. The freedom of such an individual to be himself was somehow of inalienable worth, and Mill in the end could not subscribe to the view that this should be overridden by any specious claim about the greatest happiness of the greatest number.[25] As Donald MacKinnon says, 'it is the seemingly self-justifying character of the life of the saint which sets a question-mark against the utilitarian programme; it is such a life that suggests that the whole problem of human conduct requires discussion in a different style.'[26]

Once exceptions to the rule have been admitted, whether they be actions deemed right although they do not contribute to enlightened self-interest or to the sum total of human happiness, or

23. For a convenient synopsis, see E. F. Carritt, *The Theory of Morals* (London, Oxford University Press, 1928), pp. 37-44.

24. H. Sidgwick, *The Methods of Ethics* (London, Macmillan, 1907).

25. Cf. J. S. Mill, *On Liberty*, The Harvard Classics (New York, Collier, 1909), pp. 227-30; and *Mill on Bentham and Coleridge*, ed. F. R. Leavis (London, Chatto & Windus, 1950), pp. 65-72.

26. MacKinnon, op. cit., p. 59.

lives which have the stamp of uniqueness about them, utilitarianism as a theory has been decisively undermined. For many the *coup de grâce* was delivered by that formidable group of British moral philosophers who in the earlier decades of this century subjected the whole reductionist case, as hitherto presented, to withering criticism. For instance, the impression left on students who had the privilege of attending H. A. Prichard's lectures at Oxford was that of an excited ferret remorselessly nosing out and destroying utilitarian rats! Sometimes one felt that innocent victims, such as Bishop Butler and Professor G. E. Moore, were included in the hunt; for Prichard scented the enemy everywhere. But by the time that he had finished, nothing seemed to be left of the utilitarian position, and the concepts of right and good were enthroned in splendid isolation, irreducible to one another or to anything else.

Prichard was probably the most extreme and uncompromising of the anti-reductionists, though he was run a close second by W. D. Ross,[27] while G. E. Moore, though castigated by Prichard for reducing duty to goodness, defined the latter as a quality of excellence, which was *sui generis* and intractable to translation into any other terms. We need not concern ourselves here with the differences between these distinguished philosophers nor with the question whether 'right' is reducible to 'good' or whether both are ultimates. For our purpose we need only note that, while their appeal to the data of moral experience had apparently enabled them to refute all attempts of their predecessors to explain ethical concepts in terms of self-interest, pleasure, happiness or anything else, they left a legacy of abstract ideas and unrelated obligations which constituted a most puzzling enigma. Meanwhile, the advent of logical analysis, though its initial attack was on metaphysics, presaged a far more radical reductionism in the field of ethics than had hitherto been envisaged: a reductionism which was to build upon and flourish in the critical atmosphere to which the anti-utilitarians had so largely contributed.

It was some time before the impact of this novel technique was

27. Cf. W. D. Ross, *The Right and the Good* (Oxford, Clarendon, 1930).

felt in the realm of moral philosophy, but its application event-
ually gave a completely new twist to the question which Prichard
had asked in 1912: 'Does Moral Philosophy Rest on a Mistake?'[28]
Prichard and all who had argued like him for the ultimacy of
ethical principles were themselves accused of perpetrating a
gigantic logical 'howler' and thus creating a spurious philosophical problem. The principal exponents of this new approach[29]
have in general contended that ethical judgements, while grammatically phrased as descriptive propositions, are logically of an
entirely different order. They are translatable into commands,
emotive outbursts, expressions of approval, proposals or decisions
to act in a certain way, which are mistakenly thought to attribute
certain qualities, called 'goodness' and 'rightness', to certain
people or things. When I say that the dress my wife is wearing is
red, I am properly attributing the quality of redness to the gar-
ment in question: the proposition is descriptive of a state of
things which is verifiable by observation. If I wonder whether I
am wrong, and it is after all purple or maroon, I can make sure by
looking at it again in a clear light or by checking my estimate
against a colour chart. The problems of moral philosophy, it is
argued, have arisen when the assumption has been made that
value judgements are logically parallel to descriptive propositions
whereas in fact they are nothing of the kind. Goodness is not a
quality like redness, even though it is the same kind of word
grammatically, and the puzzles are resolved when we realize
that value judgements are either expressions of personal attitudes
or proposals that we or other people should act in specific
ways.

This approach to ethical questions and the status of values in

28. H. A. Prichard, 'Does Moral Philosophy Rest on a Mistake?' *Mind*,
N. S., Vol. XXI (1912), pp. 21-37. Cf. his *Duty and Interest* (London, Oxford
University Press, 1928).

29. e.g. C. L. Stevenson, *Ethics and Language* (New Haven, Yale University
Press, 1944) and P. H. Nowell-Smith, *Ethics* (Harmondsworth, Penguin,
1954).

general has one great advantage over earlier types of reductionism in that it avoids the systematization of whatever people
account good or right or obligatory, which proved so vulnerable to the criticism of neo-Kantians like Ross and Prichard.
Values do not have to be reduced to any single common denominator, such as pleasure or happiness. Indeed, modern analysts
would have no difficulty in allowing for the heterogeneous catalogue of duties which Bishop Butler found it impossible to bring
together under any single principle save the rational nature of
man—a faithfulness to the data of ethical experience which makes
him one of the most perceptive writers on the subject.[30] Nor
would they quarrel with Ross or Prichard in their criticism of
those who in the interests of a tidy theory fail to take seriously
those actions men deem worth doing for their own sake or their
duty *per se*, undirected to their own advancement or the promotion of the happiness of others. For them, ethics is concerned
solely with man's attitudes and practical activities. It transgresses
its proper boundaries when it purports to deal with objective
qualities, laws or principles.

Leaving aside the question whether the paradigm of descriptive
statements with which analysts are accustomed to contrast ethical
prescriptions and emotive expressions is as straightforward as it is
often assumed to be, the virtual dismissal of objective[31] values on
logical grounds seems to me to be vulnerable to an attack in three
waves. To begin, it is surely obvious that, although ethics is
concerned with practical activity, and although commandments,
proposals and decisions play a large part in determining conduct,
such attitudes are adopted on the basis of convictions that a
certain state of affairs is what it is. R. M. Hare is doubtless right in
saying that indicatives cannot logically be deduced from im-

30. Cf. MacKinnon, op. cit., pp. 176-9.

31. It will be observed that I am using 'subjective' and 'objective' in the
earlier part of this chapter in the context of the controversy which regards
these two words as battle-cries, standing for the only alternatives open to us.
As I hope will be clear from what follows, I believe this to be an over-
simplification of the issue and that a third alternative is possible.

peratives or vice versa,[32] but imperatives are *based* upon factual judgements; and when people are bidden to treat others generously, or when a man decides to forgo wealth and comfort for a life of service on the African continent, it is quite unrealistic to suggest that these are arbitrary decisions. Decision follows upon judgement of what is good and right, not the other way about.

The reply of the critical analyst to this objection is to claim that, while we ordinarily suppose that factual judgements are basic, we are actually mistaken. There are no objective standards of right and wrong. Goodness is what we approve, evil what we disapprove, and nothing more. So-called moral principles and ethical standards are simply generalizations from everything towards which we happen to have a 'pro-attitude', and our duties are just those actions which we decide to perform. Clearly this abandonment of standards, which we have already criticized in the case of aesthetics, is even more contrary to common sense in the realm of morals. Its logic is that we should forswear condemnation of any attitude or activity. We may dislike it, but that is all we are entitled to say. Every man is justified in calling whatever he pleases 'good' and whatever he dislikes 'bad', and on this basis there is really nothing to choose between the Jew-baiting Streicher and the humanitarian Schweitzer. The one liked hounding those of another race to death; the other preferred to heal and educate backward Africans. It is simply a matter of the glands or upbringing or inherent prejudice or what have you that leads most people to esteem the one above the other. But from the standpoint of the detached philosopher in his thoroughgoing tolerance there is not really a pin to choose between them.

When baldly stated, such a conclusion seems too paradoxical for words, and hardly anybody is likely to accept it in this form. Nevertheless, attempts to make the underlying assumption more palatable simply gloss over the real difficulty, thrown into sharpest focus by the contrast between Streicher and Schweitzer. Two

32. Cf. R. M. Hare, *The Language of Morals* (Oxford, Clarendon, 1952) p. 28.

examples of 'rescue operations' may be cited, both of which preserve the subjective, relativist premise and at the same time try to avoid anomalies of the kind instanced above. The first of these is found in A. C. Graham's treatment of morals in his discussion *The Problem of Value* to which we have already referred. He holds that the concept of 'good' embraces all the ends which I and other people set before ourselves, while our duty is to promote these ends so far as they do not conflict with one another.[33] Thus the paradox of Streicher and Schweitzer would be resolved by saying that the former wilfully obstructed the ends of the Jews whom he baited, whereas the distinguished Alsatian missionary spent his life in precisely the opposite way.

Superficially such a solution seems to have saved the day by getting rid of the more obvious absurdities that arise if the relativist principle is pressed to the limit. But it does so at the cost of importing an unacknowledged alien value judgement: that it is good to promote the ends of other people as well as those of ourselves, and that we are under obligation to do whatever is conducive to such a result. Is this merely Graham's 'pro-attitude'? If so, what is he to say to Streicher other than 'I don't like what you do'? This apart, it is not self-evident that we have any reason to approve equally all human objectives which do not clash with one another. A man may be eaten up with pride and give himself to philanthropy or public service to feed his own egocentric ambition. This may or may not conflict with the ends of other people, but in certain circumstances the ends of other people may actually be promoted through such a self-advertising display. Our moral sense is offended by any suggestion that we should separate act and motive, and, while the results may be beneficial, we would ordinarily deem the man's conduct unworthy and his character reprehensible. Conversely, it is not at all clear that Albert Schweitzer set out to promote the chosen ends of those to whom he devoted his life. Indeed, humanitarian activity, not to mention missionary enterprise, has often depended upon the belief that certain ends were inherently good,

33. Graham, op. cit., pp. 41 ff.

whether they were recognized or not. Is it justifiable to leave an African tribe to its primitive beliefs and practices? Obviously the examples I have chosen could be debated at length, and many interesting points would emerge about the relationship of motive to action and the justifiability of overriding the ends of other people in the name of what is held to be good in itself; but the contention I wish to press is that Graham's formula does not cover all the facts. We may go even further, and urge that ethical questions arise in their most acute form when the ends that people set before themselves do in practice conflict. How, then, are we to settle the issue, except by an appeal to standards which Graham's *laissez-faire* toleration does not appear to allow?

The last point is to a considerable degree met in an article by P. F. Strawson in which he distinguishes between social morality and individual ideals.[34] Ethics, he holds, are, strictly speaking, concerned with the claims and counter-claims arising out of membership of the groups to which we belong and the legislation which provides for their cohesiveness; whereas we are free to set before ourselves any personal ideals we like, as long as they do not conflict with the rules governing social behaviour; and these ideals are good because they are what we desire. The trouble about this proposal is that the basic ethical issues are at stake not in the conventions which hold society together, still less in those matters regulated by law, but in the sphere of what Strawson describes as private ideals. Just where he allows free rein to individual preference and is neutral in his judgements, questions of right and wrong, good and evil, are in the end found to matter most. Strawson, Graham and all who share their point of view leave the impression of being unduly preoccupied with the conventions of society rather than with the inner springs of human conduct and the actions that result therefrom. They side with the legalistically-minded Pharisees against the more radical ethical teaching of Jesus of Nazareth. The warning of Christ against superficiality in concentrating upon externals needs to be care-

34. See P. F. Strawson, 'Social Morality and Individual Ideal', *Philosophy*, Vol. XXXVI (1961), pp. 1-17.

fully heeded: 'out of the heart proceed evil thoughts, murders, adulteries, fornications, thefts, false witness, blasphemies: these are the things which defile a man: but to eat with unwashen hands defileth not a man' (Matt. 15:19). Another way of putting the same thing is to ask whether the theoretical relativists have ever really considered the heights and depths of virtue and depravity of which man is capable. One sometimes wonders whether they have ever encountered a saint, or looked into the heart of human weakness and recognized the meanness, cruelty and self-indulgence which mar the lives of so many. St Paul's penetrating self-analysis in Romans 7 seems to be a closed book to them. In the last resort they seem to be dealing with a sort of moral suburbia where everything is very respectable, nothing adventurous is attempted, and the grosser passions are camouflaged and held in check. The polite conventions of academic society are taken as the norm, and their dependence on a funded ethical tradition conveniently ignored. The type of subjectivism we are discussing seems strangely out of touch with life, for instance, in an army barracks, in a large industrial concern, or in the Protestant religious community at Taizé.

In short, the case against this new form of reductionism seems overwhelming. It is difficult to see how ethical judgements can be reduced to decisions, commands or expressions of approval or disapproval when these in turn depend on some prior valuation. As A. C. Ewing so pointedly remarks in his own critical review: 'If "ethical judgements" are expressions of feelings of approval or disapproval, this is incompatible with my feeling guilty about an action; and yet believing it right, as may well be the case if I have been brought up to condemn such actions and since changed my mind. Again, if "ethical judgements", as on some naturalist views, assert that people in general approve of certain things, then that of which most people disapprove could never be right.'[35]

35. Ewing, *Second Thoughts in Moral Philosophy*, p. 19. Cf. also the detailed and trenchant criticism of Emotivism and its refinements by Brand Blanshard in *Reason and Goodness* (London, Allen & Unwin, 1961), pp. 194-265. While I am in substantial agreement with Ewing's critique of 'the New Subjectivism',

The position can only be rendered at all plausible by denying our right to any rational discrimination between one course of conduct and another. This abandonment of standards is rescued from manifest absurdity only by concentrating on conventional morality to the exclusion of man's inward struggle, and by ignoring instances of outstanding virtue on the one hand and degrees of depravity on the other.

As for truth, the third conventional category of value, reductionists would simply deny that it should be classified in this way at all. According to many modern philosophers truth is a function of propositions, denoting the way they are used in certain contexts. It may refer to logical implication, to verifiability by observation or to conventional description. Thus it is true that if Socrates is a man and all men are mortal, then Socrates is mortal. It is true that if you put your hand into the fire, you will be burnt. It is true that John is a fool to give away his money when the society to which he belongs encourages thrift, though the same proposition would be false in another context where

---

I find his proposal of 'a middle way' between this and the objectivism which characterized his earlier views quite unintelligible. Following suggestions by Toulmin, Hare and others, he maintains that ethical judgements are neither true nor false, though they may be valid or invalid. To use his own words, we shall be able to cognize 'that certain factual properties or circumstances constitute a reason why certain attitudes ought to be adopted or certain actions done' (p. 66). Behind this curious and obscure distinction lies the grudging admission that ethical judgements are not descriptive propositions, subject to the verification principle, but that they are more like decisions or commands, though they are not reducible to these. From this Ewing concludes that such judgements are *sui generis*, and thus objectivity is saved and the logicians placated. But what does this distinction amount to in the end? All that Ewing appears to be saying is that descriptions of objects are not like ethical judgements. But whoever supposed that they were? Goodness is clearly not a quality like redness, but neither is redness like heat. Of course, Ewing's intention is to deny that ethical concepts refer to qualities at all, but if they do not, how on his showing can they characterize reality at all? In the last resort, the difference between truth and validity is left entirely obscure. We want to know wherein lies the radical difference between descriptive propositions and ethical judgements. Simply to say they are different does not get us anywhere.

the possession of personal wealth happened to be regarded as disgraceful. Now if the position taken at the beginning of this chapter was right, namely that truth is called a value in the sense that knowledge is an end in itself of inherent worth, the proposal to restrict the word to its functional usage simply by-passes the issue by ignoring it. Certainly it is advantageous to know some things in order to achieve particular goals, and the ignorant will be left far behind in the struggle for wealth, prestige or even a reasonable livelihood. But that is far from being the whole story. Anyone who has pursued academic research or investigated any subject that has aroused his interest recognizes that this is an end in itself. One of the principal tasks of the teaching profession is to persuade students that higher education is not primarily a means to securing a well-paid job, but worth while for its own sake. A university is not meant to be a technical training school, important as that is in modern society. It is a community of learning in which truth is prized above everything else. One of the main reasons for fearing industrial or political control of universities is that it may lead to the prostitution of education for alien pur-poses. This is surely taken for granted by many of those who argue most forcibly for a reductionist theory of value. In so far as they are serious scholars and not mere dilettantes, knowledge is valued for itself; and this, I submit, reflects on the validity of their entire approach to ethics and aesthetics. In the last resort, however awkward and intellectually untidy it may appear to be, value judgements confront us with ultimates which cannot be ex-plained away.

The burden of the argument thus far has been that both the objectivist and the reductionist accounts of value present serious difficulties: the former because it apparently leaves us with a set of ill-defined qualities or unrelated abstract ideas, inviting the criticism that they are either figments of the imagination or pro-ducts of muddled thinking; the latter because it fails to allow for genuine standards of judgement, and, when exposed for what it is, flatly contradicts the dictates of common sense. The outline of an alternative approach has already been adumbrated by the argument of the preceding chapters. Instead of maintaining that values have any objective existence in themselves or, on the other hand, that they are the product of human thought and imagination, I am prepared to contend for a *via media*, which seems to me to avoid the principal difficulties in both the objectivist and subjectivist approaches. My suggestion is that values arise in an interrelational context, and are, with one vitally important qualification,[36] the product of man's interaction with his environment. This means that beauty, goodness and truth are not qualities inhering in anyone or anything considered in artificial isolation; nor are they human inventions. They designate a certain kind of dynamic relationship in which human beings stand with one another and with the world of which they are part. In the words of William Temple, 'it is in that interplay of mind and environment that Value resides.'[37]

The initial plausibility of the reductionist case rests upon the fact that values depend upon appreciation, which is another way of saying that they cannot be defined except in relation to an evaluating subject. As Carritt rightly says, 'there is certainly something strange about the idea of a beauty which nobody has ever seen or will see.'[38] On the other hand, values vanish when insufficient attention is paid to the distinctive characteristics of whatever stimulates an appreciative response in us. It is doubtless anomalous to dub the objectivist a realist in this respect, and the reductionist an idealist; and yet, in so far as realism denotes the primacy of the given and idealism the primacy of subjective construction, the labels are justified—perhaps a further indication of their uselessness for precise philosophical classification and their

36. The qualification is the attribution of values to God in and for himself. This is possible on the basis of a Trinitarian doctrine which allows for relationships within the Godhead.

37. William Temple, *Nature, Man and God*, p. 135. It will be obvious that I owe a great deal in what follows to Temple's treatment of the subject, although I believe that he introduces the theistic hypothesis too soon and with insufficient philosophical preparation to carry conviction.

38. Carritt, *What is Beauty?* p. 57.

inadequacy for delimiting the alternatives in metaphysical controversy. But it does focus attention on the peculiar paradoxes into which current discussions of the theory of value have led us. A fresh approach may enable us to steer our way through Scylla and Charybdis, allowing full weight to both objective stimulant and subjective response.

I propose to consider the three categories of beauty, goodness and truth in the reverse order, beginning with truth understood in terms of knowledge as contrasted with ignorance. I have already argued that knowledge arises through the adaptation of the human organism to its environment.[39] In the early stages of biological evolution the senses were predominant and were, as they still are, practical tools enabling the organism to adjust itself to everything around, avoiding danger and mastering whatever contributed to its comfort and survival. Out of this, and supervening upon it, emerged the capacity for conceptual thinking, and with it the possibility of a progressive understanding of the nature of the universe. The fact that man is not isolated, but lives his life in responsive interaction with an environment which impinges upon him wherever he turns, constitutes the condition for stimulating in him the capacity and desire to comprehend. Such understanding is itself a more comprehensive form of adaptation not only because it enables man to achieve a more effective mastery of his environment, but because he finds himself entering into a deepening harmony with the universe of which he is part. When he entertains a false proposition, he discovers that he is clashing with things as they are. In as much as he is right in his beliefs, his theories and his predictions, he is at home with reality, in tune with his surroundings. Herein lies the origin and meaning of value: the achievement of harmony which is the ultimate goal and destiny of mankind. Knowledge is the touchstone of value just because it is the basic means whereby we become related to our environment, and it is in this deepening and widening relationship that value is ultimately found. This is what is of intrinsic worth. Archbishop Temple intended much

39. Cf. *supra*, pp. 177 ff.

the same when he wrote: 'Value arises through Mind's discovery of itself in its object',[40] though the theistic implications of such a quotation seem to me to be premature from the standpoint of my own argument. Therefore, I conclude that Ryle is mistaken in drawing a sharp distinction between 'knowing how' and 'knowing that'.[41] The one arises out of the other and finally embraces it. The modern tendency to depreciate understanding in favour of practical techniques is a malaise of the times, threatening a reversion to the Dark Ages, if not total self-destruction. Progress is measured in terms of wisdom, not technological cleverness; and at no point does the teaching of Plato seem more relevant than this. The reinstatement of wisdom at the heart of our conception of values is the *sine qua non* of any satisfactory theory.

Turning to ethics, it is surely obvious that morality originates in interpersonal relationships: an axiom illustrated by the remark that Robinson Crusoe could not have been a Christian without Man Friday. The notions of obligation and duty come to birth in the realm of claim and counter-claim, and this is where moral philosophy must begin. Man is a social animal, from infancy to old age required to work out his adjustment to those around him, in the family, in the community, in groups of all kinds, in business and industry, in the nation and in the world at large. This is a living milieu in response to which he grows and develops; it is never static nor completely amenable to his control. His manhood is denigrated whenever he tries to retire into his shell and shut himself off from his fellows; and the same is true when he attempts to dominate them, treating them as things rather than as persons. He is confronted and surrounded by other people who have similar adjustments to make to his own, and the claims he makes on them and they on him are inherent in the fact that life is lived in interdependence, no man being a law unto himself.

Herein lies the principal merit of all those philosophies in the

40. Temple, op. cit., p. 219.
41. Gilbert Ryle, *The Concept of Mind*, pp. 25 ff.

Kantian tradition which have insisted on the primacy of obligation and duty in morals, refusing to allow that the concept of 'right' should be reduced to 'good' or to anything else. Whatever their defects (and these, as I shall try to show, are serious), they do at least focus attention on the fact that morality is essentially a response to claims, and that to deny this is to go badly astray. Here, surely, is the basic fallacy in the subjectivist position. When Strawson, for example, confines social morality to the laws and conventions governing man's communal life, he is unduly restricting the scope of human claims. Certainly, the laws of the country to which we belong and the written and unwritten rules of the societies of which we are members constitute prima facie claims we ordinarily feel bound to respect. But these are merely generalizations embracing a very limited range of claims that make social life tolerable. Subscription to them is the lowest common factor of moral obligation. Over and beyond this, we have to recognize that the *whole* of life is in community, and all that we do, still more all that we are, is in response to other people. A good example of this is the family: husband, wife, and children develop and mature in response to one another through claims and counter-claims which cannot possibly be reduced to rules, even though these may have a limited usefulness. In less obvious and direct ways the same applies to our relationship with people at large. When, therefore, Strawson proposes to set private over against public morals, he is drawing an artificial distinction which will not stand up to examination. Indeed, his suggestion that, after allowing for the laws and conventions of society, in private life we may set before ourselves whatever ideals we like and call them good, is a misuse of words. He is contracting out of the ethical situation, taking refuge in an individualistic escapism. The response to claims, not the adoption of ideals, is the essence of the good life.

This brings us to the relationship between the right and the good, and to the point where we part company with the neo-Kantians. One of the principal legacies which Immanuel Kant left to subsequent generations of philosophers was his concept of the moral law, defined in terms of the universal law of man's reason. It will already have become plain where this conflicts with the position here being advocated. Once morality is reduced to law, whether it be the law of the State, the law of nature, or the law of man's reason, we find ourselves left at best with a generalization, at worst with an abstraction. If the claims of persons are fundamental, and if persons and personal relationships are unique, then moral rules are but rough-and-ready generalizations; they can never be absolute. To quote an apt aphorism, the only rule to which there is no exception is that every rule has an exception. One of the most striking things about the ethical teaching of Jesus is the consistent way in which he refused to legislate, choosing to lay down principles for individual application according to the circumstances of the case. To use the terminology we have adopted, for him the particular claims of particular people were paramount. This was why he so often found himself in conflict with the Scribes and Pharisees who were the champions of the Mosaic Law with its numerous embellishments, designed to cover every conceivable contingency. Similarly, one of the objections that may legitimately be directed against the neo-Kantianism of Ross and Prichard is that their absolutism leads them to concentrate more on the nature of the claim than on the claimant. This is inevitable if 'right' and 'good' are both *sui generis*, as they maintain; for then the whole range of prima facie duties will have to stand on their own, irreducible to anything else. The question, 'What makes x obligatory?' is, on this view, unanswerable. All that we can say is that it just is so, and this makes every duty an ultimate. The case is different if the claims that men make upon one another are to be justified or otherwise in terms of some concept of goodness. The net result of the neo-Kantian view is to leave us with a set of abstractions, ontologically ungrounded, which is one of the most cogent reasons for rejecting an objectivist theory of ethics. But once claims are recognized as deriving their validity from the nature of the claimants, the argument against abstractions is undercut.

In the second place, the grounding of morality in duty and obligation lays itself open to the charge of ignoring motives by placing too much emphasis on the performance of specific acts. This is the besetting temptation of legalism. In a court of law the responsibility of judge and jury is principally to determine whether something has been done or not. The motives behind the offence are of secondary importance, to be taken into account later as extenuating circumstances in fixing the penalty. The fact that a man intended to commit a murder and failed is less serious in the eyes of the law than manslaughter, especially if the failure was so complete that the intended victim escaped all bodily injury. It is the outward effect which counts, not the inward disposition. This legalistic outlook has so influenced the thinking of ordinary people that 'ethics' is commonly held to be concerned with overt acts, whereas motives and dispositions are regarded as comparatively unimportant. The worst offence is popularly believed to be murder; pride does not really matter.

Of course Kant himself cannot be accused of neglecting the inwardness of ethics, but the attempt to define obligation in terms of universal law almost inevitably led to an artificial separation between overt acts and hidden motives, as well as between claims and claimants. This is exemplified in the distinction which W. D. Ross draws between act and action, the former denoting the observable performance of one's duty, and the latter the outward act together with the often hidden motive.[42] According to him, acts may be right, though they have no value unless they are also good, i.e. undertaken from a praiseworthy motive. The example he takes to illustrate the point is that of the creditor and debtor. A has a prima facie duty to repay a certain sum of money that he has borrowed from B. Suppose he returns it, not because he acknowledges a personal obligation, but through fear of the consequences if he fails to do so. Has he done his duty or not? Ross answers that he has done what is right, but not what is good. There seems to be something strange about this, and we are inclined to feel that Ross has given a highly attenuated version of

42. Ross, op. cit., p. 7.

what a right act really is. Surely, the error lies not, as Temple suggests in discussing the argument,[43] in a failure to recognize value in meeting the claim of the creditor, but in the unwarrantable restriction of the notion of claim (and, therefore, of obligation, duty and right) to the outward performance of overt acts. Whatever for practical purposes may satisfy the requirements of a court of law should not be sufficient for the moral philosopher who is required to take all the factors into account. Claims are claims upon *persons*, and to separate act from motive or intention is an abstraction as far as the performer is concerned. When someone owes me money, my legal claim may simply be that he should repay the debt. My *moral* claim is that he should respond to me as the sort of person who honours his financial obligations. A wife's moral claim upon her husband is not just that he should provide sufficient funds for housekeeping and her own expenses, and that he should not commit adultery, but that he should love her above all other women and give himself to her in deepening devotion. In the sphere of ethics personal relations are all important, and this is obscured when acts are artificially separated from motives. Contrary to the views of neo-Kantians and many other moralists besides, claims upon people are in the last resort *to be* rather than to do.

The most serious difficulty of all for anyone who proposes to make claims ultimate, whether he takes motives into account or not, is that some way has to be found of settling between them. Frequently they conflict, and even when they do not, we do not regard all of them as equally justifiable. Indeed, we consider some to be completely unwarrantable. An example of conflicting claims is the tension a man feels between the demands of his business or profession and those of his family. Is he to sacrifice time spent in recreation with his wife and children to the interests of his employer or his client? Some sort of balance has to be achieved, but on what basis? More difficult still is the case of the conscientious objector in wartime, who has to reconcile his sense of loyalty to the State with his conviction that he owes a duty

43. Temple, op. cit., p. 171.

to the enemies of the State as well; and the dilemma becomes all the more complex if his refusal to bear arms entails imprisonment with consequent suffering by his wife and family. Many opponents of the Nazis in Germany had to face just such an agonizing conflict. Again, no one supposes that the claims of a kidnapper for ransom money or of a blackmailer for the price of silence are in any way justifiable. And what about the demands of children which parents rightly refuse? Where are principles of discrimination to be found?

Considerations of this sort make it virtually impossible to rest content with a theory of obligation unless it is grounded in some comprehensive principle which affords a theoretical rationale for discrimination as well as guidance for practical decisions. This is why many philosophers have insisted on the integral connexion between 'the right' and 'the good': what makes a right action right and justifies any claim is whether it is conducive to goodness. But does this do anything more than push the problem one stage further back or even rephrase it in different language? For, once utilitarianism or any other kind of ethical reductionism has been rejected, goodness turns out to be an ultimate, whether it is regarded with G. E. Moore as indefinable,[44] or with J. H. Muirhead as a quality of life.[45]

Nevertheless, in spite of the fact that Muirhead leaves us in the air and does not bring us down to solid earth, he does, I believe, point the way to as satisfactory a theory as we are likely to reach; for, as Temple says, 'there is a sense in which the word "good" belongs to the good character as it belongs to nothing else at all.'[46] If the contention is valid that morality arises through the claims and counter-claims of persons on one another, and if these are not to be limited to claims for certain overt acts, but for a certain response involving the whole of a man's being, then

44. G. E. Moore, *Principia Ethica* (Cambridge, The University Press, 1960), p 17.

45. J. H. Muirhead, *Rule and End in Morals* (London, Oxford University Press, 1932), pp. 102 ff.

46. Temple, op. cit., p. 167.

goodness must be identified with a certain kind of life which is progressively evoked. This does not get us very far until we designate a good life as that which contributes to the emergence of a community of persons, each of whom is enabled thereby to develop and express his own particular gifts to their fullest capacity. To work out a detailed casuistry on the basis of this principle is beyond the scope of the present discussion. Suffice it to say, by way of illustration, that it provides grounds for condemning cruelty, avarice, selfishness and pride as wrong, and esteeming generosity, patience, consideration and humility as praiseworthy. Above all else, the crowning virtue is love, understood not in its depreciated sense of sentimental feeling or erotic desire, but as a consistent resolve, expressed in action, to treat other people as ends in themselves. This is the antithesis of individualism. To quote Temple again, 'we are from the beginning, and by the very constitution of our nature, bound up with one another, so that the weal and woe of each is in itself the weal and woe of all others within the circle of intimate relationships. . . . In early stages the community of which membership is recognized is small and sharply limited. Moral progress consists largely in the widening of the area in which the obligations of membership are recognized.'[47]

My conclusion, then, is that moral goodness is a value which arises in interpersonal relationships through response to the claims of other people. It cannot be achieved in isolation or by withdrawal from the pressing demands of those around us. Nor, in spite of arguments to the contrary,[48] can it be externalized in the performance of acts artificially abstracted from the motives or disposition of the agent. The objection that a man may act from good motives and do the bad thing or act from bad motives and do the good thing is to tear apart what cannot properly be sundered. The 'good' motive does not make a 'bad' act good, nor does a 'bad' act make a 'good' motive bad. The inverted commas

47. Ibid., pp. 185, 187.
48. Cf. H. D. Lewis's criticism of T. H. Green in *Freedom and History* (London, Allen & Unwin, 1962), pp. 25-36.

are intended to draw attention to the abstraction that the use of these words involves when applied to acts or motives in isolation from one another. A 'good' motive only becomes unequivocally good when it inspires a 'good' act. In other words, the criterion of goodness in the moral sense is the informing of act by motive in response to the claims of other persons. The most that can be said of dispositions, motives and acts considered in isolation from one another, is that they may be partially good when measured against a standard of unequivocal goodness. In turn this raises the question whether the 'good' act inspired by the 'good' motive has not itself to be measured against a standard of perfection which is beyond human attainment.

Thus my contention is that ethical value is derived from the total context of personal relationships in all their interconnectedness. This means that the proposal to separate the concepts of 'right' and 'good' is a mistake, and moral value is not to be attributed *simpliciter* either to claimants or claims or the persons on whom the claims are made. Indeed, on the view I have been advancing, all three are abstractions considered by themselves. Obligation involves at least two parties in relation to one another, and a complete account of goodness cannot be given apart from the interwoven complex of relationships which form a community. Perfection is, therefore, the ideal of a comprehensive fellowship which has never been realized on earth.

What about beauty? Does the principle of interaction help us to understand how this most elusive of all values originates? As we have already seen, everyday language ascribes beauty to objects, qualitatively inhering in them, but any attempts to define it and compare it with other qualities such as colour simply break down;[49] and we have to face the added difficulty that the experience of beauty seems inescapably to depend on the stimulation

49. Though the difficulty is, I believe, aggravated by a failure to see that so-called secondary qualities, such as colour, do not inhere in objects, but arise out of man's interaction with the world around him (*vide supra*, pp. 117 ff.). Ewing's inability to locate goodness anywhere partly arises out of what seems to me to be this cardinal mistake.

of emotion in the experient. On the other hand, the subjectivist point of view which purports to find beauty in the expression of feelings alone can only do so at the sacrifice of any objective standard of comparison; and this clearly runs counter to common sense and the critical appraisal to which the proponents of the theory, as much as anybody else, are actually committed in practice. The major objections to both alternatives would appear to be avoided if some kind of interrelational theory of beauty could be devised, allowing full weight to the objective character of nature or works of art in virtue of which we call them beautiful, as well as to the emotional satisfaction of the appreciating subject. I have already argued that this is to be found as far as truth and goodness are concerned in the harmony of man with reality and the community of persons. Is beauty similarly to be found in the harmony of man with certain aspects of his environment?

Earlier in this chapter I maintained that man's appreciation of nature is fundamental to his experience of beauty, criticizing philosophers like Carritt for basing all their arguments on the creative arts. While not departing from this conviction, for practical purposes of exposition I propose to take music as an example, which at least has the merit of meeting those from whom I differ on their own ground.

Everyone would doubtless agree that the enjoyment of listening to a Beethoven symphony is dependent upon a number of factors: the developing design of the composer, the communication of his composition in written and later printed notation, the interpretation of the conductor, the performance of certain actions of scraping, plucking and blowing on the part of the members of the orchestra, the vibrations resulting from this concerted activity, and finally the pattern of sounds in which the listener delights. Wherein does the beauty of the symphony lie? Surely not merely in the emotional satisfaction of the audience, which is not aroused in a vacuum. Still less in the scraping of catgut and blowing of wind through holes which is the immediate cause of the experience. Nor is it plausible to isolate beauty in any one of the other factors mentioned above. The truth seems to be that it lies in the complex of their interconnexions. In the example chosen this includes the intention of the composer and the interpretation of the conductor, though it is possible for an imaginative person to appreciate the beauty of the Fifth Symphony in C minor simply by reading the score, an experience that is qualitatively different from listening to a performance of the work, but one that is none the less genuinely aesthetic. It is, therefore, just a case of loose usage to apply the word 'beauty' to the musical score alone. Interplay between at least two factors is necessary before any value comes to birth: a condition satisfied in the more limited case of someone reading the musical score no less than in the more complicated one of the audience listening to an orchestral performance.

Carritt is, therefore, justified in quoting with approval the words of an eighteenth-century writer when he says: 'It seems impossible to conceive objects themselves to be endowed with more than a particular order of parts, and with powers, or an affinity to our perceptive faculties, thence arising; . . . surely order and regularity are more properly the causes of beauty than beauty itself.'[50] But he is wrong in drawing the conclusion that beauty is to be defined as the expression of feeling. Without the particular order of parts in the Fifth Symphony, the experience of beauty which audiences derive from listening to it would not be possible. Any arrangement of notes would not suffice.

This brings us to the most difficult aspect of the whole problem: how we are to differentiate between the Fifth Symphony and the latest popular song? Why do we claim that the one is of more value than the other, and on what grounds are we justified in doing so? From what has been said thus far we have no more reason than the extreme subjectivists for claiming that there are any criteria in aesthetics. The solution seems to lie in a consideration of all the different factors which contribute to the creation of what is widely recognized to be a great piece of music.

50. R. Price, *Review of the Principal Questions in Morals*, quoted by Carritt in *An Introduction to Aesthetics*, pp. 25 f.

First of all, through the works of a composer like Beethoven we are privileged to encounter a man of genius, someone who towers above his fellows, and in contact with whom the imagination is stretched to compass wider horizons. The great majority of people never meet the men and women of genius face to face, but do so through their creative works in music, painting, sculpture and most commonly literature, whereby they become citizens of the world; but then there is no mistaking them. There are many Cole Porters, but only one Beethoven.

In the second place, a great musical composition introduces us to someone whose range of comprehension far exceeds the average, enabling us to enter the storehouse of his experience and explore the sweep of his imagination. This means that we cannot afford to discount the didactic character of artistic works, provided we give the word its widest connotation and do not insist that all artistic expression must exemplify this characteristic in any precise way. Expression of feeling on the part of a man who has entered deeply into the frustration and tragedy of life may not be didactic in the narrow sense of saying something that can be put into words, but our sensitivity may be increased and our sympathy enlarged in proportion to the extent of our responsive appreciation. Has not this happened in the case of any number of people who have listened to the final chorus of Bach's 'St Matthew' Passion?

Third, a great musical work is marked by the breadth of its conception. Contrast 'Three Blind Mice' with Bach's Mass in B minor, the hymn tune 'Pentecost' with the *Passion Chorale*, or 'Chopsticks' with Chopin's Waltz in C sharp minor. The actual compositions, quite apart from the personalities and range of comprehension of the composers, exhibit the most obvious differences. 'Three Blind Mice', 'Pentecost' and 'Chopsticks' are all trivial, a set of notes strung together in the most pedestrian fashion, whereas the three famous works are the products of highly developed imaginations.

Fourth, nearly all critics are agreed that symmetry and proportion have something to do with the experience of beauty.

Alexander, as we have seen, believes that this is read into nature by the selective and ordering tendency of the human mind; but this cannot possibly be applied without radical qualification to a work of art, wherein the artist himself produces the pattern for the viewer to grasp as best he may. Likewise the composer enunciates his themes and develops his variations with regard to the balance of the whole, and the apprehension of this is implicit in musical appreciation.

Finally, there is the mastery of technique, which enables the outstanding craftsman, usually through the discipline of very hard work, to handle his medium with a facility and dexterity that is denied to the mere hack.

The interrelationship of all these factors varies and is highly complex, which accounts for the difficulty of defining why one work of art should be esteemed more beautiful than another. Nevertheless, broad standards of comparison are possible, and we can at least begin to understand why most artefacts are ephemeral, titillating the senses for a time, and then passing into the limbo of obscurity. They fail to endure because they do not introduce us to wider horizons and deeper dimensions of experience than the humdrum routine of life provides. By contrast, works of art are justifiably deemed beautiful in proportion to their potentiality for creating abiding and ever growing satisfaction as the listener or viewer is drawn into harmony with that which stretches his imagination and enlarges the range of his emotions. 'Men may be uncertain in this second quarter of the twentieth century', says William Temple, 'about the aesthetic rank of Epstein as a sculptor or of T. S. Eliot as a poet. But there is no serious dispute about Pheidias or Aeschylus, about Giotto, or Piero, or Botticelli, about Velasquez or Rembrandt, about Dante or Shakespeare . . . every name thus mentioned is securely established in the list of Masters; and the actual works of the earliest touch us now as they touched the hearts of those who knew them first. Still for sheer pulverising pathos we turn to the twenty-fourth *Iliad*, still for tragic sublimity to the *Agamemnon*, still for the calm of "port after stormy seas" to the *Oedipus Coloneus*. What scientific theory has the security of these works of art? The Newtonian Law of Gravitation seemed till yesterday to be assured beyond the risk of modification. Yet now, though the repute of Newton himself remains as well assured as that of Milton, his system is displaced by those of curvilinear space; while no amount of modern free verse displaces Milton's *Sonnet on his Blindness*. It takes longer for the aesthetic judgement to become stable than for the scientific, but when it reaches stability it also achieves finality as the other does not.'[51]

Appreciation of natural beauty may be explained in much the same way. Theists do, of course, argue that this is evidence of the handiwork of the Master Artist, and, if this is so, all the factors mentioned in the discussion of musical composition and the like would be applicable to an even more marked degree. In passing, it is perhaps to the point to ask whether the reason for the neglect of natural beauty on the part of philosophers unsympathetic to the theist position is that their theories of beauty are so tied up with creative artistry that even to admit the possibility of experiencing beauty in nature is embarrassing. However that may be, without introducing the theistic hypothesis at this juncture, we may contend that in the proportion of line and colour which man finds in mountains, lakes, rivers, waterfalls, trees and flowers, there may be deep emotional satisfaction, which is another way of achieving harmony with an environment that transcends our passing likes and dislikes.

To sum up, we may conclude that aesthetic appreciation is a kind of knowledge, whereby man reaches emotional harmony with his surroundings. Just as truth is the fundamental value in that genuine knowledge brings us into harmony with reality as such, so goodness and beauty are comparable in that the one is the harmony of man with his fellows in growing community, and the other is emotional harmony with his environment through a widening range of sensible experience. Perhaps we may differentiate between truth and beauty in the light of our earlier dis-

51. Temple, op. cit., pp. 158 f.

cussion of sense perception by saying that, while truth is harmony with reality as such, beauty is harmony with the way in which our environment impinges upon us through the senses. Thus, however satisfying the experience of beauty may be, it always points beyond to a reality that transcends the sensible. Truth, therefore, understood as wisdom, is the supreme value, and in this respect we find ourselves returning full cycle to the fundamental position of Plato.

The interactionist principle, then, provides us with a theory of value which enables us to allow for both the subjective and the objective factors in our experience without being compelled to deny the one in fidelity to the other. Value consists in the degree of harmony man achieves in rapport with his environment. This conclusion, as I shall argue later, is of cardinal importance for metaphysics, bringing to focus the nature of our experience as a whole and pointing towards its ultimate integration. At the same time, our appreciation of value more than anything else drives us to recognize the essentially mysterious nature of reality. If Marcel is right in holding that we are never so aware of mystery as when we acknowledge the claims that are made upon us, then we shall not be surprised to find that the grounding of our sense of value in the dynamic interrelationship of man with his environment, while exposing the nature of this crucial aspect of our experience, compels us to acknowledge a dimension to it which is entirely beyond our power to fathom. Mystery lies in that which we are in principle unable to master because of our finitude. In the realm of values this is not merely an intellectual issue: our inability to comprehend the fullness of truth, goodness and beauty *sub specie aeternitatis*. It is much more than that. It is our progressive awareness, as we become more sensitive, that we fall far short of attainment in our total response to the claims that are made upon us. Indeed, the fact that we have to speak of claims at all when analysing the meaning of value indicates the gulf which separates us from perfection. Therefore, from the standpoint of philosophical analysis, we are faced with profound mystery not only because a complete conspectus of the realm of value is hidden from us, but also because we are unable to know whether the experience of limited attainment is anything more than a pathetic attempt to grasp what inevitably slips through our fingers in a universe destined to disintegrate. The ultimate grounding of the values we begin to cherish is the most poignant of all mysteries.

CHAPTER SIX

THE DISCLOSURE OF THE TRANSCENDENT

The preceding chapters have been concerned with the philosophical analysis of our common experience, leading to the recognition of the mysterious depth of everything we try to understand: a depth utterly unfathomable and beyond our powers of comprehension, and yet inescapably the dimension of everything that is, forcing itself upon our attention wherever we turn. The acknowledgement of this dimension gives rise to what may be called the 'why' questions, which are nothing but attempts to push back the metaphysical frontiers and see mystery in at least a more coherent form. Why is there anything at all? Why is there individuation and spontaneity? Why does not the universe disintegrate? In particular, why should claims be made upon us in response to which we find value? Why in any case should we consider value, defined as intellectual, aesthetic and moral harmony with our environment, to be grounded in the very structure of things? Why should not our quest for value be regarded simply as evidence for the tragic pathos of man's predicament—his vain attempt to make an insignificant existence meaningful?

A time-honoured answer to these questions is, of course, the argument to a transcendent ground of finite existence. The being of everything we experience is contingent, and when this is apprehended, we are driven to Necessary Being as its *fons et origo*. Individuation is explained as due to the creative act of God and spontaneity as participation in his own freedom. The coordination of the universe, in spite of the manifest signs of randomness and dysteleology, is attributed to the divine purpose, and value is rooted and grounded in the divine will. Although there are some theists who still believe these are valid lines of argument and are prepared to defend them with skill and persuasiveness, the whole approach has been subjected to devastating criticism, and the difficulties inherent in it are formidable to say the least.[1]

In the first place, it has been argued that the appeal from the so-called contingent world to that which lies beyond it rests on a logical mistake, whereby rules applicable to propositions are un-critically transferred to the realm of fact. Kant is generally held to have exposed the fallacy of the traditional ontological argument when he showed that existence is not a predicate, and therefore that propositions about the existence of God do not establish the reality of a divine Being outside the realm of thought: a con-clusion reached by St Thomas Aquinas several centuries before in his criticism of St Anselm's original formulation.[2] But St Thomas's own argument from the contingency of finite being to its ground in necessary being has been similarly attacked for the transference of logical implication to the world of fact to which it has no reference.[3] While the objection stands as a warning against the illegitimacy of assuming that the laws of abstract thought apply to what exists in independence of the thinking subject, St Thomas would not have agreed that he was using contingency and neces-sity in the logical sense at all. It is possible to maintain, writes John Hick, 'that there is factual contingency as well as logical con-tingency and factual necessity as well as logical necessity';[4] and it is to what he believes to be the contingent *being* of everything in the universe that St Thomas appeals. All the same, the question remains whether we are justified in applying to the realm of

1. Cf. John Laird, *Theism and Cosmology* (London, Allen & Unwin, 1940), pp. 85-112, 261-321.

2. St Thomas Aquinas, *Summa Theologica*, Part I, Question ii, Article 1, Objection 1.

3. Cf. J. N. Findlay in *New Essays in Philosophical Theology*, ed. Antony Flew and Alasdair MacIntyre (London, SCM Press, 1955), pp. 47 ff.

4. John Hick, 'God as Necessary Being', *The Journal of Philosophy*, Vol. LVII (October-November 1960), pp. 725-34.

being what are basically logical categories, even though we are deliberately using the concepts in a different sense.

This brings us to the second and more serious criticism levelled against those who reason *a contingentia mundi* and its classical statement in the *Quinque Viae* of St Thomas Aquinas. The difficulty about these arguments, as both Hume and Kant saw, is that they appear to involve us in the attempt to get outside the prison-house of our experience, which in the nature of the case it is impossible for us to do. The argument to a First Cause, for instance, implies the use of a category which is applicable only to the world of our experience and becomes unintelligible once it is employed outside this frame of reference. For example, Laird castigates John Locke for drawing the conclusion that God exists from assertions like 'I exist' or 'something exists'. The fact that I am not self-dependent may be attributed to many finite causes, but 'this cause-cluster . . . is but a tiny part of the universe, and the entities on which I depend, or have depended, are of the same order as I am myself. Nothing in the argument shows that any of them operates on a cosmic scale.'[5] Accordingly, Laird concludes that the premise has to be the contingency of the *universe*, not of its constituent parts, and to this the category of causation is inapplicable. The same point is expressed in another way by Karl Heim when he says, 'we cannot, in any question we may put, step outside the primal relation to which we are confined.'[6] In other words, for the traditional arguments to have force, it is held that they would have to lead us to One who was part of the world of finite experience and not transcendent to it; and the purport of the 'proofs' is certainly not this.

The third difficulty inherent in any attempt to go beyond the world of finite experience is the problem of finding a language in which anything significant can be expressed about it. If our language is inherently confined to talking about the universe as presented to us through the senses and is built up through our interaction with our immediate environment, how can we hope to say anything meaningful about the Transcendent even if the

5. Laird, op. cit., p. 88.   6. Karl Heim, *God Transcendent*, p. 48.

Transcendent exists? And does not such a way of putting the difficulty illustrate our bankruptcy in that the word 'exists' refers to that which falls within the non-transcendental frame of reference?

Fourth, there is the problem of the apparent irrationality of so much that we have to take into account. While, as we have already noted, the teleological aspect of the universe is inescapable and has to be included within any comprehensive metaphysical analysis, this is not the whole story. Nature displays a prodigality which has all the marks of randomness and is extremely difficult to bring within the framework of any purpose whatsoever. Moreover, we have to reckon with the grim fact of evil, whether this be understood as moral corruption or the negating of any teleology by disease, destruction and death. Of course, the problem of irrationality and evil does not arise for anyone other than those who wish to maintain that God is the ultimate ground of all being; but it is obviously a serious obstacle for those who do.

Clearly, the crucial issue is the question of contingency. Is Laird right in concluding that no meaning can be given to the idea which justifies us in arguing from the finite to the infinite, from that which we apprehend through the senses to that which is transcendent? Modern Thomists would certainly want to challenge this conclusion, and, in particular, they would reject the equation of contingency with dependence on a finite cause. The cosmological argument, or, as E. L. Mascall would prefer to call it, the cosmological approach,[7] does not assert that God is the last link in a chain of finite causes, but that he is the metaphysical ground of being. In so far as 'cause' is used at all in this connexion it has to be distinguished from its general connotation *within* the world of finite relationships, and it is perhaps better to avoid needless confusion by employing different terminology altogether. Hence the reference to the ground rather than the cause of being. At all events, Mascall's belief in the validity of the

7. This redefinition was suggested in a private conversation for reasons which will become apparent later.

cosmological approach turns upon the conviction that the being of everything is contingent in the sense that it can be apprehended as non-self-sufficient, which carries with it an apprehension of God as its ontologically necessary ground.

We should note the precise significance of this claim. Mascall's contention is not that we may *infer* the existence of God from the apprehension of being as contingent; the essential Being of God is presented to us directly in the contingent *qua* contingent. Following the scholastics in their '*adaequatio intellectus ad rem*', he maintains that 'the human mind, by its very constitution, is capable of penetrating beneath the phenomenal surface of finite beings and of grasping them, however imperfectly and partially, in their ontological nature and so apprehending them in their dependence upon an infinite Being, which, as St Thomas says, all men call God.'[8] In his exposition of this intuitive faculty of the mind, Mascall draws freely on Father D'Arcy's development of Cardinal Newman's treatment of the 'illative sense' in *The Grammar of Assent*,[9] though D'Arcy prefers the word 'interpretation' to intuition,[10] maintaining that this is our capacity for knowing without inference the nature of that with which we are confronted. Taking Newman's example of our knowledge of Great Britain as an island, he says that 'the mind is here eminently engaged on its proper business, reading through data to the meaning revealed, and, in the examples of absolute certainty, seeing infinitely complex and consistent data, *by means of indirect inference*, in terms of unity.'[11] It is this capacity of the mind to 'read through data to the meaning revealed' which, according to Mascall, enables us to apprehend God in finite being, and in so far as the so-called 'proofs' are of significance, they simply explicate what this

8. E. L. Mascall, *He Who Is* (London, Longmans, 1943), p. 83.

9. M. C. D'Arcy, *The Nature of Belief* (London, Sheed & Ward, 1931), pp. 165 ff.

10. Ibid, pp. 272 f.

11. Ibid., p. 274. The italics, which are mine, serve to underline the ambiguity in this approach, where the difference between intuition and inference has not been clearly drawn. Hence the arguments are retained while suggesting that they are superfluous in view of intuitive comprehension.

apprehension is. They do not add anything to what is intuited, and are superfluous once we have grasped the contingent as grounded in the Being of God.

A major objection to this refashioned Thomism lies in the ambiguity of the word 'contingent'. If the traditional arguments are to be discarded in favour of an immediate intuition, then it would be better to refrain from using language drawn from the context of inferential argument. The word 'contingent' suggests an inference to that which is not directly given in the premise, and certainly St Thomas and the scholastics in general believed that they were reasoning from finite data to the Infinite. Mascall does not really escape from the inferential purport of his language, as can be seen from the attention he pays to the exposition of the arguments of the Five Ways; and it does not help to say that the arguments explicate the intuition; for either the intuition is direct and immediate, in which case no argument is to the point, or else an argument is involved and the intuition is not of the meta-physical premise, but of all the steps leading to the conclusion. As long as the initial apprehension is restricted to finite being, is en-closed within the confines of what is called the contingent, I do not see how the philosophical objections to arguing beyond these limitations are to be avoided. The field is left to Hume and Kant. But once the connotation of inference has been excluded from contingency, it is hard to understand what 'contingent' can mean apart from what is expressed in purely negative terms. The most that we can say is that the being of everything apprehended through the senses is self-insufficient and not self-explanatory, which is another way of saying it is profoundly mysterious,[12] and we are back where we started.

The situation, however, is radically changed if we take Marcel's contention seriously, that the transcendent is given *in* our ex-perience of the world in which we live; for then it is possible to

12. Cf. Paul Tillich's conclusion that the traditional arguments for the existence of God are not so much arguments as questions: *Systematic Theology* (London, Nisbet, 1953), Vol. I, pp. 231-3.

ask whether we have knowledge of God directly and not by inference. To put the matter in another way, the question arises
whether God is apprehended through the revelation of himself
in terms of finite experience. If it be true that he has taken the
initiative in meeting with us on our own ground, speaking to us
in our own language, breaking down, as it were, the walls of our
prison-house, then the Transcendent can be known in the finite.
No longer is it necessary to suppose that man should exceed his
powers by reasoning to the self-sufficient ground of being; the
precise reverse is the case. God has translated himself into terms
that man can apprehend *within* the realm of finite being, and this
is what distinguishes the God who acts from the God of the
philosophers—the *terminus ad quem* of metaphysical argument. It
is in this sense that we can echo the lines of Dryden:

> Thy throne is darkness in th' abyss of light,
> A blaze of glory which forbids the sight;
> O teach us to believe Thee thus conceal'd,
> And search no farther than thy self reveal'd.[13]

This does not necessarily involve, as some have supposed, immediate concentration on the pattern of events to which the
Bible bears witness, though ultimately that is involved. In the first
instance it is to raise the issue of natural theology in a different
form: not as an inference to the Transcendent beyond the frontier
of human experience, but as the apprehension of the Transcendent
disclosed *in the total range of human experience.*

Whether God is so disclosed remains to be seen. All I am concerned to establish at the moment is that the possibility of the
revelation of the Transcendent within human experience turns
the flank of those arguments which both biblical theologians and
sceptical philosophers have advanced to show that natural theology
is an illegitimate enterprise. On the one hand, if God does reveal
himself in the natural order, who are theologians to say him nay?
Even Karl Barth concedes the point when he says, 'God may speak
to us through Russian communism or a flute concerto, a blossom-

13. John Dryden, *The Hind and the Panther*, ll. 66-9.

ing shrub or a dead dog. We shall do well to listen to him if he really does so.'[14] Certainly it is plausible to argue the impiety of supposing that man by the unaided light of reason and in his sinful condition can attain to the knowledge of God, and on this premise the so-called 'proofs' of his existence may be pretentious —the attempt of the creature to bring his Creator within the framework of his own limited powers of thought. But if God graciously discloses himself for man to apprehend, that is another matter altogether. It is no more and no less paradoxical that God should reveal himself and be apprehended as revealed in the natural order in general than that this should happen through the occurrence of a particular sequence of events. Indeed, to suppose otherwise is to carve up reality in a wholly artificial manner and to confine God's effective action to a miraculous intervention in a world that has been left to its own devices. This just will not do. As William Temple so powerfully urged, 'unless all existence is a medium of Revelation, no particular Revelation is possible . . . Either all occurrences are in some degree revelation of God, or else there is no such revelation at all; for the conditions of the possibility of any revelation requires that there should be nothing which is not revelation. Only if God is revealed in the rising of the sun in the sky can He be revealed in the rising of a son of man from the dead; only if He is revealed in the history of Syrians and Philistines can He be revealed in the history of Israel; only if He chooses all men for His own can He choose any at all; only if nothing is profane can anything be sacred. It is necessary to stress with all possible emphasis this universal quality of revelation in general before going on to discuss the various modes of particular revelation; for the latter, if detached from the former, loses its

14. Karl Barth, *Church Dogmatics*, Vol. I, Part 1, p. 60. But he qualifies his admission by saying that we have no commission to spread what is addressed to us in this way. The distinctive Christian revelation stands on its own, and, in his view, to allow any place to natural theology would be to make room for 'an anthropological prius to faith' (see pp. 38-47). However, the assumption that natural theology is 'the basic science of human possibilities' (p. 45) is just what I am questioning.

root in the rational coherence of the world and consequently becomes itself a superstition and a fruitful source of superstitions.'[15]

On the other hand, the philosophical criticism that the inference from the natural to the supernatural, from contingent to necessary being, is illegitimate is seen to be beside the point, once the case for natural theology is restated in terms of the Transcendent disclosed within finite experience. No longer is it being alleged that reason takes us beyond the given to a realm where finite categories and concepts turn out to be inapplicable. On the contrary, the supernatural is held to be disclosed within the natural order and in terms of that order; it is a translation into finite experience of what would otherwise be totally incomprehensible—incomprehensible in the sense of being utterly beyond human reach. Thus it may be claimed that we are confronted with the mystery of the Transcendent in the only way in which it can be recognized as such.

The edge is also blunted of another kind of philosophical criticism which has recently been levelled against the significance of natural theology. Following John Wisdom's well-known illustration of the invisible gardener for whose existence no observational data are found to be relevant,[16] Antony Flew developed the thesis that theological statements are not factually significant because there is no conceivable evidence that would be admitted to falsify them.[17] Such utterances, he holds, as 'God has a plan', 'God created the world', 'God loves us as a father loves his children', are all asserted by believers with such sublime disregard for empirical evidence that there is 'no conceivable event or series of events the occurrence of which would be admitted by sophisticated religious people to be a sufficient reason for conceding "There wasn't a God after all" or "God does not really love us then".'[18] Now it is clear from the way in which the case is

15. William Temple, *Nature, Man and God*, pp. 306 f.

16. John Wisdom, 'Gods' in *Essays on Logic and Language*, ed. Antony Flew (Oxford, Blackwell, 1951), pp. 192 f.

17. Antony Flew, *New Essays in Philosophical Theology*, pp. 96 ff.

18. Ibid., p. 98.

stated that it rests on the assumption that belief in God can only depend on an inference from natural phenomena, which may count for or against the belief in question. Indeed, some of those who have criticized Flew's thesis have themselves proceeded on the same assumption, seeking to show that theism is compatible with inability to suggest evidence of the kind Flew desiderates.[19] My contention, on the other hand, is that the assumption itself is mistaken. Belief in God is not to be validated by an inference from phenomena considered to be exhaustively defined as natural occurrences; they may be apprehended in their own mysterious depth as occasions for the disclosure of the Transcendent, and unless God is to be known in and through them, unless they cannot be fully apprehended except in a divine-human encounter, there is no possibility of knowing God at all. To put the point in provocative fashion, if the theist position is to stand, the very events which Flew adduces as counter-evidence for the existence of a loving God, like a child dying of inoperable cancer, no less than events conducive to happiness and well-being, must be interpretable as occasions for encounter with the God whose existence or goodness they are supposed to deny. If they are not open to this interpretation, if in fact people did not claim to encounter a loving God in tragedy and suffering, then instances of this kind would count decisively against divine providence. Flew is simply wrong in saying that there are no conceivable events which would be held to falsify theological assertions. If human experience consisted of unrelieved suffering of which no one could make any sense at all, if no one had ever claimed that his suffering had been redeemed through encounter with God in it, then Flew would be right. Indeed, I am prepared to go further and admit that the cases of apparently unredeemed suffering and despair do constitute counter-evidence, though they are not decisive just because others in similar situations claim to have met with God in the depth of their own experiences.

19. e.g. Gareth B. Matthews, 'Theology and Natural Theology', *The Journal of Philosophy*, Vol. LXI (January 1964), pp. 99-108. Cf. John Hick, 'Theology and Verification', *Theology Today*, Vol. XVII (April 1960), pp. 12-31.

One of the major weaknesses in Flew's thesis is that, besides taking for granted that belief in God is an inference from natural phenomena, he implies that he has *a priori* knowledge of what kind of events would validate or falsify such inference. In other words, he seems to think he knows what God would permit and what he would disallow if he exists. The objection may be raised that this is unfair to Flew's position, since he is asking theists to tell him what *they* would take to be falsifying evidence, but the whole tenor of the discussion gives no indication that the author has ever seriously considered the possibility of what may be called a 'redemptive depth' to tragic occurrences. In particular, he ignores the biblical events to which Christians attach particular significance and in which they find the crucial clue for the interpretation of human experience in general. Flew has, in fact, ruled out any interpretation in depth by his naturalistic treatment of all events and his assumption that theological assertions must rest upon inference and nothing else. It is just this which the concept of revelation renders problematical. God may disclose himself in ways entirely confounding man's preconceived ideas. Whether he does so or not is another matter. All I am concerned to maintain at this point is that the superficial reading of events is not sufficient either to verify or falsify religious belief, depending as it does on hidden *a priori* assumptions about the ways of God and the supposal that belief in his existence is an inference drawn from those events thus regarded. Natural theology in no sense hinges upon such suppositions. Once we recognize the possibility of the disclosure of the Transcendent in finite terms, Flew's whole argument becomes irrelevant.

But does God really disclose himself? Is this more than a theoretical possibility? There are, of course, those who, without appealing to any special revelation, would claim that he does, and that this can be apprehended by paying attention to the nature of man's total experience as viewed in its mysterious depth. In particular, our awareness of value, especially if this is understood as the claim upon us to achieve harmony with our environment, appears to afford persuasive evidence of a divine encounter from which we cannot escape if we are truly sensitive. All the same this does not carry conviction to the sceptically minded, and the suggestion that it will if they are sufficiently attentive seems somewhat cavalier to say the least. Admittedly, as Leonard Hodgson has argued, some men have a 'flair' for seeing what others do not see, and he is undoubtedly right in finding illustrations for this everywhere: in science, mathematics, medicine, art and music, where particularly gifted people 'open the door through which the others may pass and have their eyes opened to see it too. Their vision is accepted as genuine insight into objective truth by those who say: "Yes, now that you have opened my eyes to it, I can see that it is so".'[20]

This account of the matter has close affinities with Mascall's discussion of intellect and intuition, to which reference has already been made, though Mascall lays more stress on the importance of attention in the belief that everyone has the capacity for the penetrative apprehension of God in finite being if only he will take sufficient pains. This is open to anyone who will allow his mind to dwell on the nature of things with sufficient attention, and the failure of many to discern God in the world around is attributed to the bustle of modern life and undue preoccupation with the passing show. 'Even if', says Mascall, 'they can be got to listen to an exposition of the Five Ways and to follow the steps of the argument, they are frequently quite unmoved. This is, it may be suggested, mainly due to the fact that, under modern conditions of life, people very rarely give themselves the leisure and the quiet necessary for the straightforward consideration of finite being. They never really sit down and look at anything. This diagnosis is borne out by the common experience of people making their first retreat, that after the first day or so natural objects seem to acquire a peculiar character of transparency and vitality, so that they appear as only very thinly veiling the creative activity of God.'[21] Thus, when he is asked why many

20. Leonard Hodgson, *For Faith and Freedom* (Oxford, Blackwell, 1956), Vol. I, p. 100.
21. Mascall, op. cit., p. 80.

intelligent people do not recognize what he claims to see as self-evident, Mascall is inclined to reply that the faculty of intuition may become atrophied by preoccupation with the superficial, and even amongst philosophers practice in the technique of linguistic analysis may blunt the capacity for metaphysical thinking.[22] Similarly, Ian Ramsey argues that if we pursue our philosophical inquiry in the most rigorous fashion, selecting models for our discourse which seem most appropriate to the analysis of our experience and qualifying them in so far as they are inadequate, we may reach the point of disclosure at which 'the penny drops' and we see what has hitherto been hidden from us.[23] But if that is as far as we can go, theist and sceptic must simply beg to differ in their interpretation of the evidence. Of course, such a dividing of the ways is bound to come sooner or later; the point will be reached when argument ceases and an ultimate decision has to be taken. However, I question whether the argument has been carried far enough as long as it remains at the level of natural theology, and whether the issue has been focused with maximum clarity by directing attention to the mysterious depth of our experience in general. There is another step we can still take: the examination of the claims of special revelation and of the Christian revelation in particular. Are we able to discern more clearly here what we have called the dimension of the Transcendent?

Our problem at this point is to keep the discussion within reasonable bounds. Without denying or minimizing the contribution that other religious traditions may make towards answering this question, we have to face the claim that the Transcendent is revealed in the distinctively Christian mystery to which the Bible bears witness and by which the Church lives.

22. The same suggestion is made by John Baillie when he says that 'our intellectual sophistication is nowadays so great that it is difficult to achieve, or to recover, that naked contact of our minds with the confronting reality out of which true wisdom can alone be born.' *The Idea of Revelation in Recent Thought* (London, Oxford University Press, 1956), p. 141.

23. Cf. Ian T. Ramsey, *Religious Language* (London, SCM Press, 1957), pp. 19 ff.

This, too, can lead us, unless we are careful, into the ramifications of exegetical and theological controversy, where we lose sight of the wood for the trees. We are concerned with a specific philosophical issue and its implications for relating theological insight to metaphysical inquiry. Accordingly, I propose to ask two questions only: how far are we justified in discerning a disclosure of the Transcendent in the person of Jesus of Nazareth, and what are the main characteristics of that disclosure, if it is recognized as such? The necessity of raising the second of these questions will, I trust, become apparent in the final chapter, where we shall consider the possibility of the Christian revelation providing an interpretive clue to the pattern of mystery which manifests itself through the philosophical analysis of our experience in general. Obviously each of the two questions has led to libraries of books, and the debate continues; but there are certain conclusions relevant to our purpose which, I believe, are emerging with increasing clarity from the discussion, and these I wish to bring into focus in the second half of this chapter.

Nobody will dispute that a great many people from the first century A.D. down to the present day have claimed to discern the mystery of the Transcendent in the person of Jesus of Nazareth. Without this there would have been no Christian Church at all. It was simply because some of his contemporaries were convinced that in him 'God had visited and redeemed his people' that the Church came into being, and their conviction has been communicated to those who have followed them over the course of nearly two thousand years. If the first disciples had seen in Jesus no more than an itinerant rabbi, one teacher among many others or even a great prophet, that would virtually have been the end of the matter. What he had said and done might have been preserved for posterity, as in the case of the Hebrew prophets, but nothing like the explosion of faith and hope to which the New Testament bears ample testimony would have occurred. This was due to the impression he made upon his followers, climaxed in what they were assured was his resurrection from the dead. The Gospels make abundantly plain the numinous impact of his personality: 'He taught them as one that had authority, and not as the scribes' (Mark 1:22): 'Depart from me', said Peter, 'for I am a sinful man, O Lord' (Luke 5:8); and the Fourth Evangelist ventures to include even those who arrested Jesus in the Garden of Gethsemane in the feeling of awe which he evoked: according to the record, when Jesus acknowledged who he was, 'they went backward, and fell to the ground' (John 18:6). The precise historicity of these references is not immediately to the point. They simply serve as illustrations, preserved in the confessional documents of the early Church, of the kind of impact Jesus made upon some, at least, of his contemporaries.

Of course there were others, indeed the majority of those who encountered him in Palestine, who saw in him nothing out of the ordinary, regarding him either as a strange eccentric or even as a dangerous impostor. But in the nature of the case they did not leave any record behind, save the kind of jejune summary found in the *Annals* of Tacitus, where he refers incidentally to 'Christus, the founder of the name, [who] had undergone the death penalty in the reign of Tiberius by sentence of the procurator Pontius Pilatus . . .'[24] Any more detailed knowledge we have of the ministry of Jesus—and there is not a very great deal of this—comes from those who believed in him and wrote from the standpoint of faith within the primitive Christian Church. How are we to decide whether their faith was justified or not?

Questions such as this, coupled with scepticism as to the credibility of the miraculous elements in the gospel tradition, led to attempts to discover the historical Jesus in the late nineteenth and early twentieth centuries. Efforts were made to get behind the New Testament documents to the 'real figure' who walked the roads of Palestine and died at the hands of the Roman authorities in Jerusalem. It is now generally recognized that the enterprise, for all the ingenuity employed, was bound to end in failure. We are entirely dependent on the testimony of those who interpreted the life of Jesus from the standpoint of faith, from the *Sitz im Leben* of the early Church, and there is just no way of

24. Tacitus, *Annals*, Book XV, Section 44.

separating 'fact' from interpretation. It is this which distinguishes the historian from the natural scientist. The latter is certainly dependent upon the testimony of others in the sense that he accepts on trust the results of their experiments; he would never make any progress if he felt compelled to repeat every experiment himself. But there is nothing *in principle* which prevents him doing so. With the historian it is different. He cannot repeat the experiment even if he wants to do so, since he is concerned with the 'once-for-all' event, the unrepeatable happening. Therefore, he is dependent on witnesses in a way in which the natural scientist never is. As Alan Richardson points out in his Bampton Lectures,[25] this is now generally recognized amongst secular historians, and marks the crucial difference between the study of history in the twentieth century as compared with the nineteenth. The 'bare facts' are simply unascertainable. We have to reckon with interpreted events whether we are Christians or not.

This has led to the distinctively modern phenomenon of what Richardson describes as the 'disengagement from history' on the part of many contemporary theologians.[26] Emanating largely from the continent of Europe, the contention has been advanced that it is not only impossible to get back to the Jesus of history, but that it is unnecessary to make the attempt. Genuine faith turns upon an existential encounter with Christ as the Word of God, and preoccupation with historical data, even if successful in achieving assured results, would actually be a hindrance to a fully Christian commitment, since the raw material available to the historian as such conceals rather than discloses the activity of God. Tillich makes the position quite explicit when he says, 'the foundation of Christian belief is not the historical Jesus, but the biblical picture of Christ. The criterion of human thought and action is not the constantly changing and artificial product of historical research, but the picture of Christ as it is rooted in

25. Alan Richardson, *History Sacred and Profane* (London, SCM Press, 1964), pp. 154 ff.
26. Ibid., pp. 125-53.

ecclesiastical belief and human experience.'[27] Both Karl Barth and Emil Brunner, whatever their differences, have embraced essentially the same thesis, but it is Rudolf Bultmann, with his demythologizing of the gospel, who has presented the case in its most provocative form. 'To understand Jesus', he says, 'all that is necessary is to proclaim that He has come.'[28] The factual details of his life on earth are irrelevant and unimportant.

This is not the place to discuss the controversy in any detail. That has been done elsewhere, and I am in substantial agreement with those British scholars in particular, who, while acknowledging their indebtedness to the insights of their Continental colleagues, find their virtual abandonment of history totally unsatisfactory.[29] Suffice it here to make the following three comments.

First of all, it is simply not true that the actual life of Jesus on earth is of no consequence for the Christian faith. Christianity is an historical religion, not in the sense that it has a history, but that it is rooted and grounded in events which took place on the historical scene, events which were public property, even if their significance was apparent or became apparent only to a few. To divorce significance from event is the same error whether it is committed from the standpoint of nineteenth-century historicism or twentieth-century existentialism. The real difficulty about Bultmann's position is that he seems to have abandoned the historical foundation of the gospel in favour of *Geschichtlichkeit* (history as meaningful to me). But events can only have meaning if they have occurred, and it is just this objectivity of the life of Jesus for which an existentialist theology such as Bultmann's seems to find no room. From the empirical standpoint of our whole discussion this is altogether unsatisfactory. Given the claim that the Transcendent is disclosed in the person of Jesus of

27. Paul Tillich, *The Interpretation of History* (New York, Scribner, 1954), p. 34.
28. Rudolf Bultmann, *Kerygma and Myth*, ed. H. W. Bartsch, trans. R. H. Fuller (London, S.P.C.K., 1953), Vol. I, p. 117.
29. e.g., D. M. Baillie, *God Was in Christ* (London, Faber, 1948), pp. 30-58.

Nazareth, it is of the utmost importance to learn all we can about the details of his life on earth and the impact he made on his contemporaries.

Second, it appears to be taken for granted by Bultmann and those who think like him that the historian *qua* historian is simply concerned with bare facts: a nineteenth-century positivist assumption that has largely been discarded by secular historians. Richardson is surely right in maintaining that Bultmann's position stems as much from his positivist attitude to history as from his existentialist philosophy: 'The nineteenth-century conception of "facts" as the objects of historical research and the rationalist insistence upon the relativity of all historical knowledge take precedence over any twentieth-century insights concerning the nature of historical facts as judgments of evidence which are not merely conditional but actually made possible by the personal standpoint (of faith) of the particular historian. Moreover, though absolutely presuppositionless history is agreed to be impossible, "dogmatic" (i.e. Nicene or Chalcedonian) presuppositions are on principle excluded, while the old Liberal presuppositions are accepted as "scientific".'[30] There are no bare historical facts. There are only events seen from an interpretive standpoint, and this leaves entirely open the question of the depth of significance with which they are charged, from the perspective of the eyewitness no less than from that of the historian endeavouring to understand through the testimony of others. The question of the significance of events in themselves, irrespective of whether the eyewitness or the historian apprehends it or not, is easily overlooked, though it surely needs to be distinguished from subjective interpretation. While it is true that an event can only have significance for us if it actually occurred, it also has no ultimate significance unless it is charged with the significance we attach to it, unless it is what John Marsh calls 'a time-with-its content'.[31] Let us return to the crucifixion of Jesus as an example. The description of a Roman execution does not exhaust what happened for the Christian,

30. Richardson, op. cit., p. 141.
31. John Marsh, *The Fulness of Time* (London, Nisbet, 1952), p. 33 *et passim*.

though without the publicly observable fact that Jesus was crucified under Pontius Pilate there would be no point in suggesting
that his death was instrumental in accomplishing man's salvation.
But the cross cannot legitimately be interpreted as a saving act
unless atonement was actually made there for sin apart from any
understanding or appropriation of it. We cannot hold that
Christ's bearing of his cross was the accomplishment of our salvation because we believe it to have been such; we are entitled to
believe that we are saved thereby only if he himself 'bare our sins
in his own body on the tree' (1 Peter 2:24). The Christian understands the events of the gospel narratives at three levels: first, as
actual happenings; second, as happenings charged with ultimate
significance because of God's action therein; and third, as happenings of decisive importance for him. In so far as he is justified
in believing what he does, he has, of course, to admit that the full
significance of the cross cannot be grasped except in the existential encounter of faith, the faith which embraces the living
Word of God through the event to the soul; but just as this does
not warrant a dismissal of the basic happenings as irrelevant to
the experience, so it precludes the elimination of a depth of
significance from the happening itself. This further distinction is
altogether obscured by a positivist interpretation of history.

Lastly, extreme scepticism regarding the possibility of knowing anything at all about the life of Jesus on earth surely turns on
a strange misreading of the evidence. I vividly remember the
late R. H. Lightfoot, one of the pioneers of '*Formgeschichte*' in
Britain, saying during my student days that his arguments did
not lead, as many supposed, to a whittling away of our concept
of the Jesus of history, but rather to the filling out of an inadequate
picture, since his life on earth must have been at least sufficient to
support the faith of the early Church. This apart, certain more
recent criticism seems to presuppose an utter indifference to the
historical facts on the part of the Evangelists, and such on their
own showing was manifestly not the case. Luke introduces his
gospel with what can only be regarded as an explicit assertion of
his intention to tell Theophilus what had actually happened, and

internal evidence is not lacking of remarkable fidelity to the facts even when the *Sitz im Leben* of the early Church might well have influenced a reconstruction of the story. For example, the paucity of references by the synoptists to the gift of the Spirit is inexplicable except on the assumption that Jesus was actually very reticent on the subject. When one considers the importance attached to the Spirit in the Acts of the Apostles,[32] it is nothing short of startling to find so few references in all three gospels put together.[33] Even the Fourth Gospel, which in the past has been generally considered to be concerned with theological interpretation rather than with the life of Jesus as actually lived out during the years of his ministry, is now beginning to be seen as testimony, very possibly by a close acquaintance of the Beloved Disciple,[34] to those events which had brought the Church into being. Whatever may have been the didactic concern of the evangelist, and however much may be allowed to his genius as a theological interpreter, there is no reason to doubt that he himself believed that he was giving a faithful account of the ministry of Jesus. At the outset of his gospel he declared that 'the Word was made flesh', and theological credulity is stretched too far if it is maintained that he was not really interested in what did take place in the flesh. He is not just a Bultmann from the ancient world! Even as careful a critic as C. H. Dodd has committed himself to the conclusion that 'this revelation is distinctively, and nowhere

32. Cf. F. F. Bruce, *The Acts of the Apostles* (London, Tyndale, 1951), p. 30: 'In all the book there is nothing which is unrelated to the Holy Spirit.'

33. Cf. C. K. Barrett, *The Holy Spirit and the Gospel Tradition* (London, S.P.C.K., 1947), pp. 122 ff. While I agree with Barrett that the basic reason for the reticence of Jesus was the connexion between the Spirit and the Messianic secret, I find it impossible to follow him in concluding that Jesus did not promise the Spirit to his disciples; at least the saying about blasphemy against the Holy Spirit and that concerning the Spirit's guidance in the hour of peril seem unmistakably authentic; cf. Vincent Taylor, *The Doctrine of the Holy Spirit*, Headingly Lectures (London, Epworth, 1937), p. 59; and Harold Roberts, *Jesus and the Kingdom of God* (London, Epworth, 1955), pp. 86-7.

34. Cf. C. K. Barrett, *The Gospel according to St John* (London, S.P.C.K., 1955), p. 113. The literature on this subject is, of course, extensive, and every commentator on the Fourth Gospel has his own view.

more clearly than in the Fourth Gospel, an historical revelation. It follows that it is important for the evangelist that what he narrates happened.'[35] The fact is that the writers of the apostolic age had a profound stake in the immediate past, and not merely in the present. Certainly they were bearing witness from the standpoint of the faith of the early Church, but they were concerned that the world should know that what they declared had most surely happened, and their testimony deserves treating with respect. They may have been wrong in what they believed they had discerned in Jesus of Nazareth, but that is very different from supposing that they were unconcerned with what happened or were unreliable witnesses. This is increasingly coming to be recognized, even amongst some of the disciples of Bultmann himself; though it should be noted that British and American New Testament scholars in general have never embraced the extreme scepticism of their European counterparts, and their caution seems to be increasingly justified. Donald Baillie speaks for many when he sums up his own conclusions by saying, 'I cannot believe that there is any good reason for the defeatism of those who give up all hope of penetrating the tradition and reaching an assured knowledge of the historical personality of Jesus. Surely such defeatism is a transient nightmare of Gospel criticism, from which we are now awakening to a more sober confidence in our quest of the Jesus of history.'[36]

But when all this has been said, it remains true that we cannot reconstruct the ministry of Jesus in such a way as to become acquainted with it at first hand for ourselves. We can never be the eye-witnesses of his majesty—at least so far as his earthly life is concerned. For this we are dependent on the apostolic testimony, and we can see only through their eyes and hear only through their ears, relating to our own situation what they sought to relate to theirs. To that extent the Form-critics and their more extreme existentialist successors have been fully justified: no return is

35. C. H. Dodd, *The Fourth Gospel* (Cambridge, The University Press, 1953), p. 444.
36. Donald Baillie, op. cit., p. 58.

possible to the confident historicism of a bygone day. Nevertheless, there is a continuity between the testimony of the apostolic
age and the standpoint of those who try to interpret the same
events in the middle of the twentieth century—the uninterrupted
life of the Christian Church, persisting through changing times
and circumstances, but united in a common faith in the risen
Christ. The early Christians claimed to be eyewitnesses of his
majesty in more than one sense. Those who had known him in
the flesh no longer knew him only as such. Now they were
assured of his unseen presence, which constituted for them and
for all subsequent generations of Christians the essence of the
Church. Thus it is faith in the risen Christ which unites men
and women of the first and twentieth centuries with one
another, validated for all alike by the continuing ministry of
Word and Sacrament whereby the Church is nourished and
sanctified.

The sceptic will doubtless remain unconvinced. Just as the outward phenomena of the earthly ministry of Jesus seemed to many
nothing more than a passing curiosity, so the liturgy of the
Church will appear to be merely the celebration of empty rites, a
'mumbo-jumbo' of mystifying words and superstitious actions,
with no significance beyond their bare performance. Yet countless people, both learned and unlettered, have found in these rites
the means whereby life has been lifted onto a new plane and has
become growingly coherent. However they might variously express it, the experience is substantially the same: the Transcendent
has been disclosed in the exposition of the Scriptures and the
observance of the sacramental acts. For them these are no mere
words, no ordinary water, bread or wine. They have become the
channels of divine grace, and the recreation of life resulting therefrom is the most powerful and persuasive evidence that this is
what they really are. Admittedly, by no means all who call themselves Christians display the fruits of the Spirit for everyone to
see; far too often divine grace is concealed by human sin. But
there are the saints of ancient and modern times, the quality of
whose lives demands explanation and who constitute for many

one of the most cogent reasons for believing in the reality on which they claim to depend. In short, then, the Christian of today, in professing to discern the Transcendent in the sacramental life of the Church, takes his stand on the basis of his own experience with those of the apostolic age who bore witness to the historical origins of the primitive *koinonia* in the transcendental person of Jesus Christ.

But it is when we ask what was the nature of the mission which Jesus believed himself called upon to fulfil that we find ourselves face to face with the issue in its most challenging form. Was his ministry of such a character as to halt us in our tracks, to call in question all our naturalistic presuppositions, and to leave us over-whelmed with awe and wonder before the disclosure of the living God? This is the point at which our whole discussion reaches its sharpest focus.

In the earlier reference to Antony Flew's argument about the falsification of religious statements, we have already noticed that the dimension of divine activity may be missed through anthro-pomorphic presuppositions about the ways of God. We are never so certain to miss the one thing needful as when we are convinced that we should be looking for something else. If this is true of our experience as a whole, it is equally likely to be the case with the crucial event which for Christians constitutes the very essence of divine revelation. And of all the general impressions left by the gospels, the one that stands out most clearly is that Jesus, in so far as he claimed to be the fulfilment of God's purpose, behaved in a way at total variance with anything that was anticipated.

> They all were looking for a King
> To slay their foes, and lift them high;
> Thou cam'st, a little baby thing,
> That made a woman cry.[37]

The background and context of the ministry of Jesus is to be found in the expectations of the Jewish people, crystallized through centuries of testing in which the hope was never

37. George Macdonald, 'That Holy Thing'.

quenched that one day Yahweh would decisively intervene in the affairs of men, confounding the nation's enemies and vindicating Israel's faith in her divine destiny. Yahweh was above all else the God who acts, and his action was primarily seen in the events of history. At first he was conceived to be no more than a tribal god, solely concerned with the fortunes and destiny of Israel; but with the consolidation of the tribal confederacy and under the threat of foes on every side, the Israelites came to believe that Yahweh was powerful above all other gods and in direct control of everything that touched the life of the nation. Ultimately he came to be regarded as God alone, creator of the heavens and the earth (Ps. 96: 5), divine disposer of the affairs of nations, whose rulers, even in their wilful arrogance, could be made the tools of his purpose (Isa. 44:28; 45:5 ff.). Certainly he was the Lord of nature, but above all else he was the Lord of history, by whose outstretched arm nations rose and fell, and through whose chosen people the reign of righteousness and peace was to be established on the earth.

But while the whole of history was regarded as the sphere of God's activity and his over-arching providence was believed to govern everything that happened, the life and religion of the nation came to be centred around certain specific events of decisive importance. These were the landmarks of Israel's history: the deliverance from Egypt, the covenant at Sinai, the golden age of David, the bitter humiliation of the Babylonian exile, and the restoration of the ransomed of the Lord to the land of their fathers. Prophets and psalmists alike appealed to the past not so much in its broad sweep as in those great events in which God had decisively acted in judgement and mercy. In fact, it is not going too far to say that the activity of Yahweh was conceived in terms of dramatic interventions, focused in those happenings which were the turning points in the life of the nation. And when God acted, he acted by divine fiat. Nothing could resist his will. 'He spake, and it was done' (Ps. 33:9).

The appeal to the past was the basis of Israel's hope for the future. Arising out of the nation's unique sense of election to a glorious destiny,[38] each succeeding generation believed that there would soon be a dramatic intervention by which the forces of evil would be overthrown and the reign of righteousness begin. The achievement of unity and prosperity under David and Solomon seemed to be but a foretaste of what Yahweh would do for his chosen people, and, in spite of the break-up of the kingdom after Solomon's death and the threat of foes from without, the hope remained that the day of Yahweh would come, the day of Israel's greater glory. This was the star that guided the nation through many dark periods of her history.

The hope in its earliest form was linked with the accession to the kingship of a prince of the Davidic line; and, in whatever way the role of the Messiah was later conceived, the idea of a kingly ruler after the familiar pattern remained determinative. The Messiah would be of the royal lineage, his authority sanctioned and up-held by Yahweh himself. In the words of Isaiah, 'there shall come forth a rod out of the stem of Jesse, and a Branch shall grow out of his roots' (Isa. 11:1).[39]

The experience of the exile in Babylon inevitably meant a re-thinking of Israel's hope, and two prophets of immense signifi-cance sought to grapple with the problem. Ezekiel, who had accompanied the first group of deportees with King Jehoiachin to Babylon in 597, unequivocally declared the judgement of God on Jerusalem and the certainty of its fall. When his prediction proved correct, and the last vain hopes for the preservation of the city were brought to nothing, he turned to the future and began to direct the thoughts of his fellow exiles to the eventual restora-

38. For a detailed treatment of this subject, see H. H. Rowley, *The Biblical Doctrine of Election* (London, Lutterworth, 1950).

39. Cf. Isa. 9:4-7; Mic. 5:2-4; Jer. 23:5-6; 33:15-16; Ps. 2:6-9; 110:1-4. It has recently been argued that this expectation was constantly kept to the fore by the ritual of the New Year Festival of Enthronement, in which Yahweh was pictured as triumphing over all his foes; a ritual in which the king was the leading figure: a reminder to him of the ideal of his office. See A. R. Johnson, *Sacral Kingship in Ancient Israel* (Cardiff, University of Wales Press, 1955); Helmer Ringgren, *The Messiah in the Old Testament* (London, SCM Press, 1956); and S. Mowinckel, *He That Cometh* (Oxford, Blackwell, 1956).

tion of the kingdom. His vision, as set forth in the closing chapters of his prophecy, is that of a theocratic state with the temple at the centre, from which would flow a river of life-giving water to fertilize the whole land. Ezekiel's outlook was nationalistic, but in a religious sense. He was concerned with Israel's destiny as a unique people pledged to the service of God. The nations of the earth were seen as subject to the divine sovereignty, falling into their place as they recognized the vindication of the name of the Lord in the establishment of a holy people in a holy community (36:22 ff.). The vision was idealized in the extreme, though it had considerable influence on the separatist movement in post-exilic Judaism.

The second prophet was the unknown writer whose work was later incorporated in the book bearing the name of Isaiah. In him monotheism reaches its most complete formulation thus far, a monotheism which passes beyond Yahweh's exclusive concern for the welfare of his people to the vision of a world united under the rule of one God.[40] More important still, he foreshadows a strikingly new and revolutionary conception of Israel's role in the divine purpose. For the first time the idea of a servant nation is adumbrated, with a world mission on behalf of all peoples, a mission in some way realized through redemptive suffering.

This theme may be found in the so-called Servant Songs, though the interpretation of the passages concerned is notoriously difficult and controversial, and we must be careful not to press their exegesis too far.[41] Israel is nowhere referred to as the servant

40. Even the earth itself participates in the promised fulfilment (e.g., Isa. 41:18-20; 43:19-20), and Mowinckel has drawn attention to the cosmic character of the prophet's vision: ibid., pp. 138 ff.

41. The crux of the problem lies in the identity of the Servant. Reams have been written on the subject, and the original author would have been astonished if he could have foreseen the speculation to which his work has given rise. For a thorough discussion of the different theories, see C. R. North, *The Suffering Servant in Deutero-Isaiah* (London, Oxford University Press, 1948); and H. H. Rowley, *The Servant of the Lord* (London, Lutterworth, 1952). My conclusion is that the corporate identification of the Servant with Israel seems

of anyone but Yahweh. Nor can we be sure that her sufferings, or indeed the sufferings of any individual who was held to epitomize the nation, had any future reference, except in the sense that the period of tribulation was drawing to a close.[42] Nevertheless the Servant Songs are pregnant with an entirely new conception of Israel's destiny:[43] one which perhaps the prophet himself did not

---

to be amply attested outside the poems, while in the second of them the association appears to be quite explicit: 'Thou art my servant, O Israel, in whom I will be glorified' (Isa. 49:3); and attempts on textual grounds to excise the word 'Israel' from this crucial verse savour too much of special pleading. On the other hand, the language and thought of the Songs strongly suggest that the author had an individual in mind, or at any rate a group which is to be sharply differentiated from the nation as a whole. How else can we make sense of a passage like 49:5-6 where the Servant is said to have a mission to Israel and thereby to be a light to the nations? Still more difficult for the corporate interpretation is the portrayal of the sufferer in chapter 53. The most probable solution of the dilemma is that which is generally associated with the names of Wheeler Robinson and Eissfeldt. Basing their arguments upon the Hebrew idea of corporate personality, they held that the poet made no sharp distinction between the nation, the group within the nation, and the individual; he could jump from one to the other without the difficulty that this involves for the twentieth-century Western reader. The concept of the Servant is, therefore, a fluid one: the mission of the nation is thought of as focused in a representative individual and sometimes perhaps in a group, while, whenever the individual is in the forefront, his representative character is always implicit; see H. Wheeler Robinson, *The Cross of the Servant: A Study in Deutero-Isaiah* (London, SCM Press, 1926); and O. Eissfeldt, *Der Gottesknecht bei Deuterojesaja (Jes. 40-55) im Lichte der israelitischen Anschauung von Gemeinschaft und Individuum* (Halle, Neimeyer, 1933).

42. The emphasis, even in the fifty-third chapter, seems to be on the past or the present, and only vindication is clearly for the future: a viewpoint which accurately reflects the situation at the end of the Babylonian era, with Cyrus already on the march. Of course, it is notoriously difficult to interpret Hebrew tenses. Grammar apart, Rowley goes so far as to express himself convinced that the Servant in Isaiah 53 is a future figure; he considers it incredible to suppose that such sufferings and achievement could have been ascribed to any historical figure of the poet's past or present; see *The Servant of the Lord*, pp. 52 f.

43. Though it should be noted that the concept of the Suffering Servant was not peculiar to Deutero-Isaiah. Much work has recently been done on the

fully recognize. At any rate, it is arguable that the implications were not worked out by him or by anyone else until Jesus of Nazareth came on the scene, patterning his own mission on the role of the Suffering Servant, and thereby becoming the inaugurator of the universal reign of God. In the post-exilic period this revolutionary idea was entirely submerged. Ezekiel was easier to accept; for he had spoken to Israel's traditional hope, and promised a return to something of her former glory. The restoration of the Israelite nation was more congenial than the vision of a world-wide kingdom in which all peoples would play their part, and the role of a favoured religious aristocracy more palatable than that of a Suffering Servant.

This explains the post-exilic development of Israel's hope. It took several forms. The first was that of a separated people, constituted as a specifically religious community, which through its faithfulness would inherit the promises of old, vindicated by the advent of God's open reign on earth. Thus Isaiah's faithful remnant became a purified nation, Ezekiel's transformation of the message of the eighth-century prophet. Haggai, Zechariah, Malachi, Nehemiah, and particularly Ezra, were all heirs to this vision of a people set aside for God, a people who would be recognized as triumphant when the day of the Lord arrived.[44] Fidelity to the Torah was the principal concern of those who so conceived the calling of Israel, and thus the era of the prophets gave way to that of the exponents of the law, the Scribes and

---

elucidation of this motif in the so-called 'royal psalms'; cf. Ringgren, op. cit., pp. 54-64.

44. Of course, no clear-cut distinction can be drawn between the religious and political forms of the post-exilic hope. In Hebrew thinking as a whole the two spheres could not be separated; the one was the expression of the other; and it can be argued, for instance, that there is obvious political content in the prophecies of Haggai and Zechariah. All the same there is a difference of emphasis between those who followed Ezekiel in the vision of a theocratic community characterized by holiness and the later advocates of a politically powerful kingdom.

Pharisees, in whom the distinctively religious mission of the nation was kept alive and perpetuated.

The second form of the hope was political rather than religious. It arose out of the attempts of the ruling authorities in Jerusalem to preserve the national independence in the face of external pressure from imperial powers, first from the Ptolemies and the Seleucids, and later from the Romans. The Maccabean revolt, with the considerable measure of success it for a time achieved, led to a resurgence of the aspiration to restore the former glories of David and to make Israel a world power, God's chosen people the rulers of the nations. The Sadducees and the Zealots represented opposite poles in regard to the method of achieving the desired end. The Sadducees were calculating politicians, realistically appraising the possibilities of the situation and playing a somewhat cautious hand; while the Zealots were the hotheads, the revolutionary party, which finally gained the upper hand and brought total destruction upon Jerusalem at the hands of the Romans in 70 A.D.

The third form of the hope arose out of the dark days of persecution and defeat. It was apocalyptic in character, looking to a divine intervention of a catastrophic kind to rescue Israel from intolerable humiliation and usher in the reign of 'the saints of the Most High'. No longer was any reliance placed upon what the nation could do either religiously or politically to prepare for the day of the Lord. The outlook was too black for that. Men were helpless; it was for God to act. Such was the message of the book of Daniel and the book of Joel, as well as of an increasing number of writings from the second century B.C. onwards, not included in the canon of Scripture. The worse the disasters that befell the Jewish people, the stronger burned the hope of a dramatic last-minute intervention. Apocalyptic is always the child of dark days.

Now whatever differences there may have been between the different forms in which Israel's hope was expressed after the exile, they all had one thing in common: the expectation of a dramatic intervention in which all enemies would be routed by overwhelming force, and the faithful honoured. The words of the *Magnificat* perfectly illustrate what every devout Jew believed: God would bring down the mighty from their seats and exalt the humble and meek. The picture was one of an irresistible conqueror coming to the rescue of a hard-pressed garrison, fighting for its life against insurmountable odds. God was conceived in terms of a supernatural Alexander. In so far as the Messiah featured in these expectations he was imagined as an eschatological figure, modelled on the kingly ideal, but no longer identified with any historical ruler.[45] This was the hope of Israel when Jesus was born in Bethlehem of Judea.

Now I believe it to be of crucial importance to recognize that the advent of Jesus of Nazareth constituted a radical challenge to the whole conception of God as rooted in the dominance of supernatural power; and unless this is admitted, it is extremely difficult to make any sense of the gospel records. Of course, any statement about the ministry and mission of Jesus is liable to be controversial, and it is necessary to proceed with caution. Nevertheless, I am prepared to maintain that from a patient examination of the evidence available to us certain broad conclusions emerge which will stand up to the most searching criticism. Basic to everything else is this: with the advent of Jesus of Nazareth there came one claiming to be the divine representative and the fulfilment of all the promises of God, and yet adopting a role totally at variance with anything expected. In other words, Jesus revolutionized the Hebrew conception of divine power, and, while tacitly assuming the long-awaited Messiahship, adopted the role of the Suffering Servant rather than that of the political or apocalyptic potentate.

That Jesus did claim to be the Messiah would seem to be one of the most obvious facts to which the gospel records bear witness, though this has been strongly challenged by those New Testa-

45. Cf. Mowinckel, op. cit., p. 123. The point at which the expectation of a prince became that of an eschatological figure is impossible to define with any precision. The one shades into the other.

ment scholars who believe that it is impossible to get behind the faith of the early Church to anything that Jesus actually said or did. Accordingly, it is not surprising to find Bultmann arguing that the Messianic role was ascribed to Jesus after his death.[46] This is surely a point at which the theory we have criticized in general is stretched beyond the limits of credibility; altogether too much originality is attributed to the apostolic Church and the evangelists in particular. Not only are they made to superimpose the role of the Messiah on Jesus, but they are thereby credited with the undoubted transformation of its character to which the records bear ample testimony. The wholly credible pattern of a gradual disclosure to the disciples of their Master's understanding of his mission gives place to a fantastically ingenious reconstruction of the story by the synoptists. Bultmann's theory implies a subtlety and inventiveness on their part which are well nigh inconceivable.

Once this has been granted, we are faced with another controversy of the first importance about the way in which Jesus conceived of his mission. From Schweitzer onwards, many New Testament scholars have taken the frequent use of the title 'Son of Man' to be the key to understanding the role which he chose to adopt, generally interpreting the ascription in terms of Jewish apocalyptic. Thus, in sharp contrast to the nineteenth-century liberal picture, Jesus is seen as the herald of a catastrophic intervention of God whereby the historical order would be swept away and the new age would begin. At long last the day of the Lord was to come, ushered in by an overwhelming display of divine omnipotence.

This is surely to misread the evidence altogether. It fails to make adequate allowance for the originality of Jesus' conception of the nature and purpose of God, the course that his ministry actually followed, and the bewilderment of his most intimate followers when their expectations were progressively confounded. T. W. Manson seems to be much nearer the truth when he argues that

46. R. Bultmann, *Theology of the New Testament* (London, SCM Press, 1952), Vol. I, pp. 26-32. Cf. John Knox, *The Death of Christ* (London, Collins, 1959).

Jesus undertook the daring identification of the Messiah and the Suffering Servant, thereby totally transforming, while fulfilling, the hope of Israel.[47] Here was one who came to summon his people to the high destiny adumbrated by the poet-prophet of the Babylonian exile,[48] and, when they turned away in disappointment and even his most intimate followers forsook him and fled, he went to the cross alone, the suffering representative of Israel and of all mankind.

How else are we to interpret the story of the temptation in the wilderness which sets the scene for the unfolding of the public ministry? It means nothing if it does not imply that at the very outset Jesus faced and abandoned the traditional form of Israel's hope. For him it would have been to fall down and worship Satan if he had tried to bring in the reign of God by sheer force; and so the idea of a kind of Jewish emperor, wielding great power and

47. See T. W. Manson, *The Servant Messiah* (Cambridge, The University Press, 1953). Cf. A. T. Hanson, *The Church of the Servant* (London, SCM Press, 1962). I am quite unconvinced by recent attempts to demonstrate that the majority of alleged references to the Suffering Servant in the New Testament are not directly traceable to Deutero-Isaiah and that Jesus derived the idea of his mission from the apocalyptic figure of the Son of Man: see Morna D. Hooker, *Jesus and the Servant* (London, S.P.C.K., 1959). The argument turns on a detailed comparison of the texts which often results in losing sight of the wood for the trees. Precise quotation and exact reproduction of thought are too much to demand before any allowance of connexion is granted, and in any case undue preoccupation with linguistic questions is to underestimate the importance of the shaping of thought and action by a highly original conception. It is hard to believe that Jesus ignored such a revolutionary idea as that contained in the Servant Songs when he was reinterpreting the Messianic mission. We are left with the surprising conclusion that *we* can see the significance of Deutero-Isaiah, whereas Jesus did not!

48. Surely C. J. Cadoux was right in maintaining that Jesus initially summoned the whole nation to assume the role of the Suffering Servant, pointing to such passages as Matt. 11:20-24 (|| Luke 10:13-15); Matt. 23:37 (|| Luke 13:34); and Luke 19:41-44 as confirmation of the belief that the nation was meant to be involved in the Messianic mission; *The Historic Mission of Jesus* (London, Lutterworth, 1941), pp. 183 ff. Cf. Roderic Dunkerley, *The Hope of Jesus* (London, Longmans, 1953), pp, 23 ff.

overthrowing Roman domination, was one that he decisively rejected. God did not act in that way to bring his purposes to pass. He would coerce neither individuals nor nations into submission to his will; and so the appeal of Jesus had to be to the hearts and consciences of his hearers, who must be won, not overpowered. The law of love was the ultimate law of the Kingdom; and, if need be, he was prepared to submit himself to death for its establishment that way. This was the course his ministry actually followed, and it is difficult to believe that the temptation narratives do not reflect a deliberate decision Jesus took at the very outset: a resolve which governed everything he subsequently said and did.

The identification of his Messianic mission with the role of the Suffering Servant did, of course, present serious difficulties for Jesus. If he were openly to claim to be the promised Messiah, the character of his mission would certainly be misunderstood. In so far as he was believed, the people would try to make him king— something which actually happened according to the Fourth Evangelist (John 6:15).[49] Therefore he had to employ the utmost caution in the use of the title, demonstrating by his actual ministry the nature of his mission. The only way in which to establish the claim was not to make it! By seeing the role of the Suffering Servant played out before their very eyes, men might gradually come to recognize that this was the true character of Messiahship. Hence the injunctions to silence whenever there was any suggestion that he was the long expected deliverer,[50] and his reluctance

49. Is there an echo of this in Mark 6:45? My colleague, H. W. Lang, has drawn my attention to the use of the word ἠνάγκασεν which seems to indicate that Jesus felt himself under strong pressure from the crowd, and so 'compelled' his disciples to get away and sail with him to Bethsaida.

50. Mark 1:25; 1:34; 3:12; 8:30; 9:9; Luke 4:41; cf. Mark 7:24 and 9:30. The commands to silence have long been a matter of debate. In the case of those following the healing miracles, T. W. Manson has convincingly argued that Jesus wished to keep the *method* secret, lest it should be thought there was a magical formula which brought them about. *Studies in the Gospels*, ed. D. E. Nineham (Oxford, Blackwell, 1955), pp. 211-12. In these cases the injunctions would have nothing to do with the Messianic secret. All the same they would

to attract the kind of attention which might lead to him being acclaimed in a way he was resolved to avoid.

The outlook of Jesus was beyond the grasp of his disciples. In spite of all that they had learnt from him, they were unable to escape from the traditional Jewish framework of thought. Here is one of the keys which must be used for interpreting the gospels, bearing witness as they do to the consistent misunderstanding on the part of his immediate followers which Jesus had to face.[51] T. W. Manson points out that the three Passion predictions in Mark (8:31; 9:31; 10:33) all produce reactions which show that the disciples were not in the least ready to listen to what Jesus was really saying (cf. Luke 9:44-45). They were interpreting his Messianic mission in accordance with traditional ideas, and these allowed no room for suffering or death, only for triumphant success. In so far as they had come to terms with his estimate of the future, they may have recalled the apocalyptic passages in the book of Daniel, and anticipated that they would have to share with him hardship, persecution, and even death before the rule of the saints of the Most High should begin. 'They are willing to postpone the glory and humble themselves to the role of the servant in the meantime. They are not ready or willing to find the supreme glory in the role of the servant.'[52]

Manson is surely right in concluding that this is the real

---

still indicate Jesus' concern not to be misinterpreted; and the bearing of Mark 8:30 and 9:9 seems clear enough.

51. Morton Enslin has vigorously protested that the thesis of the Messianic secret and the misunderstanding of Jesus on the part of the disciples is wholly mistaken. He maintains that it leaves us with the unalluring alternatives of an inept teacher or such obtuse followers that 'we have no just ground for assuming the reliability of any part of the record'. Enslin's argument is unconvincing and fails to take into account the common experience that unfamiliar ideas, especially those which challenge long established ways of thinking, are rarely absorbed but gradually and with great difficulty. ''Twixt the Dusk and the Daylight', *The Journal of Biblical Literature*, Vol. LXXV (1956), pp. 19-26.

52. Manson, *Studies in the Gospels*, p. 219.

Messianic secret. It is an open secret. Though Jesus speaks plainly, his disciples are not ready to understand; for 'no secret is ever so well kept as that which no one is willing to discover'.[53] So when Jesus asked them on the way to the villages of Caesarea Philippi whom they believed him to be, Peter answered, 'Thou art the Christ', but immediately showed that he was thinking in traditional Jewish terms by his horrified reaction to the explanation that the Son of man must suffer and even be killed (Mark 8: 27-33).[54] Jesus had at length ventured to speak quite plainly to his intimate circle, but in spite of all that he said and all that they knew of him, they were completely unprepared to accept the role he had chosen for himself. To those steeped in the Jewish tradition, the cross was indeed a stumblingblock, a sheer scandal (I Cor. 1:23).

This conception of himself as the Servant Messiah dictated the whole course of Jesus' ministry. Wherever there was human need he was to be found; for the Kingdom was open to everyone, not only to a religious or moral élite. His message was all-inclusive, breaking down conventional barriers and cutting across the boundaries of social privilege and respectability. Jesus was concerned that all who were willing to hear, whoever they might be, should know that they were the heirs to the promises of old and accepted into the family of God. That is why he identified himself with the penitents whom John baptized in the river Jordan, and throughout the subsequent three years consorted with the outcasts of society, offering his friendship and help to those who were most conscious of their need. Scandalous though this seemed to the religious leaders of the day who regarded themselves as the custodians of public morals, Jesus himself was convinced that his mission was to proclaim by deed and word the love of God for all men, not least for those who had apparently rejected his law and

53. Ibid., p. 220,
54. Bultmann's dismissal of this incident as 'an Easter-story projected backward into Jesus' life-time' is a particularly striking example of forcing the narrative to fit a preconceived theory: cf. *Theology of the New Testament*, Vol. I, p. 26.

placed themselves beyond what was commonly believed to be the reach of his mercy. The parables of the lost sheep, the lost coin and the lost son in the fifteenth chapter of Luke's gospel perfectly epitomize not only what he had to say, but what he actually did. And at the last he was crucified between two thieves, in the centre of human rebellion and despair, identified to the very end with those rejected by their fellow-men, declaring the forgiveness of God for executioner and victim alike. Looking back on it all, the apostle to the Gentiles found himself driven to exclaim, 'God was in Christ, reconciling the world unto himself' (2 Cor. 5:19).

This is the crux of the matter. How far are we justified in discerning, as Paul did, a genuine disclosure of the Transcendent in the life and ministry of Jesus the Christ? Many, of course, would say we are not, interpreting the evidence purely phenomenally and arguing that at most we are presented with a picture of a strange idealist who mistakenly believed that he was the representative of God and whose death was the pathetic, if not tragic, end of an illusion. But is this not to remain curiously satisfied with the superficial surface of things? Is there not a reconciling passion of such dimensions displayed in the life and death of Jesus, such an utter confounding of all man-centred, naturalistic presuppositions, as to cause us to pause and ask again whether in him we do not begin to see the mystery of reality breaking through and shattering our artificially limited world? This, at least, has been the basic conviction of Christendom, whatever its changing formulations through centuries of reflection. A distinguished modern theologian speaks for Christians of every generation when he says: 'At Gethsemane and Calvary most of all, faith discerns such an exhibition of Divine reconciling passion, such a tragic tension in which God spares Himself nothing, as makes our heart faint within us and stops every mouth before God. . . . It is the cardinal point at which we stand confronted with the ultimate and recurrent paradox of religious thought—that the God who stands infinitely above human life is yet deeply and decisively implicated in our most inward experience, and that to see into the unchanging heart of things we must gaze upon the travail of a cross.'[55] For Christians, this is the ultimate value judgement, the touchstone for interpreting all experience, and the decisive disclosure of the Transcendent Mystery on the human scene.

55. H. R. Mackintosh, *The Christian Experience of Forgiveness* (London, Nisbet, 1927), p. 190.

CHAPTER SEVEN

THE ILLUMINATION OF MYSTERY

The last chapter ended with a value judgement: the conclusion that in the person and ministry of Jesus of Nazareth we are confronted with the disclosure of Transcendent Mystery breaking through the purely phenomenal surface of those events to which the New Testament bears witness. There the case might rest, with the issue open between those who claim to discern a genuine dimension of depth in these events and those who remain unconvinced that this is anything but self-deception. Herein, I believe, lies the nodal point of decision to which finally we have to return, but the argument may first be carried one stage further in illuminating the question at issue by relating the Christian value judgement to the philosophical considerations advanced in the earlier chapters. We may profitably ask how far all that baffles us when we reflect on our experience as a whole is illuminated by the conviction that God has in fact revealed himself in Jesus the Christ, and inasmuch as the mysteries of metaphysics find a coherent interpretation in the reconciling mission of the Suffering Servant, we shall to that degree have persuasive confirmation of the validity of the basic Christian affirmation.

Before proceeding, however, we should make clear precisely what it is we intend to do; for it is all too easy to lose sight of the wood for the trees. Gathering the threads of the earlier discussion together, we find ourselves faced with four areas of mystery: (1) the fundamental nature of being; (2) the antinomy of spontaneity and coordination; (3) the related antinomy of teleology and dysteleology; (4) the ultimate grounding of value. In other words, the mystery of reality may be delineated as the mystery of being, exhibited in contrasting tensions. Being is diversified in manifold expressions, and yet value is discerned in deepening unity. Spontaneity, as fundamental to everything that is, makes for disintegration, but coordination is equally a characteristic of the universe. Purpose, understood in the broadest sense as organization towards certain ends, has to be balanced against the randomness and sheer dysteleology everywhere apparent. Some may see in this nothing save bewildering disorder; but the tension between opposites does suggest some kind of pattern, even if the philosopher as such cannot do more than indicate that this is so. It is, however, possible that the revelation of God in finite terms in which Christians believe may enable us to discern this pattern more clearly and find reason for suggesting that the mysteries of metaphysics, even if they cannot be penetrated from the finite standpoint, do hold together in a fashion that begins to make sense, directing us to the reality of a transcendental perspective from which everything is ultimately translucent.

Thus the purpose of this final chapter is to bring the insights of the Christian revelation to bear on each of the four areas of mystery mentioned above, with a view to seeing how far they may be illuminated thereby. Obviously, this is likely to open up a wide range of theological questions which cannot be explored in any detail without throwing the whole discussion out of balance. Accordingly, we shall limit ourselves to the question of the *relevance* of the Christian revelation to these areas of mystery, concentrating on such themes as Reconciliation, Grace and Freedom, Providence and Miracle only in so far as they illustrate this particular concern. In this way we may begin to discern how philosophical and theological inquiry can most fruitfully meet.

We begin, then, with the nature of being. From the philosophical standpoint I have argued that being presents itself as active, whether we look inwards upon ourselves or outwards to our extending environment. This at once suggests a striking affinity with the biblical testimony to the nature of God. It is recorded that when Moses asked to know the name of God, he was told that it was Yahweh, usually rendered 'I am what I am'.

But if we give full weight to the alleged dynamic overtones of the Hebrew verb 'to be', we should probably alter the translation to 'I cause to be what happens',[1] and the whole story of the Bible is concerned with what God has done in and through the life of the Israelite nation, culminating in the reconciling mission of Jesus. The key word in expounding this theme is ἀγάπη basically used to denote the self-giving of God for the salvation of the human race, of which Christ's earthly mission was held to be the embodiment. 'God commendeth his love towards us, in that, while we were yet sinners, Christ died for us' (Rom. 5:8). 'Herein is love, not that we loved God, but that he loved us, and sent his Son to be the propitiation for our sins' (1 John 4:10). Unfortunately, the word 'love' is open to serious misunderstanding, which a great deal of recent theological work has been at pains to eradicate.[2] Hollywood, the sentimental novel and pop culture have popularized an erotic interpretation far removed from the usage of the New Testament, and even the more sophisticated find it difficult to rid their minds of the notion that love is basically a feeling aroused by the attractiveness of its object. Accordingly, people commonly talk about loving antique furniture, ice-cream, football, and a thousand and one things which excite desire and the anticipation of pleasurable satisfaction. Indeed, it is to be feared that for a growing number of our contemporaries loving other people means little more than that: a disastrous misconception which accounts in large measure for the breakdown of many marriages. Let the attractiveness of an object or a person diminish with the accompanying weakening of desire, and 'love' evaporates. Of course, there is a strong element of desire involved in the marriage partnership, but unless this is undergirded by the outgoing practical concern of each partner

1. Cf. B. W. Anderson, *Understanding the Old Testament* (Englewood Cliffs, N.J., Prentice-Hall, 1957), p. 34. On the other hand, James Barr warns against pressing the philological point too far and argues that the Hebrew verb 'to be' cannot by any means always be interpreted in a dynamic sense. See *The Semantics of Biblical Language* (London, Oxford University Press, 1961), pp. 50 ff.

2. e.g., Anders Nygren, *Agape and Eros* (London, S.P.C.K., 1932-9), 3 vols.

for the other, there is likely to be little stability in the relationship.

By contrast, the New Testament writers speak of the ministry of Jesus, directed at whatever cost to the rescue of man from his state of alienation from God and from everything that hinders the full expression of his potentialities, as evidence of the divine love. We have to choose our words carefully in this connexion; for it is all too easy to convey the impression that God has a sentimental feeling towards man which is demonstrated in the life of Christ. Far from that being so, the claim is that his life *is* the love of God, a self-giving commitment even to the death of the cross. In the full New Testament sense, love is deed, deed on behalf of man. That is why Nathaniel Micklem writes: 'Only when we have said that God *so* loved, do we know what it means that God is Love, for this is not an abstract proposition in philosophy, but the adoring apprehension of a saving act.'[3] Therefore, when we say that God is Love, we mean his nature is to act in the way Christ acted in his mission of reconciliation.

How far does this illuminate the mystery of being as such, the sheer givenness of everything that is, before which both scientist and philosopher find themselves completely baffled? Attempts, like those of the Thomists, to argue beyond contingent being to a transcendental ground in necessary being fail, as we have seen, to carry complete conviction, and in any case lead us to unfathomable mystery one stage further back: a mystery, moreover, which appears to many philosophers to be one of abstraction and to confuse rather than illuminate the problems confronting them. What happens when we take the Christian revelation seriously and affirm that the Transcendent has been disclosed in the activity of reconciling love? It is then impossible to think of Divine Being in any other terms. For God, to be is to love.[4]

3. N. Micklem, *What is the Faith?* (London, Hodder & Stoughton, 1936), p. 201.

4. This conviction forms the basis of Nels Ferré's *The Christian Understanding of God* (New York, Harper, 1951), though I should not wish to follow him in his highly speculative exposition of the subject.

Once this has been granted, at least two important consequences follow. First, if God is Supreme Being and his nature is active love, then some light is cast on the reason for finite existence. One of the difficulties about the Thomist approach is that, even if we admit the validity of the argument from contingent to necessary being, it does not apply in reverse. There is nothing in the concept of necessary being which provides any ground for understanding why there should be anything else. On this basis alone the existence of the universe is an irrational surd, and another principle—the gratuitous love of God—has to be introduced to make room for the doctrine of Creation with which the scholastic emphasis on the divine self-sufficiency stands in somewhat uneasy alliance. If, however, it is of the essence of Supreme Being to love, if this is where we start, then his outgoing activity may be recognized in the creation of the universe. Such a statement is, of course, open to dangerous misunderstanding. The famous Whiteheadian dictum that the universe is necessary to God,[5] goes much too far, denying in effect the doctrine of sovereign grace. We do not have to maintain that the creation of this particular universe was necessary, or even that divine self-sufficiency having no need of creation is inconceivable. Did not St Augustine, and St Thomas after him, argue that the divine love is expressed within the Blessed Trinity?[6] All I am saying is that, given the definition of Supreme Being in terms of active love, the existence of the universe as the established object of that love does not appear to be the completely irrational surd with which the philosopher *qua* philosopher is bound to leave us.

In the second place, the nature of finite being itself is to some degree illuminated. We have already seen reason to believe that the universe is best described as a system of interacting centres of energy, but the expressions of that activity appeared to be

5. Cf. Whitehead, *Process and Reality*, pp. 523 f. It should, however, be noted that this radical departure from classical Christianity is not simply a twentieth-century phenomenon; it was adumbrated much earlier by Hegel.

6. Augustine, *De Trinitate*, Book VI, Chap. 7; Aquinas, *Summa Theologica*, Part I, Question 37, Article 1.

so variegated that we were unable to go further than a purely phenomenal analysis. Reviewed in the light of the Christian revelation, is it not reasonable to suppose that created being partakes of the nature of its divine originator? At any rate this is the biblical doctrine of man, who is declared to have been made in the image of God, and St Paul, in his picture of the whole universe in travail waiting for the adoption of the sons of God, at least implies the extension of the doctrine to the whole of creation. For us the analogy is rendered initially plausible by the definition of being in terms of activity. But perhaps we may go further. If the activity of God is love, seeking to establish man and all creation in perfect harmony with himself, may we not suggest that this is essential to the nature of finite being as well? At first this will doubtless appear highly paradoxical, if not wildly improbable. What about man's disruptive tendency? What of nature, red in tooth and claw? The inescapable fact of disharmony, or what has been called the problem of evil, seems to put the whole idea completely out of court. And surely it is nonsense in any case to talk about *things* achieving harmony.

Before dismissing the suggestion as utterly fantastic, we should ask whether we are really seeing the issue in its proper perspective. The problem of evil is certainly a formidable one, not on any account to be minimized by those who are concerned to take a fully realistic view of things. But we are mistaken if we make it the corner-stone of our thinking. Strictly speaking, as we have already noted, there is no problem at all for those who do not believe that the universe admits of any ultimate explanation. If that were so, destruction, depredation, as well as all forms of human tragedy would be irrational surds, but no more so than the noblest of human achievements and the most complete and satisfying of human relationships. Everything would simply be given in its irreducible distinctiveness. It is only when we are impressed with the overcoming of evil—the positive adaptation and coherence of everything in the universe as its fundamental characteristic—that the problem of disharmony arises. Therefore, in so far as we are inescapably aware of the adaptation of different expressions of being to one another, whether this be at the human, the animal, the organic or the inorganic levels, we have a presumption in favour of treating this as basic; while all that disrupts and destroys the achievement of harmony is to be regarded as a problem which somehow has to be resolved in the light of a more comprehensive viewpoint. How this can be is a question to which we shall return. At the moment all that I wish to affirm is that finite being displays a striking propensity towards some kind of harmony, exemplified by mutual adaptation at all levels and most conspicuously by man in his striving for fellowship and community. If we share the conviction that the being of God is disclosed in the love of Christ, then to be is in some sense to love, and a defect in love is a defect in being.

What shall we say about the principles of spontaneity and coordination? After analysing the total range of our experience, both of ourselves and of the universe around us, we reached the conclusion that faithfulness to the data demanded a pluralistic description, which would allow for the initiation of the manifold variety of phenomena evident on every hand. Determinism is a tidy theory, but one that in the last resort leaves room for nothing to happen. Its plausibility is derived from combining a closed logical system, wherein one proposition entails another, with our experience of coercion and regularity of sequence. On reflection, however, we see that when its implications are pressed, it either has to be modified to make room for the initiation of the whole process or else abandoned; and, as we have argued, once a single exception has been made to the determinist rule, we are entitled to ask why there should not be more, especially in the light of emergent novelty and the extraordinary variety and prodigality that the universe everywhere displays. To say that things spontaneously happen seems to stick much closer to observed facts than to posit a dubious metaphysical principle, which turns out to be a thinly veiled logical abstraction.

At first glance, the theistic hypothesis appears to be the one way of rescuing the determinist hypothesis from its otherwise insoluble dilemma. If God be the creator and sustainer of the whole temporal process, does not this mean that he is the sole initiator of everything, and everything happens as a result of the divine 'fiat'? Such a belief certainly animates a good deal of popular theology and has been a basic principle of those systems of thought which have emphasized the sovereignty of God and the doctrine of predestination. But unless qualifications are introduced which virtually undermine the theory, we are left with an intractable problem of evil or with a tyrannical God who treats his creation like a plaything and is utterly indifferent to value as we understand it. If this is where supernaturalism leads us, it would be better to opt for some form of polytheism, to which belief in the Devil as the originator of evil is but a halfway house. Such a suggestion is hardly likely to be taken seriously. The fact is that the universe does not look in the least like a glorified puppet-show with a concealed performer or performers pulling all the strings. Surely nobody would suppose that it is, unless he saw no alternative to the tidiness of a determinist system. In the last resort, there is nothing to commend such a theory except a revolt against the apparent anarchy of freedom which man finds it too hard to bear. Determinism is fundamentally a negative hypothesis.

All the same, the monotheistic version has one distinct advantage over the secularist: it does at least allow for spontaneity in God. He takes the initiative in creation, providence and redemption, and at any rate this allows for things to happen. But the difficulties arise when that is held to foreclose the issue, and spontaneity anywhere else is virtually denied. It makes nonsense of man's awareness of freedom and moral responsibility, besides attributing directly to God's agency the occurrence of a multitude of events which cannot be harmonized with any tenable doctrine of his nature and in any case have the manifest marks of spontaneity about them.

But spontaneity is only one aspect of the mystery with which the philosopher is faced. He has to reckon with coordination as well. Given a pluralistic analysis of the universe in terms of centres of energy, we are bound to ask why there is a universe at all. The principle of spontaneity by itself would inevitably imply complete chaos, but this is clearly not what we find, and the mutual adaptation of one thing to another is partly the reason why so many thinkers have felt compelled to deny the evidence of spontaneity in favour of a determinism that contradicts the plain facts of experience. How can the two principles be held together in a single framework of thought without in the end sacrificing one to the other?

The philosopher can begin to answer the question, as we have already suggested, by directing attention to the checks and balances which result from a system of interaction. Clearly one thing limits another, and the possibilities of destructiveness are to that extent automatically controlled. Again, the instinct for self-preservation may be cited as a reason for various types of association to ward off common dangers, while the herd instinct is introduced to account for cooperation in the achievement of certain ends: a phenomenon apparent in the insect world, as exemplified by ants and bees, no less than amongst the most highly civilized human beings. At first sight, a fairly complete explanation of mutual adaptation seems to be available, which also allows for the degrees of spontaneity we have posited. On further reflection, however, the combined weight of all these considerations does not amount to very much. They do little more than plaster over the cracks in a pluralistic universe. The appeal to the herd instinct is superficially the most cogent reason for explaining the fact of coherence. But introducing the word 'instinct' actually explains nothing. From the critical point of view it is simply a convenient way of describing the regularity of observed behaviour, and raises the metaphysical question as to the grounding of mutual adaptation in the essential nature of things. In any case, why should we suppose that the universe as a whole is favourable to cooperation, especially when principles such as a system of checks and balances and the tendency towards self-preservation are invoked to bolster up the argument? The first of these is fundamentally negative, resting on the more basic fact of conflict, while the tendency towards self-preservation is ultimately disruptive, only contributing to uneasy alliances when the threat of danger is sufficiently apparent. At most the phenomenon of cohesion in a universe riddled with spontaneity raises an ultimate metaphysical question about its possible grounding.

The gospel of reconciliation leads us to the conviction that the principles of spontaneity and coordination are confirmed in the very nature of God's activity in Christ, and the tension between them thereby resolved. To speak of reconciliation at all implies the counterpart of alienation and the freedom of man to reject the claims of God. This has always been a problem for those who have interpreted divine sovereignty after the manner of imperial dictatorship. We have seen that the Hebrews by and large could not conceive how God could be creator of the world and Lord of history unless everything conformed to his decrees. This applied no less to the apparent frustration of his purpose than to its fulfilment. The rebellion of his chosen people and the arrogance of pagan powers were awkward facts which had to be explained away as due to temporary forbearance or to the utility of unwitting instruments of his discipline. Whatever the difficulties in maintaining this position, the Hebrews were basically convinced that everything was directly under the divine control and that this would be manifest at the coming of 'the day of the Lord', when his purpose would inevitably be brought to fulfilment.

I have argued that the way in which Jesus conceived his mission was in radical contrast to any such belief about the relation of God to the historical process. From the temptation in the wilderness to the cross on Golgotha he steadfastly refused to play the part of vice-regent to a supernatural dictator. He claimed to be the representative of God on earth and the inaugurator of his kingdom, but he used the language of family life to expound the nature of man's intended relationship with God, and followed the path of suffering service as the expression of the Father's will. Men were to be won, not coerced, whatever the cost to God; for only thus could fellowship on a fully interpersonal basis be realized. In other words, the mission of Jesus was directed towards the establishment of spontaneity, not its destruction. At the same time the disintegration of society at all levels and the alienation of man from man consequent upon his fundamental character as a free agent or centre of spontaneity was to be overcome by the good news of the Kingdom: the new commonwealth of reconciled humanity achieved through the reconciliation of man to God.

In this process of recreation the redemptive suffering and sacrifice of the Servant Messiah played a decisive part. The bruised reed he would not break, nor quench the smouldering wick (cf. Matt. 12:20), but he was prepared for his own body to be broken and his own life to be snuffed out that man might be brought back to God. We are not concerned here with an exposition of the doctrine of the atonement. It is sufficient to observe that a completely paradoxical way was chosen for overcoming the disharmony of creation: paradoxical in the sense of being utterly contrary to anything man would naturally have expected. God did not act by sovereign 'fiat' or irresistible compulsion, which would have entailed the negation of freedom and would have made nonsense of the spontaneity characterizing the universe as it had been constituted. On the contrary, Christ accepted the fact of sin and its cosmic counterpart in disintegration as a burden to be borne and a tendency to be broken from within the framework of the historical process. In his person the human race was representatively and vicariously united to God through the sacrifice of a dedicated life. Thereby he made the benefits of his life and Passion available to all, and this became the redemptive feature of a situation otherwise marked by disruption and disintegration. The positive deed was done. The rot was stopped. The tide was turned. And this without the unmaking of things as they were. The cross and the events surrounding it established the condition for a new harmony between God and his creation, the healing influence of which cannot be measured. For Christians this is the clue to everything, to human history and the natural realm alike: the evidence of hope in a context of despair. The cross of the Servant Messiah is the tree for the healing of the nations, and his outpoured blood the river of life renewing the parched and broken ground of the world.

It is, of course, notoriously difficult to hold together the idea of the sovereign freedom of God with the spontaneity of finite being and not imply that God has abdicated from the control of the universe. This is the problem forced upon us not only by Jewish expectations and the incredulous hostility of Christ's contemporaries, but also by the mature Christian experience of owing everything to the divine activity, illustrated in Harriet Auber's well-known lines:

> And every virtue we possess,
> And every victory won,
> And every thought of holiness,
> Are His alone.

How are we to reconcile such an authentic expression of indebtedness as this with the conviction that we are morally responsible for what we do, and that therefore we are fundamentally free agents? This is the problem of grace and freedom which has vexed the history of Christian thought, and the theological counterpart to the philosophical antinomy between spontaneity and coordination. Inasmuch as grace and freedom can be held together in the unity of Christian experience, we shall have further reason to believe that what we have found to be sheer mystery for the metaphysician is thereby illuminated and from the transcendental point of view transparent.

No easy solution is available, as the history of the Pelagian and Arminian controversies amply demonstrates. If with Augustine and Calvin we hold that salvation is the work of sovereign grace alone, we seem to be landed with the terrible doctrine of double predestination:[7] those who are created for an inheritance in the family of God and those who are foreordained to damnation; and we are bidden to believe that the inscrutability of God's will is his glory. Such a conclusion reduces man to the level of a

---

7. Augustine did not teach predestination to evil in so many words, though this was implicit in his doctrine. Cf. J. P. Bethune-Baker, *An Introduction to the Early History of Christian Doctrine* (London, Methuen, 1903), p. 325. It was left to Calvin to draw out the full implications of the Augustinian theory of grace.

plaything, without responsibility, worthy of neither praise nor blame. Moreover, so far from this view of sovereign grace reflecting the majestic glory of God, it does in fact cast doubt upon his efficiency, let alone his omnipotence. As John Oman says, 'we have the uncertainties of revelation and the divisions of the Church, which, if grace be irresistible power acting so individually and impersonally that a prophet may be a pen and a pope a mouthpiece, are mere scandals of God's negligence.'[8] The extreme Pelagian alternative, whereby man's destiny is made dependent on his own choice, virtually makes human beings the authors and perfectors of their own salvation, relegating God to the role of a helpless spectator, observing from afar the fate of his creation from the effective control of which he has abdicated.[9] This would place an intolerable burden on man, and runs counter to all genuine religious experience, the consciousness that we are dependent upon God for the achievement of our highest aspirations.[10]

8. John Oman, *Grace and Personality* (Cambridge, The University Press, 1925), p. 70.

9. While this is the logic of the position adopted by Pelagius, it must be remembered that he was protesting against a doctrine which was itself full of difficulties. Still more was this the case with Arminius who had to face a starker form of predestination than did the fifth-century divine, and his teaching was based not so much on a doctrine of man's freedom as on a rejection of the views of the extreme Calvinists. How far the latter went in following the implications of pre-natal damnation can be seen by referring to a letter Arminius wrote to Uitenbogaert, setting forth the views of his New Testament colleague at Leyden: see A. W. Harrison, *Arminianism* (London, Duckworth, 1937), p. 29. Actually Arminius was concerned to preserve the biblical paradox with its double emphasis on divine grace and human responsibility. He almost bent over backwards to emphasize his orthodoxy, as when he wrote, '*Et addo illum doctorem mihi maxime probari, qui gratiae quam plurimum tribuit: modo sic causam gratiae agat, ne iustitiae Dei noxam inferat, et ne liberum arbitrium ad malum tollat. Quid amplius a me desiderari possit non video.*' *Epistola ad Hippolytum*, iv (Frankfurt edition, 1635), p. 772. Short of a thorough-going Calvinism it is difficult to see what more could have been required of him.

10. I am completely unconvinced by the argument that the admission of a doctrine of grace makes nonsense of human freedom and moral responsibility, as W. G. Maclagan contends in *The Theological Frontier of Ethics* (London,

Clearly a course must be charted between the Scylla of thorough-going predestinationism and the Charybdis of man-centred voluntaryism. This alone accords with the teaching of the New Testament in which divine grace and human responsibility are held in tension, as most notably in Philippians 2:12, where the apostle exhorts his readers: 'Work out your own salvation with fear and trembling. For it is God which worketh in you both to will and to do of his good pleasure.'[11] It was the intention of the so-called semi-Pelagians, John Cassian and Faustus of Rhegium, to hold both aspects of the truth together,[12] though at most they only succeeded in stating the paradox without indicating any way in which it might be resolved; but that is better than falling into manifest error.[13]

Augustine's real problem lay in the equation of sovereignty and power, both conceived in limited political terms. Perhaps such a sweeping generalization does less than justice to the profundity and complexity of the thought of someone who was undoubtedly a religious genius. But he was a denizen of the Roman world, and in spite of the depth of his insight into the Christian mysteries, his thinking was influenced by common presuppositions about the exercise of imperial power. He could not conceive of a king or

---

Allen & Unwin, 1961), pp. 108 ff. His case seems to me to rest on a view of man as an atomic individual which runs counter to all we know about our biological interconnectedness, let alone our more general experience of mutual interdependence. Maclagan himself begins to recognize the difficulties into which his theory lands him when he allows the artificiality of isolating the will from the rest of the personality as if it were an independent entity (ibid., p. 126).

11. Cf. the discussion of 'election' in C. Ryder Smith's *The Bible Doctrines of Grace* (London, Epworth, 1956), pp. 141 ff.; though the Pauline epistles are made to appear more consistent than in fact they always are. This is particularly the case in the exposition of Romans 9-11 (pp. 177-86).

12. Cf. Bethune-Baker, op. cit., pp. 321-4.

13. Oman is more critical, and argues that semi-Pelagianism can provide no satisfactory basis for religion because it implies that God will act only when we begin to do so, or continue acting only as we fulfil certain conditions (op. cit., p. 29).

emperor who did not govern by force; and therefore he assumed that the reign of God could only be interpreted in the same way. His was an error common to men of all ages: what H. H. Farmer calls 'a projection into God of our own egotistic and mechanized conception of will-power as power to ignore or override other wills.'[14] But if a man is to be a person and not a thing, the appropriation of salvation must be genuinely his own, however difficult that may be to relate to the doctrine of sovereign grace.

The essence of what takes place when someone responds to the gospel is vividly expressed in the words of a Swiss theologian, recounting what happened to him. 'I was following out my life, pursuing my own desires, when Christ advanced to meet me, placed himself before me, and barred my way. He stopped me; he made a silence in my heart; and then he held with me a solemn interview in which he spoke as he alone can speak. For long I disputed the case in a revolt of mingled anguish and bitterness; for I could not consent to renounce everything which till then had seemed to me precious and desirable; and yet I felt it to be a question of life and death, and that to disobey would have been to pronounce sentence upon myself. When at last I gave up the struggle and accepted God's will for my life, I was no longer free. I was a bondman, the bondman of Jesus Christ.'[15] There can be no doubt that this was a genuine personal encounter in which the initiative was God's and yet the writer played a decisive part. Had his personality been overruled, it would have been necessary to give an entirely different description of the experience.

What, then, happens to the doctrine of sovereign grace? The question is unanswerable as long as we persist in using subpersonal categories and talk of grace as if it were a substance or a liquid, donated to or infused into man: an error to which theologians of every generation have been curiously blind. Grace is descriptive of the reconciling activity of God, and must be con-

14. H. H. Farmer, *The World and God* (London, Nisbet, 1935), p. 139.
15. Gaston Frommel, quoted by H. R. Mackintosh, *The Divine Initiative* (London, SCM Press, 1921), p. 54.

sistently conceived in the highest personal terms. Only so can we hope to hold divine sovereignty and human freedom together. How this can be is indicated by our general experience of inter-personal relationships. The more intimate such relationships, the more one person is influenced by another and yet becomes more truly himself. Sometimes our half-conscious imagery deceives us, making it difficult to interpret what happens. All too readily we are inclined to imagine that influence is exercised by external pressure, much as a billiards cue propels a ball towards its object; or else—and this is the form in which we most often think of the relationship between God and man—we assume that the central motivating force of the personality is supplanted by another after the manner of the change of drivers at the wheel of a car. Neither metaphor is applicable to strictly interpersonal relationships. We have to give up the notion altogether that a person is rightly thought of as a thing to be pushed around or driven from within. Nor is personality to be likened to an enclosure from which other centres of consciousness are excluded or within which they may be allowed to take up a separate abode: a figment of the imagina-tion which leads to the conception of a work of God super-imposed on the activity of man, analogous to the adding of an upper storey to the ground floor of a building. 'In a right relation of persons', says Oman, 'especially of father and child, the help of one does not end where the effort of the other begins.'[16]

Personality is a unique centre of consciousness, an increasingly self-determining individual, who is yet constituted as such in virtue of the interpenetrating relationships in which he stands to other human personalities and to God. There is no such pheno-menon as an isolated individual. We are what we are because of a sort of cross-fertilization which is a never-ending process. Locke was completely wrong in holding that man is self-contained, only open to external influences through the senses.[17] So far from that being true, personalities are more correctly designated as

16. Oman, op. cit., p. 87.
17. Locke, *An Essay Concerning Human Understanding*, Book III, Chapter xi, Section 23.

'por-ous',[18] capable of the interpenetration which allows for the contribution of others without destroying the self-determinative centre of individuality.

This is sufficiently illustrated from common experience. The closer two lives are entwined in marriage, the more the values, the convictions, the aspirations of each partner become the shared possession of both; the deeper the relationship, the greater the capacity to share a common life and the more fully personal is the development of each character. We do not find that the happiest and most complete marriages diminish the individuality of the partners; quite the contrary. Again, the relationship of pupil and teacher is a case in point. The views of the teacher may gradually become part of the pupil's thinking, sometimes taken over in entirety, more often, one would hope, reshaped by the student's own intellectual efforts. At any rate in later years someone may well find himself propounding a thesis as his own which was originally that of his professor; and in some sense the teacher is living in and through the pupil.

The experience of the artist and the writer is still more striking testimony to the same undoubted fact. While plagiarism is rightly condemned, no creative work springs solely out of the depths of an isolated personality; it is in some sense the product of the artist's rapport with his environment. However outstanding a genius he may be, whatever the distinctive contribution he brings to his craft, he is engaged in communicating that which itself arises out of his capacity to receive communication. In the case of an author, no sentence can be written which does not in some measure depend on the sentences and ideas of others. Complete originality, if possible, would mean separation from the community of human thought. Original work is distinguished from plagiarism, not in virtue of its independence of the intellectual endeavour of others, but by the creative use to which the results of their thinking and research are put. As the ideas of others are made the author's own, integrated within a mental

18. Cf. N. Micklem, *Ultimate Questions* (London, Bles, 1955), p. 99.

framework which he has wrestled to produce, the charge of plagiarism falls to the ground. Dependence is then acknowledged indebtedness and participation in the commonwealth of teaching and learning.

All these are illustrations drawn from the realm of human experience; but if the interpenetration of personalities is such that we cannot isolate individual responsibility for any creative achievement, by how much more is this not the case in the relationship between man and God.[19] The analogy of the vine and the branches (John 15:1-8) is seen to be particularly apt, while the confession of the apostle Paul, 'I am crucified with Christ: nevertheless I live; yet not I, but Christ liveth in me' (Gal. 2:20), no longer appears paradoxical, but the only way of stating the facts with any accuracy. If on the human level we are more truly ourselves when we are inspired by others, we shall reach the heights of personal development only when our lives are the fruit of the Spirit's activity. Thus the individual is neither absorbed nor overridden by God. On the contrary, he becomes most fully himself, a unique self-determining personality in so far as the Spirit has free course with him.[20]

Such inward transformation and growth are rooted in an attitude of receptivity, wrongly described as passivity, if by that is meant a state in which the personality sinks to the level of a thing, to be moulded without making any contribution to the process. Receptivity is a vital attitude, proportionate to the degree of concentration on the object of inspiration. We may easily be misled by the way in which artists and writers describe what happens to them when they are vividly aware of being taken hold of by some

19. Cf. F. von Hugel, *Eternal Life* (Edinburgh, Clark, 1913), p. 229, where he takes M'Taggart to task for failing to make due allowance for what he calls 'that indefinitely penetrative and penetrable quality, that power of embracing and stimulating other minds and lives, which we know, from daily experience, constitutes the very character, actuation, and worth of these our spirits'. See too Lionel Thornton, *The Incarnate Lord* (London, Longmans, 1928), p. 338.

20. Cf. Leonard Hodgson, *The Doctrine of the Trinity* (London, Nisbet, 1943), pp. 54 f.

mysterious power beyond themselves. They are inclined to reduce their own role to one of total passivity in the interest of expressing their indebtedness.[21] But inspiration does not come to the mind that is a blank; and the moron is not more likely to become the creative artist than the aesthetically awakened and the spiritually alert. It is no part of the purpose of God that we should be reduced to mere ciphers, empty-headed and empty-hearted, without character or personality of our own. That is a travesty of the language of Christian devotion.

Once the interpersonal nature of the relationship between God and man is recognized, we are in a position to see how the power of God for salvation may be defined as justification and sanctification. If we persist in dealing in impersonal categories, speaking of grace as an infused gift, we are inevitably led either to extreme Calvinism with its logic of moral and spiritual irresponsibility, or to a dichotomy between that which is the work of man and that which is the work of God in the soul—a kind of ultimate schizophrenia! The traditional categories of Protestant theology are much more amenable to a fully interpersonal interpretation of the way of salvation. The Reformers spoke of effectual calling, justification, adoption and sanctification—all descriptive of the activity of God in recreating man; while repentance and faith define a response on the part of man which is truly his own.[22] Moreover, there is no difficulty in attributing that response to the initiative

21. Cf. Plato, *Ion*, 534; *Timaeus*, 71; Philo, *Quis Rerum Divinarum Haeres*, 53; *Migrat, Abraham*, 7; Tertullian, *Adv. Marcion*, iv, 22. J. B. Priestley gives a more balanced account in *Rain Upon Godshill* (London, Heinemann, 1939), p. 45: 'I am not claiming that a play of mine was really the work of some world-mind. This would be monstrous impertinence. The play itself, the people and scenes in it, all these are coloured and shaped by my own ego, and exhibit all my own particular weaknesses and merits. But that triumphant rush of energy and skill, enabling me to run across the dramatic tightwire effortlessly, just for this one act, was not really my own doing, and owed its existence to the fact, which might or might not be the product of chance, that this immensely greater mind could for the time being sustain my own mind. I was indeed not so much a creator myself as an instrument of creation.'

22. Cf. H. Wheeler Robinson, *The Christian Experience of the Holy Spirit* (London, Nisbet. 1928), p. 201.

and inspiration of God as well, provided that the character of interpersonal relationships is borne in mind. In this way the conviction that faith is my commitment and yet his work within me is fully preserved.

Thus we are in a position to see how the metaphysical antinomy between spontaneity and coordination begins to be illuminated in the light of the Christian revelation and the resulting synthesis of grace and freedom in the working out of man's salvation. As long as we continue to think about God in sub-Christian terms, conceiving him after the image of dictatorial man and his ways, the mysteries of metaphysics appear to be completely opaque; for on that basis the universe does not even start to make sense. Indeed, it is better to stay with irreducible metaphysical mysteries than to import a theistic hypothesis that leaves confusion worse confounded: an inevitable consequence of trying to fit the transcendent into finite categories. But once we begin from the premise that the transcendent God has paradoxically disclosed himself in finite terms, the result is altogether different. The mission of the Suffering Servant, wrought out in the Christian experience of salvation, confirms that the metaphysical antinomy between spontaneity and coordination is rooted in the very nature and purpose of God himself. The universe displays the characteristics it does because God, as revealed in Christ, is its ultimate ground and explanation.

This conclusion is further borne out by considering the other antinomy to which metaphysical inquiry leads us: between teleology and dysteleology, the widespread evidence of organization to certain ends and the apparent purposelessness of chaotic disorder, disease, suffering, death and destruction. Both alike are aspects of reality, in sharpest contradiction to one another, and defying all attempts at philosophical rationalization. At first the theistic hypothesis does not seem to help us in the very least; for once the fact of dysteleology is admitted, questions are raised not only about the goodness of God, but even about his competence. How can we hold together in a unity of thought the idea of a perfect, omnipotent being and the kind of universe in which we live?

The problem of theodicy, as it has been called, has proved insoluble at the level of rational speculation, and the reason is obvious: from within the purely finite framework of reference no adequate explanatory principle is available to us. It is only when we take the Christian revelation seriously, recognizing reconciliation through redemption as the completion of creative love, that we begin to see the possibility of resolving the metaphysical antinomy.

The issue comes to clearest focus in the attempt to relate a doctrine of divine providence to the hard facts of experience. Most thinking about the subject is at the level of Paley's watchmaker and watch,[23] the universe being considered as a gigantic mechanism, constructed and set in motion by God, who periodically interferes with it in the interest of chosen individuals. His general providence is then imagined as the maintenance of the mechanism and his special providence as interference with it and the suspension of the laws governing its operation.[24]

Such an account is open to the most serious objections. For one thing, words like 'suspension' or 'interference' suggest a deistic view of God's relationship to the universe, implying that apart from these special occurrences everything is left to its own devices.[25] This is impossible to square with the Christian revelation of God's involvement in the whole historical process, besides appearing philosophically nonsensical. If he is the origin and ground of creation it is inconceivable that he should stand aloof

23. Cf. William Paley, *Works* (Edinburgh, Brown & Nelson, 1828), pp. 435-9.

24. It is this, for instance, which vitiates C. S. Lewis's sometimes brilliant discussion of the subject. He begins by defining the word 'miracle' as 'an interference with Nature by supernatural power', and this precludes him from any thorough analysis of the way in which God encounters us in what we call miraculous events. Cf. *Miracles* (London, Bles, 1947), p. 17.

25. James Ward warns against the danger of misrepresenting the eighteenth-century deists in this connexion, who denied 'not the divine immanence *in toto*, but only such occasionalistic interference as miracles, special revelations and special providences imply'. *The Realm of Ends* (Cambridge, The University Press, 1911), p. 261.

from any part of it. 'As Lotze has well said, such a proceeding "is intelligible in a human artificer who leaves his work when it is finished and trusts for its maintenance to universal laws of Nature, laws which he did not himself make, and which not he, but another for him, maintains in operation"; but "the picture of God withdrawing from the world", the sole ground of which is himself, is incomprehensible.'[26] Moreover, if God is immanent in the whole natural process, then the conception of interference is meaningless. In the words of St Augustine, 'God, the Creator and Founder of all nature, does nothing contrary to nature: for that will be natural to each thing which is done by him from whom every kind of number and order of nature came.'[27]

Even if this were not so, the state of our knowledge would never permit us to decide whether an interference with the natural process had in fact occurred. The extraordinary is not necessarily evidence of some special divine intervention; it may simply indicate the limited range of our experience. If a student arrives late for a lecture and finds his professor standing on his head while he expounds some philosophical problem, he would no doubt consider this to be a remarkable phenomenon, probably unique in his experience! But he would never think of it as being a miracle; he would simply wonder why an otherwise normal person was behaving in this extraordinary way. To take a very different example, the resurrection of Jesus Christ from the dead, which Christians claim to have been an act of God: the unusual character of the event does not constitute the miracle. Suppose that the historicity of the empty tomb and the visible appearances of Christ could be satisfactorily demonstrated beyond any question, the unbeliever might very well say that a most surprising and to him inexplicable happening had occurred, but that would not necessarily lead him to the acknowledgement of a miracle; he would not be compelled to see in it the divine triumph over sin and death. This was surely what Jesus meant when, in response to the request for a sign, he said that people would not 'be persuaded, though one rose from the dead' (Luke 16:31).

26. Ibid.   27. Augustine, *De Civitate Dei*, Book VIII, Chap. 21.

But the most serious difficulty of all in defining miracle as a special intervention in the natural process is that it altogether fails to account for disaster. To claim, for instance, that the retreat from Dunkirk in the Second World War was a special deliverance of the Allied forces by a manipulation of the weather invites the question why God did not intervene to rescue the millions of Hitler's unfortunate victims from the concentration camps and gas chambers. If it was a miracle, as so many asserted, that two groups of miners, entombed for over a week in the winter of 1958 in the ill-fated Springhill colliery of Nova Scotia, were finally brought to the surface, why did not God intervene on behalf of the many more who were buried alive? Every day the news in the Press of some fresh disaster resulting from a fire, a car accident or a fatal illness makes it impossible to believe in a God who waves a magic wand, quenching the flames, averting a skid, or evaporating a cancerous growth.

Unless God is involved in those calamities, unless he is discernible *there*, in the end we shall not find him anywhere. The test of God's providence is not so much in the retreat from Dunkirk as in the concentration camps of Belsen and Dachau; it is less in the rescue of entombed miners than in the experience of those who lost their lives and of the families who were bereaved. Had God abdicated when fire swept through a Chicago school in December 1958, taking a toll of nearly a hundred children? Not until we can find God at work in these events, in spite of and in the midst of those things which he is often expected to prevent, will we have a tenable doctrine of providence.

We are therefore driven to the conclusion that if we are to find God anywhere, we must find him everywhere—in the midst of disaster no less than in those events which seem on a superficial reckoning to be the best evidence of his involvement in human affairs. We must go even further. It is in those occurrences which at the first glance constitute the greatest challenge to belief in God's providence that we are most likely to discern his power. That, at any rate, was the view of the apostle Paul. Writing to the Christians in Rome, who knew by what tenuous threads they held on to life and liberty, he declared: '*In* all these things we are more than conquerors through him that loved us' (Rom. 8:37). These were the men and women who before many years passed would become the victims of Nero's persecution, the human torches to light his games. Paul made no promise that God would intervene to deliver them out of the hands of their enemies, but he declared that, however serious the calamities that might befall them, they could be assured that their Lord was with them and nothing in heaven or earth could separate them from him in his resurrection. It was in his victory that they would share, even though death might overtake them.

The final seal upon this way of regarding the providence of God is the crucifixion of Jesus. He prayed in the garden of Gethsemane that, if it were possible, the cup might pass from him. And yet there was no intervention, no twelve legions of angels to rescue him. There was succour at a deeper level, deeper than the experience of dereliction. 'God was in Christ, reconciling the world unto himself' (2 Cor. 5:19). Out of the midst of his help-lessness in the hands of men he lifted the whole human race back to the Father, *because the Father was there*, implicated in the sacrifice of Calvary. There was no one, not even God himself, who stood outside and aloof from this event to intervene miraculously. In-volved in it, his power was revealed in the victory he wrought out of it through the Son.

Once the mission of the Suffering Servant is recognized as the paradigm of all God's activity, then we are given an entirely new perspective on divine providence in human life. Without the achievement at Calvary, it would scarcely be possible to imagine how the grimmest disasters could be revelatory of the providence of God, or how a miracle could be wrought in the midst of dis-aster without removing the outward appearances of calamity; but, if the redemption of the world was achieved on Calvary, then we are not justified in excluding any eventuality from his redemptive grace. He is immanent everywhere, bringing life out of death and order out of chaos, without overriding the relative independence and power of being of anything in creation.

What, then, has become of the idea of miracle? Clearly it will have to be redefined, as we move beyond the concept of an arbitrary intervention which breaks the rules and insist upon the universality of God's providence. H. H. Farmer suggests the lines along which a fresh approach may be explored when he argues that miracle is a religious category, evidenced in that which evokes awe and wonder because it is apprehended as a revelation of God.[28] It is a special instance of God's all-pervasive providence in which a man recognizes that God has met with him in saving encounter at the deepest interpersonal level. Farmer clarifies his position by suggesting that such an experience takes place when three conditions are fulfilled: an awareness of serious crisis or threat of disaster: an explicit turning to God for help: an acknowledgement of special help granted to meet this particular situation.[29] A miracle, therefore, is not a supernatural and exceptional interference with the course of events *ab extra*; it is rather an occurrence of peculiar intensity in the fulfilment of the divine will; it is a providential event raised to the highest degree, only apprehensible as such to the man of faith. The world is full of wonders, but these are not necessarily miracles or instances of special providence. An event only takes on this character when man is ready to apprehend the activity of God in response to some specific need.

That is why the same happening can be a natural event for one man and sheer miracle for another. If a passing bedouin tribesman had been attracted by the sight of a burning bush which was not consumed, he would probably have thought little of it. All he would have seen was a thicket apparently alight and a man at prayer. But for Moses this was a unique occurrence, an encounter with the living God, wherein he received the call to lead his people out of Egyptian bondage—an experience which changed the course of human history. The special providence is not to be discerned in the phenomenon of the burning bush, but in the confrontation of Moses with the divine claim upon his life;

28. Farmer, op. cit., pp. 107-27.   29. Ibid., pp. 122 f.

though it should be added that no one can tell how far external appearances may be affected by the inner meaning of a given event.

If this is the way in which we are to interpret the incident of the burning bush, how much more should we not apply the same insight to the Exodus itself, wherein the Hebrews discovered Yahweh as their Redeemer. The decisive importance of this event can scarcely be questioned. It was the beginning of Israel's existence as a nation, as the chosen people of Yahweh. Future generations believed that this great deliverance had come about through the outstretched arm of the Lord, and it was the theme of which psalmists sang and prophets spoke. 'O my people, what have I done unto thee? and wherein have I wearied thee? testify against me. For I brought thee up out of the land of Egypt, and redeemed thee out of the house of servants; and I sent before thee Moses, Aaron, and Miriam' (Micah 6:3-4). Here, for instance, was Micah's appeal to a rebellious nation at the end of the eighth century. How are we to conceive God's involvement in this great event? In what sense was the Exodus his doing, as Israelites of subsequent generations undoubtedly believed? Are we to look for his providential action in the extraordinary phenomena recorded in the narrative—the infliction of plagues, the summary destruction of a host of mothers' sons, and a series of tricks with a magic wand? Or are we to look deeper, to the identification of God with the sufferings of his people?

In this connexion Bernhard Anderson significantly draws attention to the verbs used in the account of God's call to Moses:[30] '*I have . . . seen* the affliction of my people . . . and *have heard* their cry . . . I *know* their sorrows; and I *am come down to deliver them . . .*' (Ex. 3:7-8). This is the language of involvement, strangely akin to that in which the Incarnation itself has to be affirmed. Who is to say that the lift from within and beneath cannot accomplish much more in the end than the stroke from above? The image is spatial and anthropomorphic, but it suffices to indicate the way in which we have to think if we are to

30. Anderson, op. cit., p. 32.

233

begin to view God's providence in the light of the Christian revelation.

This redemptive activity is the clue whereby we may see how the metaphysical antinomy between teleology and dysteleology is in principle resolved. The inner working of redemption may be entirely beyond our powers of comprehension, and the ultimate fulfilment of the purpose of God may be outside the range of our imagination. Nevertheless, we may venture to believe that here we are at the heart of truth, once we have grasped with the apostle Paul that nothing in heaven or earth is 'able to separate us from the love of God, which is in Christ Jesus our Lord' (Rom. 8: 38-39). And herein lies 'the victory that overcometh the world' (1 John 5:4).

What of the mystery of value? In our earlier discussion of beauty, goodness and truth we reached the conclusion that aesthetic, moral and intellectual aspirations find their common denominator in man's developing harmony with his environment. How far they are grounded in the nature of reality and are destined to ultimate fulfilment was left an open question, beyond the range of philosophical analysis. The achievement of harmony is never complete in our experience on earth and is constantly liable to frustration. Knowledge is at best partial and provisional; nothing is absolutely translucent; and the more we reflect on the problems raised by the theory of knowledge, the more bewildered we are prone to become, the more sceptical about the validity of what we claim to know, the more pragmatic in our attitude to the quest for truth. As for our appreciation of beauty, we seem to be subject to changes of mood, our criteria for judgement are elusive, and our insight is at best defective; unsatisfied aspiration rather than the tranquillity of permanent attainment marks the aesthetic experience. Occasionally we may have the sense of apprehending that which abides beyond the changes of mortal life and then we feel at peace, as when listening to a Brandenburg Concerto or when lost in the contemplation of a masterpiece of art like the Venus of Milo. But this is quickly gone, and the discords of everyday life remind us that the felt harmony of the supreme moments of aesthetic appreciation is not enough; we are only too painfully aware of deep, unsatisfied desire. But it is in the realm of ethics that we are most poignantly conscious of frustration. 'For the good that I would I do not: but the evil which I would not, that I do' (Rom. 7:19). If goodness is the achievement of harmony with our fellows, then we all fall short of the ideal; perfection is entirely beyond us, and increasing sensitivity simply leads us to a growing awareness of the disharmony in human relations: a disharmony to which we contribute in spite of our best intentions. Indeed, the better the man, the more sensitive he is to his own imperfections. It is the saint who is most likely to speak of himself as 'the chief of sinners' (1 Tim. 1:15). What grounds have we for believing that the gulf between what we are and what we would be, between actuality and ideal, will ever be bridged? Are our aspirations anything more than vain hopes, doomed to disappointment—the pathetic longings of these strange creatures who have emerged in the course of evolution, but altogether unrelated to the structure of the universe?

The view has, of course, been advanced that man's sense of value, and especially his unsatisfied aspirations, provide the key to metaphysics and to the nature of reality as a whole. The case was powerfully and persuasively argued by W. R. Sorley in his Gifford Lectures, when he took as his starting point 'the dictum that we must seek in that which *should be* for the ground of that which *is*.'[31] But in the end the argument from value suffers from the same weakness as the cosmological argument: it proceeds from the given in finite experience to that which transcends it; and we are left wondering whether the conclusion is ultimately valid. Do we know enough to be confident that the very nature of the universe conforms to our highest aspirations, or is this just a matter of wishful thinking? Certainly man's appreciation of value *may* be significant; it *may* even be the most significant aspect of human experience from the metaphysician's point of view.

31. W. R. Sorley, *Moral Values and the Idea of God*, p. 22.

But that is not enough. We need the assurance that this is so, that our quest for harmony is grounded in the ultimate nature of things; and here the Christian revelation seems to be particularly relevant.

At first sight, Christianity has little, if anything, to say about beauty and truth. Apart from his obvious delight in nature, there is nothing in the recorded teaching of Jesus to suggest that he dwelt upon this aspect of human experience; though we should not forget that the Christian tradition has inspired many of the world's greatest works of art: a clear indication that the harmony of feeling, the basic characteristic, as we have argued, of aesthetic appreciation, is consonant with, and indeed part of, a full-orbed Christian experience. Again, Jesus was not directly concerned with intellectual questions. His immediate mission was to his own people, and the Hebrews had never been given to theoretical speculation. Knowledge for them was much more a matter of the practical relationship of man to his environment than the holding of true propositions about the universe. When Hosea declared that there was no 'knowledge of God in the land' (Hos. 4:1) and that 'My people are destroyed for lack of knowledge' (Hos. 4:6), he was not complaining of the lack of 'clear and distinct ideas about God, but rather that Israel was in the wrong relationship to God':[32] a point reinforced by the promise of the new covenant in Jeremiah. 'Behold, the days come, saith the Lord, that I will make a new covenant with the house of Israel, and with the house of Judah: . . . I will put my law in their inward parts, and write it in their hearts; and will be their God, and they shall be my people. And they shall teach no more every man his neighbour, and every man his brother, saying, Know the Lord: for they shall all know me, from the least of them unto the greatest of them, saith the Lord: for I will forgive their iniquity, and I will remember their sin no more' (Jer. 31:31-34). The same word is used in this connexion as is found elsewhere in reference to sexual intercourse and the most intimate personal relations (cf. Ps. 139:1; Jer. 1:5;

32. Anderson, op. cit., p. 245.

Amos 3:2). For the Hebrews, knowledge was basically union with God and one's fellow-men. And when the Fourth Gospel speaks of Christ as the truth (John 14:6), it is quite clear that he is said to be this in his mediatory capacity.

Little imagination is required to trace the connexion of this line of thought with later Gnosticism and mysticism, but that is beyond the scope of our present inquiry. We are concerned here with the nature of the Christian revelation in its bearing upon our understanding of value. As far as we can tell from the records, Jesus had nothing to say about the question of knowledge as such, although his mission of reconciliation is entirely consistent with our interpretation of truth as intellectual harmony with reality, and in this sense as being of ultimate worth. It is, however, when we turn to ethics that his life and ministry most clearly assume decisive importance; for the idea of moral perfection is at the very heart of the purpose he came to fulfil.

At this point we have to be careful to see that our emphasis is in the right place. It is popularly believed that the unique significance of the teaching of Jesus lies in the nature of his precepts, especially as found in the Sermon on the Mount. But there was nothing particularly original about what he said if viewed as a regulative guide to conduct. Indeed, the great Jewish scholar, Joseph Klausner, claims that 'throughout the Gospels there is not one item of ethical teaching which can not be paralleled either in the Old Testament, the Apocrypha, or in the Talmudic and Midrashic literature of the period near to the time of Jesus.'[33] The most that Klausner is prepared to allow is that 'Jesus gathered together and, so to speak, condensed and concentrated ethical teachings in such a fashion as to make them more prominent than in the *Talmudic Haggada* and the *Midrashim*, where they are interspersed among more commonplace discussions and worthless matter';[34] though, in passing, we should not minimize the value of casting new light on familiar sayings through setting them in a

33. Joseph Klausner, *Jesus of Nazareth* (London, Allen & Unwin, 1925), p. 384.
34. Ibid., p. 389.

fresh perspective.[35] Nor do we find the ultimate significance of the Christian ethic in the emphasis which Jesus placed on the importance of motive and inward disposition, essential as this is to any profound moral teaching. When Klausner cites instances of parallelism between the ethics of Jesus and Jewish literature, he includes those passages in which motives are stressed over against observable behaviour,[36] even if he does not focus attention on the crucial nature of the distinction: a fact which is perhaps suggestive of a significant difference of outlook. But it is in what Jesus says about the relationship of man to God, and still more in what he did to achieve reconciliation, that the kernel of his teaching is to be found. All that he says about motives and actions has to be understood within this context. Goodness is the fruit of a right relationship with God.

This is the conclusion which T. W. Manson reaches in a well-known discussion of the subject. 'It [the teaching of Jesus] has to do not with mere acts and motives but with the fundamental relation of man's will to God's. Repentance is not a striving to bring one's conduct into line with the law or with the higher righteousness demanded by Jesus. Neither is it a painful scrutiny of one's motives with a view to substituting, let us say, unselfish for selfish motives. It is a return of the whole personality to God, a submission of the will to his will, the acceptance of his sovereignty. Now it is by this act of submission that the kingdom is entered, and it is this decisive change that is presupposed in the detailed teaching of Jesus. The change itself is made possible by the new experience of God as Jesus reveals him, that is, as the merciful loving Father who seeks and saves the lost. The transforming experience bears fruit in life and conduct; and the examples of the higher righteousness given by Jesus in his teaching are, so to speak, samples of this fruit. The word "fruit" is used advisedly, for there is a certain spontaneity and inevitableness

35. Cf. G. P. Gilmour, *The Memoirs Called Gospels* (Toronto, Clarke, Irwin, 1959), p. 131.
36. Klausner, op. cit., p. 385.

about this new behaviour that cannot be attained by mechanical obedience to rules or by meticulous scrutiny of one's motives.'[37]

From the standpoint, then, of the teaching of Jesus, religion and ethics are inseparable since the one is the well-spring of the other. Accordingly, the contrast that has often been drawn between the precepts of Jesus and the theology of Paul is entirely mistaken. The latter, in opposing faith to works, may be regarded as simply building upon the anti-legalism of his Master, and elucidating the essentially religious character of the good life in the light of the Crucifixion and the Resurrection. In his letter to the Galatians the apostle not only exalts the inward dispositions of love, joy, peace, patience, kindness, goodness, faithfulness, gentleness and self-control, but attributes them to the operation of the Spirit, the fruit of the life united with Christ in his death and resurrection (Gal. 5:22; cf. 2:20). Elsewhere it is quite clear that in the thought of Paul, and of the early Church in general, the Spirit was the gift of God to those who had been reconciled with him through faith in Christ; the new relationship was the foundation of the new life.[38]

At the same time, reconciliation was never conceived in merely individualistic terms. Out of the travail of the cross and the triumph of Easter Day a new community was born—the *koinonia* of the Spirit—whereby Jew and Gentile, slave and freeman were united in one fellowship, the *arrabon* or 'earnest' of the communion of the saints in heaven. Christ was declared to have 'broken down the middle wall of partition' (Eph. 2:14) in his death on the cross, and through him by the Spirit's agency those hitherto divided from one another were promised access together to God (Eph. 2:18). This was the foundation for Paul's doctrine of the Church, and in particular for his use of the metaphors of

37. T. W. Manson, *The Mission and Message of Jesus* (London, Nicholson & Watson, 1937), pp. 328 f.

38. See 2 Cor. 3:16-18; and cf. Acts 2:32-33. The same point is underlined in the Apocalypse, where the Seven Spirits are the eyes of the Lamb, sent forth by him into all the earth. On this, see H. B. Swete, *The Holy Spirit in the New Testament* (London, Macmillan, 1910), p. 303.

the body and the building to expound his theme. The former of these was particularly appropriate, suggesting the interdependence of Christians upon one another with Christ as the head (1 Cor. 12: 12-27), and no one can read the apostle's strictures on the divisions within the Church at Corinth (1 Cor. 1:10 ff.) without realizing how vital to his thinking was the unity of Christians within the fellowship. This is underlined in the Epistle to the Ephesians where in the fourth chapter especially unity is the recurring theme: 'There is one body, and one Spirit, even as ye are called in one hope of your calling; one Lord, one faith, one baptism, one God and Father of all, who is above all, and through all, and in you all' (Eph. 4:4-6). Only in the light of this principle does the writer go on to enumerate the diversity of gifts within the Church; it is as if he were afraid that difference of capacity and function might obscure the all-important factor of unity.

Thus, for the apostle as for his Master, the good life was founded in a right relationship between God and man in his 'togetherness' with his fellows: an ethic of religiously oriented community which has the most obvious connexions with Hebrew thought. Indeed, a continuous line of development may be traced from Judaism at its best, through the teaching of Jesus, to the theological exposition of Paul; for in Judaism the law was the expression of the covenant: a relationship binding the whole nation to God. Individualism in ethics and the separation of ethics from religion were both equally foreign to Judaism. Thus when Jesus protested against the legalism of the Scribes and Pharisees, he was standing in the tradition of the prophets of Israel, and Paul was not re-pudiating the religious heritage of his people, but showing how the work of Christ was its fulfilment, making it possible for man by faith to walk humbly with his God. The good life was the reconciled life.

The uniqueness of Christ, therefore, lies in what he achieved rather than in what he taught, or perhaps, more accurately, his teaching was the expression of all that he had come to do—the reconciliation of man with his fellows to God in the kingdom of heaven. The fact that this was simply inaugurated in his lifetime on earth and still appears far from consummation today is patently obvious. But if we believe that God was really at work in him, that conviction becomes decisive for the philosophical interpretation of value. Inasmuch as we have seen reason to hold that the progressive achievement of harmony is the essence of truth, beauty and goodness, then the work of Christ is both assurance that this conclusion is rooted in the purpose of God and is also the consummation towards which the whole historical process is moving. How this will ultimately come about and what it will be in itself remains within the area of mystery, hidden from the imaginative grasp of finite man. It is enough for us to know that here we have an anchorage in reality.

I am conscious of having done no more in this chapter than open up the subject of the bearing of the Christian revelation on the nature of our experience in general. Each of the topics on which I have touched merits extended treatment which, if attempted, would have thrown out of balance the methodological purpose of the whole book. All that I have tried to do is to show how the Christian revelation begins to illuminate the mysteries disclosed in a philosophical analysis of our common human experience: the enigma of being, the antinomies of spontaneity and coordination, of teleology and dysteleology, as well as the mystery of value. Obviously this is not the evaporation of mystery. The disclosure of the Transcendent in finite terms may provide an interpretive clue in the light of which we may fruitfully explore the meaning of our total experience; it does not enable us to escape from our finitude and involvement in the temporal process.

Here 'we see through a glass darkly' (1 Cor. 13:12). The transcendental being of God as he is in himself remains hidden from us. We cannot know him as he essentially is, but only so far as he has revealed himself; and the conditions of finite existence impose inevitable limitations on the completeness of that disclosure; otherwise man would not be finite at all. Furthermore, we cannot know ourselves or our environment from the transcendental point of view; we remain caught within the subject-object relationship of all human experience. The problem that vexed Kant is one we have to live with, and it is sheer illusion, if not pretension, to suppose that we can escape and know anything translucently from some detached Olympian height. As W. R. Sorley says, 'understanding must be from within, not from without. We are ourselves parts of the universe, or factors of it, and an outside view of it is impossible.'[39] The extraordinary thing about man is that he can know anything at all, that he can in any way apprehend that by which he is conditioned, still more that he can in any way apprehend himself. Above everything else, his capacity for reflection, whereby he becomes aware of the mystery of being, is the ultimate enigma. And yet the fact remains that he does. It is surely misleading to speak of this as transcendence—a word that is required for the unconditioned standpoint of God. We may perhaps stretch the word 'insight' to connote a deepening apprehension of ourselves in interaction and rapport with our environment, and yet as involved *within* that dynamic relationship: we see *into* the nature of reality while still *in* the finite situation.

This brings us back full-cycle to our point of departure: the context within which theological inquiry may fruitfully be pursued. All that I have said about the disclosure of the Transcendent in terms of our finite experience closely accords with the insistence of the secular theologians that God is not to be found in another world or on the periphery of this one, but as 'beyond in the midst', discerned in and through the whole of this bourne of time and space. Tillich speaks for all who take that as axiomatic when he says: 'The universe is God's sanctuary. Every work day is a day of the Lord, every supper a Lord's supper, every work the fulfilment of a divine task, every joy a joy in God. In all preliminary concerns, ultimate concern is present, consecrating them.'[40]

But if this is to be the keynote of modern theology, then the fallacy of any narrowly fenced empiricism has to be exposed. If

39. Sorley, op. cit., pp. 306 f.
40. Paul Tillich, *Theology of Culture* (New York, O.U.P., 1959), p. 41.

the Stratonician principle is upheld, that is the death-knell for theology. On the contrary, I have tried to show that thorough-going empiricism does not lead to such a closed system, but to the apprehension of the depth of mystery which characterizes everything that is. This mystery betrays a pattern to which the Christian revelation is seen to be strikingly relevant, and thus the door is open to constructive theological reflection, freed from the inhibitions that have been in danger of turning it into a meaning-less enterprise.

ACKNOWLEDGEMENTS

❈

The author and publisher wish to acknowledge their indebtedness for permission to reproduce copyright material as follows: from *Space, Time and Deity* by Samuel Alexander, published by Macmillan, London, 1920; from *An Introduction to Aesthetics* by E. F. Carritt, published by Hutchinson, London, 1949; from *Second Thoughts in Moral Philosophy* by A. C. Ewing, published by Routledge & Kegan Paul, London, 1959; from *The Glass of Vision* by Austin Farrer, published by Dacre Press, A. & C. Black Ltd., London, 1948; from *Prophets, Priests and Kings* by A. G. Gardiner, published by Dent, London, 1917; poem by G. K. Chesterton, reproduced by permission of publishers and Miss Collins; from *Reality as Social Process* by Charles Hartshorne, published by the Free Press, New York, 1953; from *Christian Faith and Natural Science* by Karl Heim, published by SCM Press, London, 1953; from *The Christian Experience of Forgiveness* by H. R. Mackintosh, published by Nisbet, Welwyn, 1927; from *The Mission and Message of Jesus* by T. W. Manson, published by Nicholson & Watson, London, 1937; from *He Who Is* by E. L. Mascall, published by Longmans, Green, London, 1943; from *Words and Images* by E. L. Mascall, published by Longmans, Green, London, 1957; from *Personal Knowledge* by Michael Polanyi, published by Routledge & Kegan Paul, London, 1958; from *Rain Upon Godshill* by J. B. Priestley, published by Heinemann, London, 1939; from *The Concept of Mind* by Gilbert Ryle, published by Hutchinson, London, 1949; from 'Meaning and Verification' by Moritz Schlick, in *Readings in Philosophical Analysis*, edited by H. Feigl and W. Sellars, published by Appleton-Century-Crofts, New York, 1949; from 'Colours' by J. J. C. Smart, in *Philosophy*, Vol. XXXVI, published by Macmillan, London, 1961; from *Nature, Man and God* by William Temple, published by Macmillan, London, 1934.

INDEX

being [*contd.*]
241; nature of, 209; propensity towards harmony, 214; respect for, 26

Bentham, Jeremy, 143

Berkeley, George, 71, 123

Bethune-Baker, J. P., 219n, 221n

Bible, 177, 183, 210

biology, 26, 69, 80, 100, 101

Blanchard, Brand, 151n

body; Cartesian view, 35, 37, 39; and person, 45-6

Bohm, David, 85

Bohr, Niels, 85

Bonhoeffer, Dietrich, 12-13

Botticelli, Sandro, 167

Bruce, F. F., 190n

Brunner, Emil, 30, 187

Buddenbrock, Wolfgang von, 125n

Bulgakoff, Sergius, 28

Bultmann, Rudolf, 187, 188, 190, 191; on Jesus' Messianic role, 201, 205n

Butler, Joseph, 145, 147

Cadoux, C. J., 202

calling, 226

Calvin, J., 219, 219n

Calvinism, extreme, 220, 226

Campbell, C. A., 43, 45n, 46n, 118n

Carritt, E. F., 144n; on aesthetics, 137-9, 140-2, 154n, 164, 165

Cartesian dichotomy, 34-40, 67, 69, 100

Cassian, John, 221

causality; connexion and, 106-7, 108-9, 126-7; Hume's critique of idea of, 106-7, 107n; problem of, 104-5, 126; three different levels of operation, 114-15

cells, 75; concept of organism and, 97-8

centre; idea of organizing, 70, 80-1, 82, 83, 84; universal reconciling, 78. *See* self

centres of energy, 99, 102; in hierarchical structure, 104, 113, 113n; interaction between, 112-13; interpretation of universe by means of, 82, 126-7; principle of individuation in terms of, 87, 93, 94-6. *See* self

Chalcedonian presuppositions, 188

chance, determinism and, 114

chemistry, 80, 81, 100, 101

Cherwell, Lord, 85

Chesterton, G. K., 121-2

Chopin, F., 166

Christian ethic, 133

Christian mystery, 183

Christianity; and beauty and truth, 236; historical religion, 187

Church, 133, 184, 191; early, 185, 189, 191, 201; origin of, 184, 190; St Paul's doctrine of, 239-40

Church of England, 10

claims; and claimants in ethics, 158, 159, 160, 162; goodness response to, 162; morality response to human, 156-7; and realm of values, 169, 171

'*Cogito ergo sum*', 43, 67

cognition, 51, 52

coherence; explanation by 'herd instinct', 216; intuition apprehension of, 61, 62; of universe, 104

colonies of monads, *see* monads

colour, 163, 163n

community; goodness and, 164; man's striving towards, 214; and moral progress, 162

complementarity, principle of, 85

conation, 51, 52

conduct, problem of human, 144

connexion and causality, 106-7, 108-9, 126-7

conscientious objection, 160-1

conscious purpose, 74

consciousness, 43-4, 46

contingency; argument for existence of God from, 172-5, 211, 212; logical and factual, 172-3

cooperation, herd instinct and, 216

coordination; antinomy of c. and spontaneity, 208, 209, 214-15, 219, 227, 241; and gospel of reconciliation, 217; of universe, 171

Copernican revolution, 72

Copleston, F. C., 85n

cosmological argument, 106n, 174-5; weakness of, 235

cosmology, 72-3

Couturat, Louis, 103

Cox, Harvey E., 10

Creation, doctrine of, 212

creativity, 59-60, 62, 64, 67

Croce, Benedetto, 137, 137n, 142

cross, crucifixion, 189, 205, 207, 217, 218, 231, 239

damnation, 219, 220n

Daniel, book of, 199, 204